# HERE'S TO THE
# WOMEN

*100 Songs for and about American Women*

Hilda E. Wenner  Elizabeth Freilicher

THE FEMINIST PRESS at The City University of New York

Published 1991 by The Feminist Press at The City University of New York,
311 East 94 Street, New York, NY 10128
Distributed by The Talman Company, 150 Fifth Avenue, New York, NY 10011
First Feminist Press edition

95  94  93  92  91  6  5  4  3  2  1

**Library of Congress Cataloging-in-Publication Data**
Here's to the women : 100 songs for and about
    American women / [compiled by] Hilda E. Wenner,
    Elizabeth Freilicher. — 1st Feminist Press ed.
        p. of music.
        Melodies with chord symbols.
        Reprint. Originally published: Syracuse, NY :
    Syracuse University Press, 1987.
        Discography: p.
        Includes bibliographical references (p.
        Includes indexes.
        ISBN 1-55861-041-3 (cloth, acid-free paper) :
    $49.95. — ISBN 1-55861-042-1 (paper, acid-free
    paper) : $24.95
        1. Women—United States—Songs and music.
    2. Feminism—United States—Songs and music.
    3. Folk-songs, English—United States. 4. Popular
    music—United States. I. Wenner, Hilda E.
    II. Freilicher, Elizabeth.
    M1977.W64H4   1991                        90-22009
                                                  CIP
                                                  M

The authors gratefully acknowledge permission to reprint these songs from the following
sources:
"To the Ladies" from *Songs of Independence* by Irwin Silber, copyright © 1973 by Stackpole
    Books. All rights reserved. Printed by permission.
"I Am a Suffragette" and "Female Suffrage" from *Songs America Voted By* by Irwin Silber,
    copyright © 1971 by Stackpole Books. All rights reserved. Used by permission.
"Brigham, Brigham Young" from *Mormon Songs from the Rocky Mountains* edited by Thomas
    Cheney. Publication of the American Folklore Society, University of Texas Press, 1968.
    Reprinted by the University of Utah Press, 1981 (paperback).
"My Country," traditional abolitionist song, from *Protest Songs in America* by David Rosen,
    copyright © 1972 by Aware Press.
"The Teacher's Lament," words by an anonymous Arkansas teacher, music by Merle Travis,
    from *Songs of Work and Protest* by Edith Fowke and Joe Glazer, copyright © 1973 by Dover
    Publications, Inc. Originally published in 1960 by the Labor Education Division of
    Roosevelt University under the title *Songs of Work and Freedom*.

Design by Mary Peterson Moore
Front cover photograph: *Womenharvest* by Jan Phillips

Printed in the United States of America on acid-free paper
by McNaughton & Gunn, Inc., Saline, Michigan

Dedicated to the memory of
Malvina Reynolds

*"She helps us face tomorrow with some muscle."*

HILDA E. WENNER began her career as a teacher of English and United States history. In the early 1970s she began performing and teaching American folk music. She plays the piano, guitar, old-time banjo (for which she arranges music), mountain dulcimer, and autoharp, and publishes articles and music arrangements, many of which are in this book.

ELIZABETH FREILICHER has been a teacher of English and speech, a published poet, and a prize-winning writer and director of children's radio drama for WNYE, the New York City Board of Education radio station. The research for her articles appearing in a feminist journal, *New Directions for Women*, spurred her interest in writing a book about women and their songs with Hilda Wenner, whom she met in 1977.

THE DIANE PEACOCK JEZIC SERIES ON WOMEN AND MUSIC publishes books that reflect women's past and present contributions to music making in all genres and in multi-cultural contexts.

# Contents

# CONTEMPORARY ISSUES

# GROWING UP

# ROLE MODELS

# Foreword

SOME of the best news in a long time is what has been happening to 51 percent of our population.

Throughout the world, women young and old are using their talents to express their feelings about the world's problems—especially those that threaten the end of the human race.

A song is not a speech. It can mean different things to different people at different times. But these are songs full of hope and affirmation of life. The best ones are passing from singer to singer, to school, to church, to summer camp, to demonstrations.

There is a new revival of topical songs afoot. Many of these songs are already recorded. Some of the best are in print here for the first time. Someday they may be known by millions.

Songs are seeds. Scatter them widely. Who knows where they'll take root?

PETE SEEGER

# The Music of This Songbook

IN 1978 and 1979, when Elizabeth Freilicher and I began to gather songs for this volume, we realized we would end up with either of two books as a result of our research. We would have a prose book *about* songs or a songbook that would refer to women's history and culture. Whichever book emerged, we would be satisfied. Betty envisioned a prose book that talked about songs, and I, as the musician, hoped for a songbook for women, without too much talk. At the end of a couple of years we had a collection of about fifty songs, mainly historical ones, a discussion of each, and an essay introducing each of seven categories of songs. The manuscript was accepted by a New York literary agent and remained with him for two years.

In 1983 I mentioned the songbook in an article written for a banjo journal. One of the readers was Pete Seeger, who wrote me to say that he would be happy to read it over for us and to publish the table of contents in *Sing Out* magazine.

On Pete's advice we began the work anew. "Like the telephone book," Pete commented, "it had a great cast of characters—but no plot." He suggested rewriting the prose and expanding the collection to include many contemporary songs. With that, the door flew open. The possibilities for songs became endless, of course, and even a "plot" emerged.

There is no doubt that other collectors would have produced quite a different anthology, although any women's songbook will necessarily contain a number of "classics": the great labor songs, for example, and the feminist songs of the seventies which had become the anthems of the women's movement. Besides the genre termed "women's music," there are many songs that United States women would enjoy having in such a collection, including certain songs written by men.

As soon as Johanna Halbeisen at the New Song Library was contacted for her suggestions, musicians started sending their songs in every conceivable form. Some on tape were recorded, I suspect, during the wee hours by earnest (if sleepy-eyed) songwriters, eager to have their work heard and acknowledged for the first time. While many of the songwriters have been professional for a long time, others sent only lyrics and a few chords with their tapes. Records, too, arrived without music, since even well-known music is sometimes not written down.

It became my job to turn over to the copyist 100 lead sheets all matching in style, at least to a degree. For help in the editing, which was far more extensive than I could have anticipated, I enlisted three San Francisco Bay area musicians/copyists who consulted with each other and with me: Janet Smith of Berkeley, Rick Walsh of San Francisco, and Ernie Mansfield of Oakland. Rick produced the camera-ready music.

Of the four of us, some were more "classically" oriented than others. I wondered, for example, if a folk musician who played these songs would know the meaning of "da capo," or "coda." Eventually we reached consensus on editing problems and made compromises which pleased all of us.

When crediting the traditional songs the question arose: when are the terms "adapted by," "arranged by," or "transcribed by" best used? They have different meanings. I prefer to use simply "American Folksong" or "Traditional," since this is the best way to keep the old songs in the public domain. We want the music to be accessible to other collectors for their own books and articles, thus I decided to use these two terms wherever possible.

"Arrangements" of traditional songs are often copyrighted in nearly the same and sometimes even identical versions as earlier ones. I believe this is usually done innocently. Nor can the copyright office examine each version of "Buttermilk Hill" or "Careless Love" that comes through its doors; consequently, duplicates sometimes receive new copyrights, as our research showed again and again.

"Adaptations" of songs nearly always lose in translation and are usually inferior. The early versions can hold charm and appeal that the adapters and arrangers fail to retain—although there are notable exceptions, of course.

In earlier decades adaptations were often used to avoid copyright infringement. Since the seventies, however, the practice is abating, probably due at least in part to the changes in the complicated copyright laws taking place at that time. We were not interested in creating new songs from old ones, and the same is true of the "composed folksongs." If the music has been changed from the original version given to us, it has been in order to move the song to another octave for easier reading, to save necessary space, or to provide a better key for the guitarist or singer.

In cases where a song is in print for the first time ("One-Hour Mama" or "I Want To Be a Real Cowboy Girl," for example), I transcribed it from the recording and attached my name only in the few instances I thought it might be important. My idea was to stay as close as possible to the original or most familiar version.

When is "American Folksong" a better term than "Traditional"? I believe that the former is better when the song originated in this country, and the latter should be used when a song was first sung on the other side of the ocean. (While only two composed songs in this collection are by overseas writers, our traditional material is often found both here and abroad.)

For corroboration on song credits and to confirm the status of public domain, I drew on the advice of some experts in the field: Irwin Silber; Pete Seeger; Jerry Silverman, whose *Liberated Woman's Songbook* was published in 1971 by

MacMillan; and Bob Reiser, the co-author with Pete Seeger of the labor songbook *Carry It On* (Simon and Schuster, 1985).

With Jerry Silverman's publications we have had a refreshing reversion of the nation's famous songs back to the people. Silverman simply uses the term "American Folksong" to credit music in the public domain. He seems to have avoided "arranged by" and "adapted by" wherever possible. One gets the impression that Silverman does not jealously guard his arrangements, and I believe it wise for us to follow suit.

I feel adamant about sharing all of my own work. It is time to stop the "ballad mongering" of the past decades—generations, in fact—and to allow the songs of the country to go free. Because we have allowed many of our oldest songs to be locked up with copyrights, collectors and publishers have long been leery of printing what truly belongs to all of us. While it is one thing to write an original song and expect recognition and payment for one's work (a legitimate and honorable practice), it is not honorable, it seems to me, to allow a dozen or more collectors of famous traditional songs, our nation's treasures, to make money from "arrangements" or "adaptations" of handcrafted songs of old balladeers who never had a thought of monetary gain from the work. These songs too often have become the business of others who have copyrighted and licensed at will. Rather, we need to appreciate and to protect the important heritage of our traditional music, and eventually assure everyone access to what is truly ours together in the first place.

HILDA E. WENNER

# Acknowledgments

THIS songbook, consuming a large portion of six years since 1978, is the result of the efforts of many people, including the work of fifty living songwriters. Many have become our friends; we thank all of them for both their music and their sustained communication with us.

A huge debt is owed to the balladeers who went on before us. The miners' bards; the writers of the old mill songs; the nameless slave women who sang in the fields and houses; the immigrant girls who produced many of our early work songs; the mothers, daughters, and wives.

We also lovingly remember the great topical songwriters of the past who are represented in this book. Malvina Reynolds died the year we began this project. Thanks are due her good friend and associate, Ruth Burnstein, for bringing some of Malvina's lesser-known songs to our attention.

Our gratitude goes to Johanna Halbeisen of the New Song Library in Massachusetts, who put us in touch with many of the songwriters. Marcia Deihl, one of the authors of *All Our Lives* (Diana Press, Baltimore, 1976), lent her moral support, knowing from experience that the job would be long and difficult. We saved her from writing a sequel, she claims.

The music of this volume was edited by three San Francisco Bay area Californians: Janet Smith, Rick Walsh, and Ernie Mansfield. Rick Walsh produced the camera-ready music pages.

A number of companies helped smooth our path to publication. The staff at Ladyslipper, the largest distributor of women's music, was always ready to assist us with addresses and telephone numbers. Redwood Records, Rounder, Folk Legacy, and other record companies also helped. TRO, Shawnee Press, Harold Leventhal's company, and Carol King at Mitchell, Silverberg and Knupp deserve our thanks for making licenses available to us.

Many musicians and performers read the manuscript. While we failed to keep a list, we gratefully acknowledge the comments of Jean Ritchie, Bruce Phillips, Cathy Fink, Sally Rogers, Oscar Brand, and Jeannie McClery. Roz and Howard Larmon, hosts of KPFK's Folkscene radio show in Los Angeles, interview and play the music of a number of the songwriters in this volume. We thank Howard and Roz for their support of this work as well.

*Sing Out,* the most important journal of folk music in the United States, is a great resource, and we highly recommend its music and articles. Important women in music are often featured, and a number of songs in this volume have appeared in *Sing Out*'s pages, some before our manuscript was completed and some after.

Experts on traditional American music were asked to comment on the crediting of old songs. Valuable advice came from Jerry Silverman, Bob Reiser, Pete Seeger, and Irwin Silber. Thanks go to all.

Our editors in the field of women's studies were Patricia Cline Cohen and Carolyn Ashbaugh, who edited the Introduction, and Barbara Lindemann, who read the song commentaries for historical accuracy. Mary Lou Thompson commented on our original manuscript. Raya Bertram read the manuscript when it was in its embryo stage and gave us helpful advice. Adrian Wenner lent us much practical publishing and editorial advice. Our gratitude to all for their help.

We also wish to thank the librarians and archivists at the various museums and historical societies who assisted us in finding illustrations. A number of government agencies and private businesses also contributed pictures. We are grateful to Edith Mayo, Curator of the Smithsonian Institution's Division of Political History, who showed us the temperance songs and other music of America's past and helped us to locate photographs.

We found some of our illustrations in a remarkable book by Cathy Luchetti and Carol Olwell, *Women of the West* (Antelope Press, Utah, 1982). We wish to thank our feminist photographer friends, Susan Jørgensen and Sandy Stone, for access to their fine work.

Our attorney, Linda Dubroof, saved us from a morass of bad legal advice; she wrote simplified songwriter contracts and all other legal documents for the project. Her expertise was extremely valuable and greatly appreciated.

We cannot say enough for the cheerfully given help of Pete Seeger, who is just as fine a man as his public image shows him to be. It is due to Pete's voluntary evaluation of our original manuscript and his encouragement that our rewriting was accomplished and the song collection enlarged. Pete's unflagging support made the seemingly endless work bearable, and we were able to "keep our eye on the prize," as the old song goes. It is appropriate to also thank Toshi Seeger, who works with him.

We hope that this volume will justify the years of love, patience, and support our families have given us, for which we will always be grateful.

Special gratitude is due Hy Freilicher for his active assistance and steadfast commitment to our book.

One of the blessings of writing for a university press is that, while many decisions (and expenses) are left to the authors, the end product usually turns out very much the way they envisioned it in the first place.

We thank Syracuse University Press for the opportunity of publishing with them and applaud The Feminist Press for reprinting this book.

HILDA E. WENNER
ELIZABETH FREILICHER

# Introduction

THIS anthology of traditional and contemporary songs for United States women is the first major volume to tie women's songs to their culture and history.

The book is the end result of several years of research and study. It grew out of our belief that an exploration of songs for and about United States women, past and present, would give us an intimate view of their feelings and thoughts.

The music of the collection features songwriters of the past and present and includes topical songs, ballads, children's songs, anthems, blues, spirituals, and hymns. They illustrate the many facets of women's lives from the earliest days of the country to the present.

The songs may be performed either alone or with others, accompanied with a guitar, keyboard, or wind instrument. Their arrangement by sections makes it easy to select music for special events. Organizations such as youth groups, women's gatherings, senior citizens' meetings, political meetings, and rallies will find the volume useful. Classes in history, women's studies, and music should also find it valuable. Some of the music is familiar, and some is in print for the first time. The accompanying commentaries will help place each song in context.

We began our song search with a trip east to Washington, D.C., and then to New York, first to visit the Smithsonian Institution's Division of Political History and to meet with Edith Mayo, its curator and an expert on United States women's history. We also spent time in the Archive of Folk Song at the Library of Congress, curious to see what feminist light might be shed on the early literature, biographies, recordings, and songbooks of women. We examined the music and rare books of the Americana Collection in the New York City Public Library.

These three libraries provided us with the primary sources for the songs of the Revolutionary War days, slavery times, the abolition movement, and the music of the temperance women and the suffragists.

While not always the intention of the singers, some of those early songs of American women are often considered today to reflect their narrowly confined roles. "Single Girl," for example.

> Single girl, single girl, goin' where she please,
> Married girl, married girl, has a baby on her knees.

Upon our return to the west coast, we continued our song search at the major California universities. The libraries of the Berkeley campus housed music of some of the student singer-songwriters of the early years of the second wave of feminism, the 1960s and 1970s. (The first wave took place during the mid-nineteenth century.)

These contemporary songs of women mirror the new women's movement. In contrast with the early ones they contain strong currents of anger and protest, whether the theme is environmental problems, women's liberation, exploitation of women and minorities on the job, or gay rights.

But a refreshing optimism is often expressed in their lyrics. In a self-published volume of songs of the early 1970s, titled *Fight On, Sisters,* Carol Hanisch writes about getting involved in the nuts-and-bolts of liberation already under way.

While her lyrics in "I Gotta Learn to Sing" begin, "I always had a weakness for a guitar man, especially if he could sing," the song concludes, "I'm gonna pluck my own banjo, strum my own guitar":

> 'Cause somehow lookin' on ain't enough
> I wanna make the rafters ring.
> I can't go lookin' on forever
> I'm gonna learn to sing.

A new sense of women's empowerment was due largely to the fact that for the first time women could make realistic long-range plans for a productive life.

Widely available birth control had facilitated the changes in the sexual mores of the nation:

> Oh, the pill, the pill, I'm pining for the pill,
> I'll never have any more because they're going to bless the pill.

("The Pill")

With women's ever-increasing participation in the labor force came the problems of inequities on the job. Far-reaching legislation was passed in the sixties and seventies, such as the 1964 Civil Rights Acts, with the provision Title VII, barring discrimination on account of sex. This did not change the fact that women were nearly always a cheaper pair of hands. Even in 1985 the American woman earned only sixty-four cents to every dollar earned by a man.[1]

> I listened to my mother and I joined a typing pool,
> I listened to my lover and I sent him through his school;
> If I listen to the boss, I'm just a bloody fool,
> And an underpaid engineer!

("I'm Gonna Be an Engineer")

The mid-century singer-songwriters, having renounced their dependency on men, were no longer trapped by marriage and childbearing and showed in their songs that they were eager to explore the world:

> There's a whole lot of places my eyes are longing to see,
> Where there is no dream cottage, no babies on my knee,
> And there's a whole lot of people just waiting to shake my hand,
> And you know a rambling woman's no good for a home-lovin' man.
>
> ("Rambling Woman")

Women sing about many aspects of their lives. In preparing this book, we wanted to hear as many of the most recent songs about women as possible. No general song anthology for women had been published in a decade, and Pete Seeger suggested that we contact Johanna Halbeisen of the New Song Library in Massachusetts. She, in turn, put us in touch with a number of topical songwriters composing music on subjects directly concerning the lives of women. These musicians suggested still other talented writers, and soon we had more than enough good songs.

Feminist music of the past decade has taken a new direction. In the 1970s and 1980s, women's songs have often expressed an exciting effort to communicate with women of other nations, cultures, and political backgrounds, extending the sisterhood they had developed during the era of consciousness-raising. This new theme of international sisterhood is well illustrated in "Hay Una Mujer," a song by Holly Near about victims of the repressive Chilean regime. It names some of the "disappeared" women of Chile:

> Michelle Peña Herrera,
> Nalvia Rosa Meña Alvarado . . .
>
> and the junta knows
> And the junta knows where she is
> And the junta knows where they are hiding her, she's dying.

Aware of the enormous pressure of a ticking nuclear clock, women are now working together, sharing with men their techniques of conflict resolution. As those who create life, women feel they have a special responsibility for insuring a peaceful world. And, while not war's perpetrators, civilians constitute the largest number of victims of contemporary warfare.[2]

The subject of peace or nonintervention appears in fully 20 percent of the music of this volume and now seems to be the priority in women's topical songwriting.

The new theme of women's leadership in this important area is a source of inspiration. These lyrics are by Judy Small:

> The first time it was fathers
> The last time it was sons

And in between, your husbands marched away with drums and guns
And you never thought to question
You just went on with your lives
'Cause all they'd taught you who to be was mothers, daughters, wives.

("Mothers, Daughters, Wives")

### Why Choose Folk Music? What Is a Folk Song?

In contrast to rock, pop, and country music in which the subject matter is essentially love or sex, folk music is enormously varied in its subject matter and is easily read, learned, and shared.

It is a mistake to adhere to the traditional definition of a folk song as music which is very old; folk music is a powerful and contemporary expression of the people of any era. Many of our early songs were indeed passed down to us through an oral tradition during the times when the printed word was not available to the masses, but people continuously write or invent new folk songs. Whether the music is old or new, however, its amateur quality remains important. "Experts" attempting to apply formal standards of high art to these gems of social comment are merely gilding the lily. Whether witty, sad, or satirical, the songs speak for themselves and need no apology, such as a children's song about sexual stereotyping:

Well it's only a wee-wee
So what's the big deal?
It's only a wee-wee, so what's all the fuss?
It's only a wee-wee and ev'ryone's got one
There's better things to discuss!

("It's Only a Wee-Wee")

A good folk song is often like a good political cartoon. It quickly sums up a subject and makes a memorable statement about it in a spicy or even irreverent style. The best folk songs can disarm even the most hard-shelled conservative. Yet many of those songs involving liberal protest are traditionally regarded as unsalable by commercial recording companies. However, we need not be afraid of social protest but rather the lack of it. As Pete Seeger once remarked during the great midcentury "folk scare," even a lullabye is a protest song if the baby doesn't want to go to sleep.

In fact, women have always protested their inequality in song, although often very quietly, just as they have in their diaries, letters, journals, manifestos, poetry, novels, historical essays, and plays. Many times it was couched in fun, perhaps more often in song than in any other form of expression:

Oh, I'm lookin' for a man to wash my clothes,
Iron my shirts and blow my nose,

Sweep the floor and wax the kitchen
While I sit around playin' guitar an' bitchin'!

("Talking Want Ad")

## The Seven Topics of the Songbook

We found that our 100 songs could be arranged into seven categories, with some bridging more than a single topic. An antiwar song might also be a love song, for example.

I sold my rack and sold my reel, I even sold my spinning wheel
To buy my love a sword of steel, Johnny has gone for a soldier.

("Buttermilk Hill")

Our seven topics encompass love, politics, work, contemporary social themes, children, and outstanding women (biographical songs). This final category presents songs of women's personal struggles toward liberation and self-awareness. We titled it "Women Emerging."

## Friends and Lovers

We chose those songs about love that we believe are representative of the various eras of our history, but their singability and timeliness were also important. And, although love songs are among the most numerous, contemporary love songs which stress *equality* in relationships are the most difficult to find.

Old love songs are seldom happy. Typically they tell the story of early marriage, poverty, and too many children, or they concern the unmarried and pregnant girl about to be abandoned. Many of the early murder ballads were based on true accounts of a villainous man (often named Willie), doing away with a pregnant lover whom he found to be too great an inconvenience.

In our research we found that people's concept of love has undergone many changes throughout United States history. For a wife in early America, for example, marriage meant many years of drudgery in the colonies or on the frontier, with few pleasures. The grim facts tell us that colonial and frontier wives were pregnant or nursing for up to twenty years. Slightly more than half of all children died during their childhood, and one of five deaths of women was attributable to childbirth.[3]

The colonial home was at the center of the social and economic system. While patriarchy was certainly at the core, the roles of husband and wife in maintaining the household and supervising the children, servants, and unmarried members of the household were not as finely separated as they later came to be. Women's skills were highly regarded.[4]

With the mid-nineteenth century's Industrial Revolution and the consequent rise of the middle class, clearly defined roles were assigned to husbands and wives. Women found themselves "potting and panning" in earnest:

> There's too much of worriment goes into a bonnet;
> There's too much of ironing goes into a shirt.
> There's nothing that pays for the time that you waste on it;
> There's nothing that lasts us but trouble and dirt.
>
> ("The Housewife's Lament")

It should be noted that men's and women's roles, or "spheres," were not as clearly separated among the lower classes, where women might work for pay on farms, in factories, or as domestics. (The country was, of course, still largely rural during the early years of the Industrial Revolution.) But with larger numbers of men leaving for factories and businesses, wives of the upper and middle classes remained at home to attend to the children and the ever more consumer-oriented and luxurious household. These women were labeled with high-flown attributes—"chastity," "purity," "benevolence," and "tenderness"—and were considered to be little lower than the angels.[5]

Men, on the other hand, were believed to have different characteristics. "Lust," for example, was believed a male trait. "Good" women were not expected to be sexually responsive, and men were sometimes referred to as "the grosser sex." Sex was too "gross," in fact, to be enjoyed by many nineteenth-century women. The myth of female frailty and sexual passivity was widely accepted. In fact, many women avoided sex, fearing pregnancy.[6]

The polarization of men's and women's essential qualities reinforced a double standard which lasted many generations. Worse, it gave men exclusive political and economic power with the excuse of "protecting" the "weaker sex." For example, an 1867 song, "Female Suffrage," expresses the typical argument against the women's vote: it would allow the "angels" to descend to the level of the ballot box.

> Then mothers, wives and sisters,
> I beg you keep your place;
> And remain what nature made you—
> The help-meets of our race.

It was not until the 1920s, fueled by an ardent crusader for birth control, Margaret Sanger, that the "sexual revolution" began. Birth control devices, diaphragms, and pessaries were actually available in the 1870s and 1880s to some women, especially in Europe, but diaphragms were not widely used before Margaret Sanger's birth control crusade in the 1920s and 1930s.[7]

Sophisticated big-city women of the 1920s and 1930s with inhibitions gone, or at least loosened, became more assertive in lovemaking. In the media urban women were shown smoking and drinking in public, and the "vamp" was the sought after female image. The blues became the rage in music of the 1920s and 1930s, and the subject of the songs was often sex:

> I'm a one-hour mama, so no one-minute papa ain't the kind of man for
>     me.
> Set your 'larm clock, papa, one hour, that's proper, then love me like I like
>     to be.
>
>                              ("One-Hour Mama")

We watched for changes in the musical expressions concerning love in the two decades immediately prior to the onset of the feminist movement but found only love songs of the moon-and-June variety. "Love" in the 1940s and 1950s meant marrying and settling down.

Middle class suburban women of the fifties had smaller families to care for than their earlier counterparts, and they were the designated consumers of men's incomes. The romantic songs of the time sound Victorian today.

The liberated college women of the 1960s "hippie era" found that the many choices made possible by the new sexual freedom often left them confused and disillusioned. Women, once best friends and confidantes, found themselves now competing with each other for men.

The "new" woman, and the man as well, received mixed messages concerning what now to expect of one another, a problem not resolved even in the 1980s. When should women be soft and gentle, and when is assertive and confident the proper style?[8]

> Well, I tried to be the kind of woman you wanted me to be,
> And it's not your fault that I tried to be what I thought you wanted to see;
> Smilin' face, and shining hair—clothes that I thought you'd like me to
>     wear,
>
>                         ("Custom-Made Woman Blues")

A high divorce rate (one in every two marriages by 1985) came on the heels of sexual liberation. Many women became aware that their hard-won independence would, in the long run, be their most important asset:[9]

> Lovers may come, and lovers may go,
> But I only have what I am,
> And I'd rather be flyin' lonesome and free,
> Than be standin' behind some man.
>
>                         ("Standing Behind a Man")

In the past decade some lesbian women—talented singer-songwriters—formed their own music collectives and record companies in order to produce "woman-identified" music. However, in this more androgynous society, their concerts and albums now attract growing numbers of straight women and men. Like their sisters, lesbian songwriters write about other subjects as well as love, and many of their songs are included throughout the book.

For this volume we chose two genderless love songs that have no victors nor victims, "Keep in Mind (That I Love You)" and "If You Love Me":

> If you love me, if you love, love, love me
> Plant a rose for me
> And if you think you'll love me for a long, long time,
> Plant an apple tree.
>
> ("If You Love Me")

## Activism

Songs of major political and social movements of United States women, past and present, are grouped together in this section.

The first two songs concern colonial women during Revolutionary War times and are followed by songs about slavery, abolition, temperance, and suffrage. Songs of the twentieth-century civil rights movement, the fight for the Equal Rights Amendment, and, finally, the quest for world peace conclude the section. (A group of topical songs under "Contemporary Issues" covers abortion, rape, and environmental problems, which are also activist subjects.)

It is incorrect to presume that all that has happened to liberate women has occurred since the beginning of the 1960s. Colonial women participated in the revolt against England and were therefore the nation's first activists. In 1766 the Daughters of Liberty organized to support the Patriots in the boycotts of English goods.[10] The group held scrap metal drives for making bullets, and their spinning together became a patriotic activity.

"Activism" begins, therefore, with two very singable broadside ballads from the Revolutionary era. "To the Ladies" encouraged colonial women to spin and weave their own cloth rather than to purchase imported textiles from the British, since cloth was Great Britain's largest export to the New World.

> Young ladies in town, and those that live 'round,
> Wear none but your own country linen;
> Of economy boast, let your pride be the most
> To show clothes of your own make and spinnin'.
>
> ("To the Ladies")

"Revolutionary Tea," which follows, is a ballad about the Boston Tea Party. It is followed by an abolitionist hymn, then a favorite slave song, "The Drinking Gourd," which was revived in the 1960s.

Until the 1830s a woman's sphere was her home, as established by the powerful Puritan preachers who, armed with Biblical pronouncements, extolled the duty of woman as man's helpmate and the mother of his children. However, in the 1830s women were encouraged to extend their attribute of benevolence out into the community in order to effect "moral reform."

Prostitution was the first major issue in women's moral reform. A relatively small number of immigrant girls were lured into the profession when they found themselves starving on the shop girls' salary. The venereal diseases brought home by husbands caused the reformers to press for a single sexual standard for both men and women.[11]

The next subject of moral reform was temperance. If an alcoholic husband could not hold a job, his family could starve. Depending on individual state law, there was often little provision for divorce or for a mother's custody of her children.

"Temperance" was not, however, an effort to encourage people to drink moderately, but an all-out campaign to prohibit the sale and consumption of alcoholic beverages in every community across the nation.

The reformers were active in the Anti-Saloon League and in the Women's Christian Temperance Union from 1874 until their goal, the passage of prohibition, was attained in 1919. The WCTU produced an interesting *Campaign Songbook,* from which we have borrowed two rousing songs for this collection.

> Vote, vote, vote for prohibition, vote to banish the saloon,
> Let us stay this awful curse growing every year the worse,
> For we have no further use for the saloon.
>
> ("Vote for Prohibition")

The long-lasting value of women's work in early moral reform, and temperance in particular, is that it honed women's ability to organize themselves, handle funds, and speak in public. The temperance reformers' experience would be crucial to their lengthy battle for the abolition of slavery and women's right to vote.

It was in 1848 that Elizabeth Cady Stanton and Lucretia Mott held the first Women's Rights Convention in Seneca Falls, New York, marking the start of the women's suffrage movement.

> "Yes, Papa votes, but Mama can't, Oh, no, not yet, not yet.
> No matter what the others think, I am a suffragette."
>
> ("I Am a Suffragette")

The original plan for the Seneca Falls convention was to press for economic, social, and legal rights, among them women's property laws, so that women could control their own money and garner some independence as adult citizens of the nation. Surprising today is that a declaration advocating the vote for women passed by only a narrow margin by the very women expressly interested in their rights. However, it was not until seventy-two years later that U.S. women's right to vote (universal suffrage) became the law of the land.

We have included two nineteenth-century songs about suffragists, as well as a modern one about Lucretia Mott, a greatly loved moral reformer of the temperance, abolition, and suffrage movements, in the section titled "Role Models."

The remaining songs in the "Activist" section are contemporary and concern war, nonintervention, and the ERA:

> Isaiah and Peter were quoted left and right.
> Pro and con, rescind or not, became the issued fight.
> "They want to draft your mother, kids, and send her off to war,
> Then you won't have a mommy to love you anymore."
>
> ("The Era of the ERA")

## Labor

Songs about the various kinds of jobs women do, whether traditional or non-traditional, and favorite union songs comprise the section entitled "Labor."

Working class women before the 1830s were generally domestics, shop girls, and farm women. Widows and spinsters were allowed to own boarding houses, inns, and other businesses; although married women did not have that right, they often worked in their husbands' businesses.[12]

The first time women were hired in significant numbers to work outside the home, apart from domestic labor, was in the cotton mills of New England beginning in the 1830s.[13] Songs of the mill workers are numerous and interesting.

> Come out of bed, little sleepyhead, and get you a bite to eat;
> The fact'ry whistle's callin' you, there's no more time to sleep.
>
> ("Babies in the Mill")

The editor of *Sing Out* magazine was curious about our reason for including Dorsey Dixon's "Babies in the Mill," a "man's song" about child labor. We pointed out that 15 percent of the songs of this collection are written by men, and that the earliest mill workers were young women and children, many of them girls.[14]

Whether women were the paid laborers themselves, or part of the workers' families, they have had a significant impact on the early labor movement in the United States. Women were at the forefront of the early mill and mine workers' struggles for decent wages and working conditions.[15] We have included "Bread and Roses" and "Union Maid" (the latter in the "Role Models" section). Aunt Molly Jackson's "I Am a Union Woman," Ella Mae Wiggins's "The Mill Mother's Lament" and Florence Reese's "Which Side Are You On?" are historic songs by women organizers who fought heroically on behalf of mill hands and miners.

Don't scab for the bosses,
Don't listen to their lies.
Us poor folks haven't got a chance
Unless we organize.

Which side are you on?
Which side are you on?

("Which Side Are You On?")


In 1900 female labor in the northern cities was mainly white, young, and unmarried. Half were immigrants or daughters of immigrants. The young women in urban clothing manufacture, the sweatshop workers, were employed under truly deplorable conditions.[16] We have included a ballad about the infamous Triangle fire, a sweatshop disaster in which approximately 146 women died for lack of safety standards.

In that firetrap away up there, with but a single door
So many innocent working girls burned, to live no more.

("The Ballad of the Triangle Fire")


By the 1920s women entered the labor market in large numbers, with a great disparity in pay between men and women. Only a small fraction of women were unionized because most were young women or girls who hoped to work only until marriage. Working mothers could not spare time away from children to participate in union activities. Unions were negative toward including women, who were viewed as a threat to male employment, driving wages down, and reducing job opportunities for breadwinners. Women's wages were regarded as "pin-money," and the jobs men did not want went to women. The needed protective laws often kept women from skilled jobs that might have admitted them to the American Federation of Labor.[17]

During the Great Depression of the 1930s, with large numbers of workers unemployed, men were given job priority. Many women were dismissed from teaching jobs, and the National Education Association reported that in 1930–31 married women teachers were asked to resign.[18] Some federal, state, and local governments refused to hire married women; however, women continued to enter the work force, especially in white collar jobs as clerks and stenographers.[19]

During World War II women comprised half of the then indispensable labor force; they took the place of the men who had gone into the armed forces. Six million women took jobs for the first time, two million in defense plants, where both black and white women learned to assemble guns, tanks, and planes.[20] "Rosie the Riveter" was the stereotypical female American patriot until after the war, when the industry jobs were given back to the men returning home, and the government once again declared homemaking a woman's highest calling.

In the 1950s middle class women obtained educations they could "fall back on," and received two conflicting messages about work: new opportunities were opening up for women, and they were needed at home.

By the end of the 1960s, more than 40 percent of the adult women were already part-time wage earners, largely because extra income was needed to keep up the family's rising standard of living. Women thus began to take their educations more seriously, and the number of women in colleges doubled.[21]

President Kennedy's Commission on the Status of Women was created in 1961 for the purpose of addressing women's issues, their rights, and their roles. The commission was proposed by Esther Peterson, the assistant secretary of labor and head of the Women's Bureau, to which the commission was advisor. Its first chair was Eleanor Roosevelt. By 1967 all fifty states had similar commissions.

The commission's premise is the goal of equality with men, although the Equal Rights Amendment did not receive the commission's support. It was believed that passage of the ERA would destroy the protective legislation for which progressive women's groups had fought. (However, the commission changed its opinion concerning the ERA a decade later.) Even in the 1960s, however, the commission pushed for day care and an end to sexual inequities in social security benefits and unemployment insurance. It paved the way for the Equal Pay Act of 1963, and, although ultimately unenforceable, it was the first federal law against sex discrimination. This was a time of massive equal opportunity legislation in Washington.[22]

A new political pressure group, formed in 1966 to work for full equality of the sexes, was the National Organization for Women (NOW).[23] Betty Friedan, the author of the landmark book, *The Feminine Mystique* (Norton, 1963), was NOW's first president. The group worked for the passage of the ERA, which had been first introduced into Congress by the suffragist Alice Paul in 1923. (In spite of a considerable effort, the ERA was rejected by only six votes in 1983.)

In the 1960s NOW organized nationwide feminist consciousness-raising to deal with sexism, using techniques similar to those used in the civil rights movement while dealing with racism. Some of the major issues the organization addressed in the 1970s and 1980s were child care reform, lesbian civil rights, the defense of abortion rights, pay equity, and sexual discrimination on the job.

Two songs feature women in nontraditional work and illustrate the latter problem:

> When you see me in the truck stop
> And my long hair hangs in curls
> Don't you try to buy my coffee
> 'Cause I ain't no good time girl.
>
> No, I'm a truck drivin' momma
> Five children waiting when I end my run . . .
>
> ("Truck Driving Woman")

> It's dark and cold and dangerous down in that dusty mine,
> And the fear of fire and cave-in are hard to leave behind;

But the life that woman faces down in that lonely hole
Would be brighter now if you'd respect that woman loadin' coal.

("What She Aims To Be")

While women have proven they can do "men's jobs," the women of the 1970s and 1980s have had difficulty persuading men to share what used to be traditional "women's work": child care and homemaking duties. Stress often results when women are not able to share their traditional roles as caretakers of the home and children, and they often find themselves working double time:

It's down at the fac'try, it's out on the line,
A woman is working from morning 'til night,
Then it's back home again to do supper and chores,
Canning and mending and scrubbing the floors,

("Here's to the Women")

It is estimated that young women will spend more than thirty years in the work force. For the working woman pay equity has been the most pressing issue of the 1970s and 1980s. It is being won on local and state levels, even without federal legislation providing for equal pay for equal work, and by 1985, nearly all states had instituted pay equity in some significant form, especially in the area of civil service jobs.[24]

### Contemporary Issues

This section, with sixteen songs on thirteen different topics, begins with two old traditional songs having interesting applications today.

"The Little Orphan Girl" considers the plight of abused and neglected children of the last century. "Brigham, Brigham Young," a song about the virile religious leader, "a shepherd of a heap of pretty little sheep ... and his five and forty wives," has passed into Mormon song tradition, possibly from the stage.

Significantly, "The Pill," a song from the 1960s follows.

Now they're talking o' the pill, they've filled my heart wi' hope;
I'm sitting here and waiting on a signal frae the Pope;
I went along to buy some at fifteen bob a tin,
I hope we hae the Pope's O.K. before me man comes in.

("The Pill")

Then comes this 1970s country song about abortion, a right that pro-choice women defended vigorously in the 1980s:

They say two point five's the limit, and I see the reason why.
Well, I hear it's legal in New York now, and I think I'll give it a try.

Well, you can leave me if you want to, take your lady and give her your all,
And when you've had enough of her, well, don't bother to give me a call.

("Something I've Been Meaning To Tell You")

Also in the songbook's *Contemporary Issues* section are an unaccompanied ballad about a welfare mother, followed by the famous "Take Back the Night." They precede three songs about aging. (One, "Maggie Kuhn," is under "Role Models.") "Coming Into My Years" is a now-famous anthem of power and assertiveness:

I'm a streetwise woman and I'm coming into my pride
I'm a fight-back woman and I'm coming into my pride ...

("Coming Into My Years")

"The Left-Handed Song for Human Rights" that follows pleads for rights of all minorities, while it parodies the hysterical rhetoric of the political right wing. Next is a witty talking blues story of a wheelchair-bound woman winning a race with an able-bodied man and raising some consciousness in the process.

The next three songs deal with environmental issues, including Buffy Sainte-Marie's "Now That the Buffalo's Gone" and Malvina Reynolds's "What Have They Done To the Rain?" Three topical songs, about health food, the Three Mile Island nuclear plant, and nuclear "preparedness," conclude the section.

I've got my Master Charge, Visa card, checkbook and mortgage,
Certificate of birth, marriage and death—
Sure is good to know we're ready for a nuclear war.

("Sure Is Good to Know")

Two extraordinarily important concerns of American women are the threat of AIDS (acquired immune deficiency syndrome) and teenage pregnancy—children having babies. Songs on these topics are now beginning to appear.

### Growing Up

Here are songs that are either for or about children. The section begins with a contemporary lullabye written in a style reminiscent of Joni Mitchell. Titled "Sleepyhead," it is followed by "It's Only a Wee-Wee," and "My Body," two songs of Peter Alsop, who writes and performs music which opens communication between parents and children.

My body's nobody's body but mine
You run your own body, let me run mine!

("My Body")

"The Family Song" honors the various ways in which a family may be constructed today. "Mario's Duck," by Malvina Reynolds, concerns a family in a developing country. "The Witch Song" tells of the historic importance of these fascinating medieval women, while "Turkeys" praises patience and forbearance:

Some days I think that everyone is out to get me down,
And I can't fight the whole darn town,
But if I can let my steam off by running half a mile,
Then I can suffer turkeys with a smile.

And it's don't let the turkeys get you down . . .
Even your best friend can be a turkey now and then . . .

("Turkeys")

The last three songs in the section are serious ballads for older children and adults, including Margie Adam's "Best Friend" ("The Unicorn Song") and Alix Dobkin's never-recorded, "My Kind of Girl."

## Role Models

Consisting of ten songs about famous women, "Role Models" begins with two modern pieces: "Harriet Tubman," in honor of the escaped slave who led hundreds north to freedom along the Underground Railroad, and "Lucretia Mott," a song about the great reformer and suffragist of the last century.

Five advocates for working people are also represented with songs: Mother Jones, Emma Goldman, Joe Hill's "Rebel Girl" (Elizabeth Gurley Flynn), and the generic "Union Maid," written by Woody Guthrie in honor of all struggling union women:

There once was a union maid who never was afraid
Of the goons and ginks and company finks
And the deputy sheriffs who made the raids.

("Union Maid")

The remaining four songs are about Amelia Earhart, the record-setting aviator; Maggie Kuhn, the leader of the Gray Panthers; Dolores Huerta, the vice-president of the United Farm Workers; and Sally Ride, the first American woman in space.

## Women Emerging

The final group of eight songs shows women's personal evolution toward self-awareness, confidence, and independence. By the same token, the songs give a historic view of American women's liberation over the generations.

We begin with an old traditional song of a woman living her life through a man and his work, and follow it with a 1930s cowgirl song about a woman planning to do the same job alongside the man. (Both songs, conveniently, are about breaking wild horses.)

Peggy Seeger's great liberation anthem, "I'm Gonna Be an Engineer," precedes Rosalie Sorrels' serious-comic "Mother's Day Song," which concerns the age-old problem of reconciling the creative life with raising children. The next four are songs of personal independence and freedom, and the book ends with Peggy Seeger's philosophical ballad, "Song of Myself."

## A Final Word

The commentaries which accompany each song provide historical background and important information about women's culture and social concerns. The discography provides audio sources for these and related songs, with information about obtaining them. The songwriters are listed in a separate section with their other work.

We hope we have conveyed to our musicians and readers the pleasure we found in researching the song book and presenting this music. We hope, too, that this anthology will give today's women a sense of community with those women of other eras in our history, and justifiable pride in all of our achievements.

## Notes

1. A 64-cent wage gap in 1985 was reported by both the United States Bureau of Labor Statistics and a Rand Corporation study prepared by economists James P. Smith and Michael Ward. These estimates agree with the figure obtained by the Women's Bureau of the United States Department of Labor, July 1985.

2. Francis A. Beer, *Peace Against War: The Ecology of International Violence* (San Francisco: Freeman and Company, 1981). More than twice as many civilians were killed as soldiers in World War II. The total of both was more than 51 million, not counting murdered Jews. [Tables 2–11 (pp. 25–26), statistics from Wood (1968) and Wright (1965).] During the war in Southeast Asia, 10 percent of all people of Laos, Cambodia, and Vietnam died between 1961 and 1975. American soldiers in at least one case shot all inhabitants of a village (My Lai, May 16, 1968). Rachelle Marshall termed the Vietnam conflict "virtually a war against civilians" in *A Brief Account of Vietnam's Struggle for Independence: America's Longest War* (Philadelphia: Women's International League for Peace and Freedom, 1975).

3. Nancy Woloch, *Women and the American Experience* (New York: Alfred A. Knopf, 1984), p. 23. See also Laurel Thatcher Ulrich, *Good Wives: Image and Reality in Northern New*

*England, 1650–1750* (New York: Alfred A. Knopf, 1982); and paperback, New York: Oxford University Press, 1983.

4. Carl Degler, *At Odds: Women in the Family in America from the Revolution to the Present* (New York: Oxford University Press, 1980), pp. 26–29. Nancy F. Cott, *The Bonds of Womanhood: "Woman's Sphere" in New England, 1780–1835* (New Haven: Yale University Press, 1977). Emily Hahn, *Once Upon a Pedestal* (New York: Thomas Crowell Company, 1974), p. 10.

5. Lois Banner, *Women in Modern America: A Brief History* (New York: Harcourt, Brace, Jovanovich, 1974), p. 16: "The middle class could afford to support the idea of the fragile female; for the working class, it was often a different matter."

6. Gerda Lerner, *The Female Experience: An American Documentary* (New York: Bobbs-Merrill, 1977), pp. 42–45. Margaret Forster, *Significant Sisters: The Grassroots of Active Feminism, 1839–1939* (New York: Alfred A. Knopf, 1984). The latter contains a section on Margaret Sanger and a discussion of nineteenth-century women fearing sexual relations because of continual pregnancy and birth.

7. At this writing there are at least fourteen biographies of Margaret Sanger, the early champion of birth control. See also Sanger's autobiography, reprinted by Dover Publications, New York, 1971. For a good discussion of diaphragms and pessaries, see Boston Women's Health Collective, *Our Bodies, Ourselves* (New York: Simon and Schuster, 1976 edition); page 182 gives 1882 as the date of the invention of the diaphragm.

8. *NOW Guidelines for Feminist Consciousness-Raising* (Washington, D.C.: National Organization for Women, 425 13th St., N.W., Suite 723: 20004, 1983), pp. 34–35.

9. The National Center for Health Statistics projected a 49.6 percent figure for divorce by 1984. The statistical abstracts of the United States listed a divorce rate for nearly half of all marriages by as early as 1980 (Bureau of the Census, United States Department of Commerce, 1983).

10. Linda Grant DePauw, *Founding Mothers: Women in the Revolutionary Era* (New York: Houghton-Mifflin, 1975). An entire chapter is devoted to the Daughters of Liberty. See also Barbara Meyer Wertheimer, *We Were There: The Story of Working Women in America* (New York: Pantheon Books, 1977), pp. 39–41.

11. One of the first surveys of prostitutes was made by the physician at Blackwell's Island Prison, New York City, in the mid-nineteenth century. William Sanger's study of two thousand women in the prostitution business is reported by Boxandall, Rosalyn, Linda Gordon, and Susan Reverby (compilers and editors), in *America's Working Women: A Documentary History—1600 to the Present* (New York: Vintage Books, 1976). Prostitutes came from many walks of life and were patronized by men of all classes; perhaps one in four men visited prostitutes. By mid-century the number of these women was astonishing. In New York, the ratio was approximately one for every fifty-seven men. In Norfolk, Virginia, one for every twenty-six men. Causes for women entering the business were destitution, abandonment by husbands and lovers (often leaving the woman with a child to support), and alcoholism.

12. Page Smith, *Daughters of the Promised Land: Women in American History* (Boston: Little Brown and Company, 1970), p. 52. Wertheimer, *We Were There* pp. 12–13.

13. Philip Foner, *The Factory Girls* (Urbana, Ill.: University of Illinois Press, 1977), Chapter 2, "In the Factories."

14. Ibid. The Pawtucket, Rhode Island, mills, of which Slater's was the first, copied the English system of labor; thus young children were the first operatives. In 1791 Slater's Mill employed seven boys and two girls under twelve years old. In 1820 the factory workers were boys and girls of nine and ten, working twelve to thirteen hours a day, for wages "ranging from 33 to 67 cents a week." The Lowell Mill added girls in the early teens through their 20s, and by the 1820s and 1830s thousands of young women had left farms to enter factories in the company towns of New England.

15. Alice Kessler-Harris, *Out to Work: A History of Wage-Earning Women in the United States* (New York: Oxford University Press, 1982), p. 153. Woloch, *Women and the American Experience*, p. 235.

16. Woloch, *Women and the American Experience*, pp. 236–37).

17. Ibid., pp. 388–89. Gerda Lerner, *The Majority Finds Its Past: Placing Women in History* (New York: Oxford University Press, 1979), p. 61. Lerner mentions the triple burden of work, housework, and children, which kept women from organizing.

18. Susan M. Hartmann, *The Home Front and Beyond: American Women in the 1940s* (Boston: G. K. Hall, 1982), p. 17. Section 23 of the Economy Act of 1932 required that when federal agencies reduced personnel employees married to persons holding federal jobs would be the first to be dismissed. Seventy-five percent of dismissed workers were women.

19. Ibid. See also William H. Chafe, *The American Woman: Her Changing Social, Economic and Political Roles, 1920–1970* (New York: Oxford University Press, 1976), p. 146.

20. Bureau of Labor Statistics, U.S. Department of Labor, Report 710, August 1984.

21. Woloch, *Women and the American Experience*, p. 508.

22. Ibid. Woloch discusses the president's commission, pp. 489–93.

23. *The National NOW Times* is a monthly newsletter detailing the activities of that organization (1401 New York Ave., N.W., Suite 800, Box 7813, Washington, D.C. 20004).

24. United States Department of Labor Women's Bureau Report (Fact Sheet M85), July 1985.

# Friends and Lovers

Country women. Photograph by Susan Jørgensen

Mrs. Smith and her wildcat. Wyoming State Archives, Museums and Historical Department

## 1. WHO'S GONNA SHOE YOUR PRETTY LITTLE FOOT?

This is considered the liberated version of the old folksong, with the last verse: "I don't need no man." (The other version says, "*You* can kiss my red and rosy lips when you come back again.") The song dates back a few centuries, says Pete Seeger.

### Who's Gonna Shoe Your Pretty Little Foot?

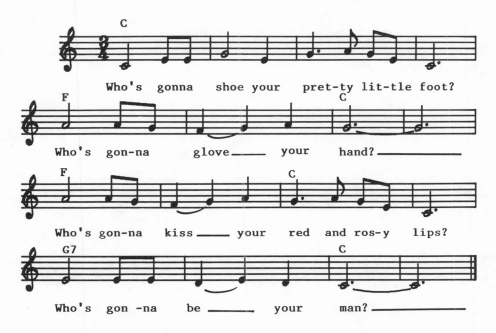

2. Papa's gonna shoe my pretty little foot, Mama's gonna glove my hand,
   Sister's gonna kiss my red and ruby lips, I don't need no man.

3. I don't need no man, my love, I don't need no man.
   Sister's gonna kiss my red and ruby lips, I don't need no man.

Traditional

## 2. THE CUCKOO

In past centuries the cuckoo bird was considered a messenger of spring and a sexual symbol favorable to lovers. It is the origin of the word *cuckold,* in old times meaning a man sexually deceived by his wife (and alluding to the bird's habit of laying its eggs in the nests of other birds).

We like both of these versions, but there are a number of others. The first is approximately the tune which came to us in the eighteenth century from the British Isles. The second is the banjo tune from Galax County, Virginia. The Galax, or "sawmill," tuning of the banjo creates a haunting modal sound.

The "beware young ladies" lyrics are found in "Come All Ye Fair and Tender Ladies," "On Top of Old Smoky," and other folksongs. There are many "floating verses" for the melody of Version II, including this one. The third verse of Version I is not well known.

### The Cuckoo, Version I

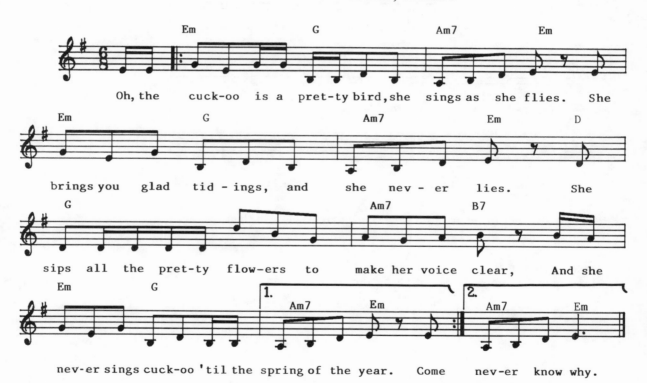

Oh, the cuck-oo is a pret-ty bird, she sings as she flies. She brings you glad tid-ings, and she nev-er lies. She sips all the pret-ty flow-ers to make her voice clear, And she nev-er sings cuck-oo 'til the spring of the year. Come nev-er know why.

Traditional

2. Come all ye fair maidens and listen to me.
   Don't hang your affections on a green growing tree,
   For the leaves they will wither, and the roots they will die,
   And you'll all be forsaken and never know why.

3. But if he will leave me, I'll not be forlorn,
   And if he'll forswear me, I'll not be forsworn.
   I'll get myself up in my best finery,
   And I'll walk as proud by him as he walks by me.

## The Cuckoo, Version II

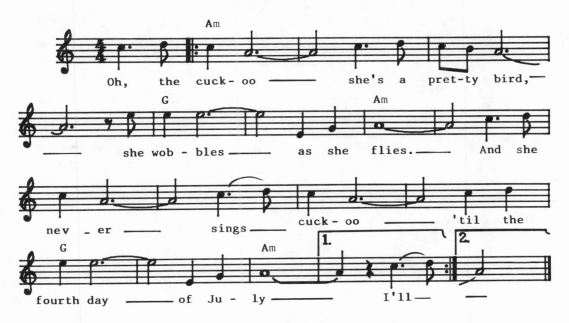

Oh, the cuck-oo ——— she's a pret-ty bird, ——— she wob-bles ——— as she flies. ——— And she nev - er ——— sings ——— cuck-oo ——— 'til the fourth day ——— of Ju - ly ——— I'll ———

2. I'll build me a mansion on the mountain so high,
   So I can see Willie as I'm riding by.

Traditional

### 3. CARELESS LOVE

In isolated mountain regions women still sing ballads of forsaken or lost love. In these old songs the girl was often pregnant, hence the words, "Now I wear my apron high." This old blues favorite has many sources.

## Careless Love

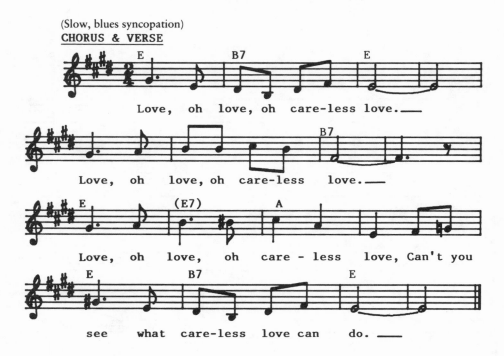

1. Once I wore my apron low, [repeat three times]
   You followed me through rain and snow.

2. Now I wear my apron high, [repeat three times]
   You see my door but pass it by.

3. I cried last night and the night before, [repeat three times]
   Gonna cry tonight and cry no more.

4. I love my mama, and my papa, too, [repeat three times]
   But I'd leave them both to go with you.

Traditional

## 4., 5., 6.  SINGLE GIRL, WHEN I WAS SINGLE MARRYING'S ALL I CRAVED, and SINGLE LIFE

No women's songbook would be complete without an Appalachian "single girl" song. Traditional banjo player and singer Hedy West performed this little medley on an early album, simply called *Hedy West* (Vanguard 9124).

According to Hedy's grandmother, Lillie Mulkey West, these songs were typically sung at social gatherings in the area where her family lived for generations. Often on a Saturday night or Sunday after church a neighbors' party would bring young and old together, and while the elders talked and sang their favorite songs, usually of a religious nature, the young people gathered in another room to sing love songs and ditties.

While these friends were certainly not expressing a particularly strong social comment when they sang these "single girl" pieces, today we see them as typical of many songs of the Southern mountains that tell of a poor girl who becomes yet poorer through marriage and childbearing. The freedom of a single life looks especially appealing in retrospect.

Hedy West is a collector of her family's music, a North Georgia singer, and banjoist of the authentic Appalachian tradition. Like Jean Ritchie, she is urban in education (with a degree in music composition from Columbia University), and she lives in New York City. She has never lost touch with her roots, however, but sings the songs of her ancestors' British Isles tradition and those of the cotton mill hands, the farmers, and the miners of Appalachia. She is the daughter of the poet and once-cotton mill unionizer Don West, director of the Appalachian South Folklife Center in Pipestem, West Virginia.

Photograph of Lillie Mulkey West taken by Hedy West, 1976

Hedy West. Photograph by David Gahr

## Single Girl

Sin - gle girl, sin - gle girl,
go - in' where she please, A married girl,
a married girl, has a ba - by on her knees.

2. A single girl will go to town and buy and buy and buy,
   A married girl, stays at home, and rocks the cradle and cries.

3. A single girl, a single girl, wears clothes so fine,
   A married girl, a married girl, wears just any old kind.

4. A single girl, a single girl, has good things to eat,
   A married girl, a married girl, has cabbage without the meat.

5. A single girl, single girl, you'd better stay,
   Don't become a married girl, to grieve your life away.

## When I Was Single Marryin's All I Craved

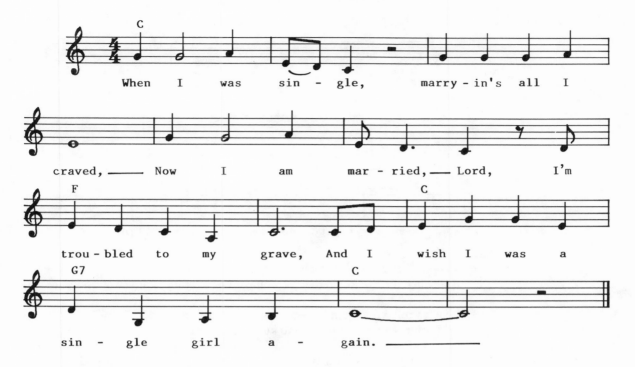

When I was sin - gle, marry - in's all I craved, _____ Now I am mar - ried, _____ Lord, I'm trou - bled to my grave, And I wish I was a sin - gle girl a - gain. _____

2. Dishes to wash, the spring to go to,
   I ain't got no one to help me, Lord, I got it all to do,
   And I wish I was a single girl again.

3. Two little children lyin' in the bed,
   Both of them so hungry, Lord, they can't raise up their heads,
   And I wish I was a single girl again.

4. I took in some washing, made a dollar or two,
   My husband went and stole it, Lord, and I don't know what to do,
   And I wish I was a single girl again.

   *(Repeat first verse)*

## Single Life

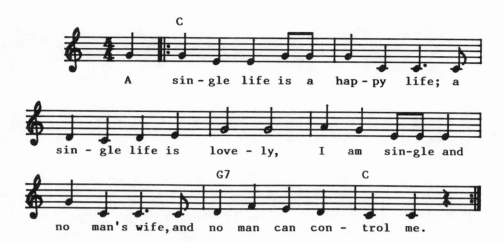

A sin-gle life is a hap-py life; a sin-gle life is love-ly, I am sin-gle and no man's wife, and no man can con-trol me.

2. Some will court you for a while, only to deceive you,
And when they've found they've won your heart, they'll run away and leave you.

3. I don't want a roving man, a man with too much money,
All I want is a nice young man to kiss and call me "honey."

4. Some will come on Saturday night, and some will come on Sunday,
If you give 'em half the chance, they'll stay with you 'til Monday.

*(Repeat first verse)*

## 7. CAL-LIB-SONG

Annette Kirk sang this song for us onto a tape, with a calypso backup, and we signed her up for this volume. However, we reluctantly had to turn away her second and third numbers: "Let's Keep the X in Xmas," and "Don't Let Your Doggie Do," a fine ecology song.

We also asked for a short biography, and we print every word of it here: "Annette Kirk was born in Brooklyn in 1937 and lived in discomfort during her post-puberty years due to wearing waist cinchers, spike heels, girdles and garter belts, crinoline petticoats, padded bras, and boned bathing suits. At twenty she married, dropped out of college, and gave up the guitar for a husband who wanted 'a feminine woman without callouses on her fingers.' "

In 1972 she learned that it was permissible to admit she had calloused fingers, and she gave up the husband (but not men). She presently works for a research laboratory at Cold Spring Harbor, New York, where she is production manager of the publications department. Before entering publishing, however, she was an elementary school teacher in New York City. Some of her children's songs have been recorded on the Creative Materials label. As for her songs for adults, the influence of Tom Lehrer's satire is evident in the lyrics; she claims to be incapable of writing a serious song.

### Cal-Lib-Song

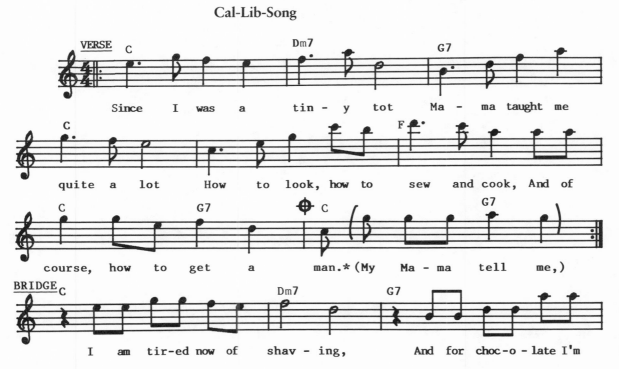

VERSE

Since I was a tin-y tot Ma-ma taught me

quite a lot How to look, how to sew and cook, And of

course, how to get a man.* (My Ma-ma tell me,)

BRIDGE

I am tir-ed now of shav-ing, And for choc-o-late I'm

*"Man" is pronounced "mon," "plan" is "plon," true calypso style.

crav - ing   Lib - er - a - tion flag is  wav - ing.

CODA  Got  to  change  my  plan.* (I  tell  my  Ma - ma, )

man,  hey!     that will  be  my  man.

Mama read the magazine
Watch the color TV screen
Each advertiser made her wiser
At how to get a man.

2. My mama tell me:
   "Don't show too much common sense
   I know from experience
   Use your head at the stove and bed
   And you'll surely get a man."

   My mama tell me:
   "Stay slender like sugar cane
   Eat no chocolate and no chow mein
   False eyelashes and perfume splashes
   Will help you get a man."

3. Soon I went on my first date
   Golly, but I could not wait
   Mama gave me every recipe
   For how to get a man.

   My mama tell me:
   "Go gargle with Listerine
   Take a bath in Mr. Clean
   Lift your dress up, spray FSD up
   That's how to get a man."

4. Don't you tippy-toe down the stairs
   'Til you clip your nose's hairs
   Shave your armpits and make them charmpits
   That's how to get a man.

Cover up with acnomel
Store-bought hair made of dynel
Lots of bother, but ask your father
That's how I got a man.

5. Finally, a man I got
   He eat and he drink a lot
   Got big belly and kind of smelly
   But still it is a man.

   I make for him chocolate cake
   Half a grapefruit myself I take
   He get fatter and I get flatter
   But still I got a man
   (Bridge)

6. I tell my mama:
   "You can keep your recipe
   For your femininity
   You may love it, but you may shove it
   And you may keep that man."

   I tell my mama:
   "When a man for me does fall
   He will love me hair and all
   He'll admire though I perspire
   And that will be my man, hey!
   That will be my man.

## 8. THE DEBUTANTE BALL

It was not long ago that girls were raised to be "husband material." Affluent families often participated in debutante balls, where an eligible daughter was presented to society. In larger cities the practice is still common, as it is in Southern society as well.

In the past, marriage was essentially an economic contract. A marriageable girl's family was often expected to contribute a substantial sum, rather like a dowry. In poorer families the girl bartered her services as a housekeeper, sexual partner, and bearer of children in exchange for financial support and security.

The writer of "The Debutante Ball," Willie Tyson, was herself raised in the South and still lives there. She considers herself primarily a lyricist, although we know her as a feminist singer, songwriter, and humorist. This is from her album, *Debutante* (see the Discography).

Misamerika I, II. Photographs by Sandy Stone.

# The Debutante Ball

Get your gold la-mé slip-pers from the clo-set, ___ The ones your ma-ma bought for you to-day. ___ Get that lav-en-der chif-fon thing you want-ed, I can't be-lieve the price I had to pay. ___ Get dressed up like a queen now, and don't for-get them fan-cy pearls. ___ Meet me di-rect-ly in the hall ___ I'm tak-in' my fine — bred, South-ern daugh-ter — girl Out ___ to the Deb-u-tante—

Words and music by Willie Tyson.
©1977 by Willola Tyson.
All rights reserved. Used by permission.

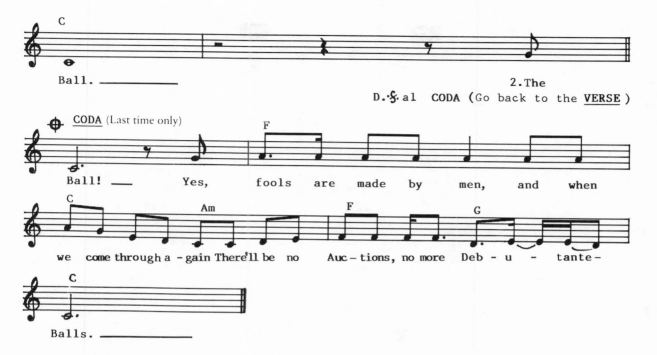

Ball. _____

D.%. al  CODA (Go back to the **VERSE**)

2.The

CODA (Last time only)

Ball! ___    Yes,    fools   are   made   by    men,    and    when

we   come through a - gain There'll be   no    Auc – tions, no more  Deb – u – tante-

Balls. _____

2. The Debutante Ball is my favorite function,
   It happens every year about this time.
   It coincides with our local cattle auction,
   The best breedin' stock in the county all in a line.
   I run back and forth between the Auction and the Ball,
   Thinkin', "Sherwood, ain't you lucky, ain't you fine?
   The best cows on four legs and the prettiest gals on two—
   Ain't nobody else's but mine."

3. Get your gold lamé halter from the tack room,
   The one you won all them ribbons in last spring.
   You been a winner in your time, Old Red Satin,
   But since you had them three calves you ain't won a thing.
   Brush up your hide now, and don't forget to trim your hooves,
   Leave behind you a clean stall.
   I'm gonna drop you off at the cattle auction,
   On my way to the Debutante Ball.

4. This year's Ball is quite a splendid occasion,
   I feel it in my bones, it's gonna be fine.
   I'm standin' here in great anticipation,
   As the time nears for my little girl to walk the line.
   What's this I see, clompin' up to me,
   Stompin' and sheddin' all over the hall?
   My God, it's Red Satin, how, how, how, how could this have happened?
   It's my cow at the Debutante Ball!

## 9. BEDROOM BACKLASH

It's interesting to compare this view of sexual politics to those of Ida Cox in the next song. (For the biography of Carol Hanisch, see p. 272.)

### Bedroom Backlash

Words and music by Carol Hanisch.
© 1978 by Carol Hanisch.
Used by permission.

CHORUS

Oh for the day— when wo-men get free. Oh for the day— when men ac-cept it. No more shames No more games Just "Yes, yes, yes!" ——————

2. Women's liberation came along
   said men can't have all the say
   of if and how and where and when
   at the end of a weary day.

   For woman wants her fair share too
   in pleasure as in pay
   but he still wants to be the boss
   so he turns away.

   With
   "No." "Yes."
   "No." "Yes."
   "Damn it, woman, I've got a headache."

   *Chorus*

## 10. ONE-HOUR MAMA

It took many women a long time and a lot of liberation to talk about sex in the terms Carol Hanisch describes in "Bedroom Backlash." It was the 1970s before female sexuality was anything but "aggressive behavior" and "bitchiness"—a turn-off to men. Love, with all its ins and outs, was the most common of the subjects of urban blues.

As the spirituals were based on heaven (religion), the blues were down to earth. The earliest rural blues came northward with the blacks from the plantations to the cities—especially New Orleans—where there was work along the Mississippi. The country (folk) blues mingled with the music of the urban, formally trained Creoles. Aspects of jazz took over the rural blues, and the folk quality of the blues largely disappeared.

Many of the early blues singers came from the black churches. (Some, like Ethel Waters, would convert and renounce their earlier blues singing.)

The minstrel shows, rather folk and rural, were popular from the civil war until vaudeville took their place twenty-five years later. The shows were badly racist, but they gave blacks the first opportunity to perform on stage. An early tent show was Ma Rainey (and her husband) and the Rabbit Foot Minstrels, which featured Rainey's protégé, Bessie Smith. Later, then-young Ida Cox would perform in the show.

The New Orleans bawdy houses where the blues and jazz singers had their start were shut down by the U.S. Department of the Navy in World War I, and the black entertainers moved up the Mississippi to Chicago and then New York, where prohibition was in full swing and black and white alike wanted to hear the music. The Chicago-style jazz era was open to women singers, but they were not allowed to appear in mixed-race stage performances. Billie Holiday and other light-skinned blacks had to blacken their faces further to play all night with the all-black bands.

One of the greatest of all the classic blues singers was Ida Cox, born in Georgia in 1896. As a child she became interested in music and sang in the African Methodist Church choir. In her teens she ran away from home to tour with White and Clark's Black and Tan Minstrels, then with the Rabbit Foot Minstrels. She also appeared on radio in Memphis and was featured on the vaudeville circuit as it replaced the minstrel shows. In 1929 and 1930 she toured in her own road show revue, *Raisin' Cain,* and in 1934 worked with Bessie Smith in a revue at the Apollo Theater in New York City. Later she performed at Cafe Society Downtown and was featured in a Carnegie Hall concert titled *From Spirituals to Swing.*

Ida Cox married at least two times, perhaps three, and she had a child. Among her many blues songs are "Wild Women Don't Have the Blues" and "One-Hour Mama." The best source of her songs is Rosetta Records. "One-Hour Mama" is arranged from Independent Women's Blues, Volume I: *Mean Mothers* (see the Discography).

## One-Hour Mama

I've al - ways heard____ that haste makes waste,— so
I be - lieve in tak - in' my time.____ The high - est moun - tain
can't be raced,____ it's some-thing you must slow-ly climb. I
want a slow and eas-y man, he need-n't ev-er take the lead,
____ 'Cause I work on that long - time plan, and I
ain't a - look - in' for no speed.____ I'm a
one - ho - ur ma - ma, so no one-min-ute pa - pa
ain't the kind of man____ for me.____ Set your

Words and music by Ida Cox.
Transcribed from the singing of Ida Cox by Hilda E. Wenner.

**LAST TIME ONLY**

One – ho – ur ma – ma,   so   no one – min – ute pa – pa

ain't  the  kind  of  man ———— for me! ————

*(Other bridges)*
I can't stand no crowin' rooster, what just likes a hit or two,
Action is the only booster of just what my man can do.

I don't want no imitation, my requirements ain't no joke,
'Cause I've got pure indignation for a guy what's lost his stroke.

*(Verse again)*
I'm a one-hour mama, so no one-minute papa ain't the kind of man for me.
Set your 'larm clock, papa, one hour, that's proper, then love me like I like to be.

*(Last bridge and end)*
I may want love for an hour, then decide to make it two;
Takes an hour 'fore I get started, maybe three before I'm through.
I'm a one-hour mama, so no one-minute papa ain't the kind of man for me!

## 11. RAMBLING WOMAN

Hazel Dickens writes many songs that speak to the sensibilities of women. In this one she speaks for a woman who is clear about her goals and knows that marriage won't allow her to do what she needs to do.

Hazel Dickens is recognized as one of the best traditional singers in the United States today. She was raised one of eleven children in the coal camps of West Virginia, where the early style of bluegrass music played an important part in her daily life. Whether singing an old English ballad, a Carter family song, a driving bluegrass tune, or one of her own socially conscious songs, she carries on the Appalachian tradition of her childhood. Her songs speak of basic bread-and-butter issues when she performs for coal miners' benefits, women's organizations, or for welfare rights groups.

Hazel Dickens composed most of the sound track of the Academy Award-winning documentary, *Harlan County, U.S.A.* Emmylou Harris, The New Riders of the Purple Sage, and many others have recorded her songs.

She was part of the famous duet, Hazel and Alice, with Alice Gerrard, and the Strange Creek Singers, with Gerrard and Mike Seeger. *Hard-Hitting Songs for Hard-Hit People* is her first solo recording. *By The Sweat of My Brow* followed. An album of women's coal mining songs called *They'll Never Keep Us Down* features four songs of Hazel Dickens (see the Discography).

Besides appearing at most of the major folk festivals, Dickens has performed at Lincoln Center in New York, the Kennedy Center in Washington, D.C., Madison Square Garden, and the White House during the Carter administration. She lives in Washington, D.C.

Hazel Dickens. Photograph by David Gahr

## Rambling Woman

You've been hand- in' me a lot ____ of sweet talk ____ ____ 'bout things ____ you want us to do, ____ Well, you're talk - in' '— bout set - tlin'__ down in a dream house built____ for two;_____ Well, I hate to dis- ap- point you, _____ but I don't ____ fit in - to that____ plan _____ For I'm a ram- bling wo- man,____ — and you're ___ a home-lov- in' ____ man. ____ Yes, I'm ____ a ram- bling wo- man, _____ but I

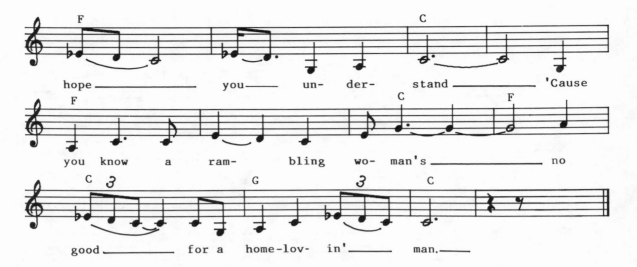

hope _____ you \_\_\_ un- der- stand _____ 'Cause

you know a ram- bling wo- man's _____ no

good _____ for a home-lov- in' _____ man. \_\_\_

2. There's a whole lot of places my eyes are longing to see,
   Where there is no dream cottage, no babies on my knee,
   And there's a whole lot of people just waiting to shake my hand,
   And you know a rambling woman's no good for a home-lovin' man.
   *Chorus*

3. Take all of that sweet talk and give it to some other girl,
   Who'd be happy to rock your babies and live in your kind of world,
   For I'm a different kind of woman, got a different set of plans,
   You know a rambling woman's no good for a home-lovin' man.
   *Chorus*

## 12. BEST OF FRIENDS

Debby McClatchy, originally from San Francisco, attended Oakland and San Francisco State College during the turbulent years of S. I. Hayakawa and the free speech movement. She now makes her home in the Appalachian Mountains of central Pennsylvania. "Times are changing, and the marriage vow is no longer the viable institution it once was," she says. "Couples are finding that compatibility, not legality, has to be the basis for a working arrangement."

McClatchy, a skilled entertainer, is equally at home with old-time mountain music as with her many topical songs and those of the California Gold Rush. (She has a forebear who was a forty-niner.) She is an accomplished instrumentalist on the banjo, mountain dulcimer, guitar, concertina, and "lost instruments," including the ukelin and the Hawaiian tremaloa.

She attends every folk festival she can, either as the caterer or a performer. "Half the time I'm there to feed the crowd, and half the time I'm there to play."

This song is from her album aptly titled *Homemade Goodies*. At this writing, she has released seven albums (see the Discography).

### Best of Friends

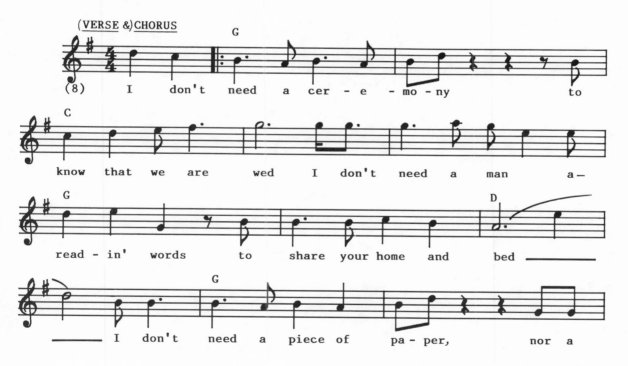

gold - en wed – ding band I just need for you to
love me, to be my sweet, sweet man. ⸺

1. Oh, people move and change a lot,
    there's no use to deny
That the ways that went in Grandma's
    day don't best suit you and I
So let's live our life now day by day,
    with no thought to the end
And if we part, we know we've gained
    by being best of friends
*Chorus*

2. Oh, the wise man said to follow your
    own heart through every day
For you need a peace within yourself
    to help others on their way
So let's live our life now day by day,
    no thought to the end
And if we part, we know we've gained
    from being best of friends
*Chorus*

## 13. ODE TO A GYM TEACHER

Alix Dobkin explains the lesbian singer's dilemma in the songbook *All Our Lives:* "It is hard for a heterosexual feminist to find traditional songs she can feel comfortable singing. It is hard for a lesbian to find traditional *or* contemporary songs that she can relate to. Lesbians share many battlefronts with all women, but there are some very real personal and political struggles that only lesbians deal with." Dealing with it here, "Ode to a Gym Teacher" is a classic of its kind, a favorite of Meg Christian fans.

Born in Lynchburg, Virginia, Christian first expressed her interest in music at age five, and as a teenager learned to play guitar from recordings of Joan Baez, the Kingston Trio, and Buffy Sainte-Marie. She studied music at the University of North Carolina, Chapel Hill, where she "discovered Doc Watson's picking and the beauty of the classical guitar." She became the school's first guitar major.

After college she began her career playing local clubs in Washington, D.C., and in 1973 was ready to record her first album, *I Know You Know.* She cofounded Olivia Records, and was their first performer to cut an album for the company. Since that time three solo albums followed, then the live recording of the two concerts celebrating the tenth anniversary of Olivia: *Meg and Cris at Carnegie Hall,* with Cris Williamson. The hall was sold out both nights.

Meg Christian. Photograph by Irene Young

# Ode to a Gym Teacher

She was a big tough wo-man, the first to come a-long That showed me be-ing fe-male meant you still could be strong. — And though grad-u-a-tion meant that we had to part — She'll al-ways be a play-er on the ball-field of my — heart. FINE (umMmm) I wrote her name on my note-pad, and inked it on my dress. And I etched it on my lock-er, and I carved it on my desk. And I paint-ed big red hearts — with her i-ni-tials on my

Words and music by Meg Christian.
©1974 by Thumbelina Records.
All rights reserved. Used with permission.

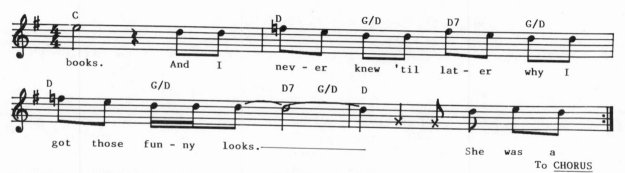

books.    And   I   nev - er   knew 'til   lat - er   why   I

got   those   fun - ny   looks.———————— She was a
To **CHORUS**

2. Well, in gym class while the others talked of boys that they loved,
I'd be thinking of new aches and pains the teacher had to rub.
And when other girls went to the prom, I languished by the phone,
Calling up and hanging up if I found out she was home.
*Chorus*

3. I sang her songs by Johnny Mathis, I gave her everything—
A new chain for her whistle, and some daisies in the spring.
Some suggestive poems for Christmas by Miss Edna Millay,
And a lacy, lacy, lacy card for Valentine's Day.
*Chorus*

4. So you just go to any gym class and you'll be sure to see
One girl who sticks to teacher like a leaf sticks to a tree,
One girl who runs the errands and who chases all the balls,
One girl who may grow up to be the gayest of all.
*Chorus*

## 14. CUSTOM-MADE WOMAN BLUES

Alice Gerrard's blues song speaks to many women disappointed in love when they have done "all the right things" to please a man. As Alice says, this is due to the confusion and ambivalence of changing roles and values.

Gerrard is originally from California, and comes from a musical family. Since 1954 she has lived in Ohio and then on the East Coast; during the mid-50s she became interested in folk and country music, taught herself guitar and banjo, and settled in the Washington-Baltimore area where many Southern people live. The musicians among them found a friend in Alice, whose living room became famous for all-night picking parties, and where she learned their styles.

Gerrard worked for two years with Hazel Dickens and recorded two duet albums with her. She was part of two other renowned groups: The Strange Creek Singers and the Harmony Sisters (see the Discography). She sings and performs at concerts and festivals all over the United States and occasionally abroad. Her songs, like "Custom-Made Woman," make powerful statements.

### Custom-Made Woman Blues

Well, I tried to be the kind of wo-man you want-ed me to be, And it's not your fault that I tried to be what I thought you want-ed to see; Smi-lin' face, and shin-ing hair, clothes that I thought you'd like me to wear,

Made to please, and not ____ to tease— it's the
cus - tom — made wo - man blues. ____

2. Yes, I tried to be the kind of woman you wanted me to be,
   And I tried to see life your way, and say all the things you'd like me to say;
   Lovin' thoughts, gentle hands, all guaranteed to keep ahold of your man,
   Made to please and not to tease—it's the custom-made woman blues.

3. And now you say you're tired of me, and all those things I thought you wanted me to be,
   Is it true you want someone who knows how to think and do on her own?
   Lord, it's hard to realize the lessons I learned so young were nothing but lies,
   Made to please, and not to tease—it's the custom-made woman blues.

## 15. WE DON'T NEED THE MEN

Malvina Reynolds wrote this song in 1959, a few years before "women's liberation" or *The Feminine Mystique* were heard of. Over the years she wrote about several of the topics relating to the women's movement, including a song about rape ("The Judge Said"), one about a homeless flower child ("The Rim of the World"), and one concerning a mother who finds herself pregnant too many times ("Rosy Jane").

It was Malvina's policy never to be vindictive against men in getting equal opportunities for women. She said it never did the cause good. She was married to one of her best admirers, and the man who encouraged her to sing her own songs, even though her voice was not pretty.

Humor is a fine weapon. Malvina Reynolds's cracked and crotchety voice did fine justice to "We Don't Need the Men." The introduction needs to take its time (ad lib for effect), and the verses assume a calypso beat. Her own version of the song appears on *Malvina—Held Over* (the Discography lists all of her records and songbooks).

Malvina Reynolds. Photograph by Alejandro Stuart

# We Don't Need the Men

INTRO. (Ad lib)

It says in Cor-o-net Mag-a-zine, June nine-teen fif-ty six, page ten, That mar-ried wo-men are not as hap-py as wo-men who have no men. Mar-ried wo-men are crank-y, frus-trat-ed and dis-gus-ted, While sin-gle women are bright and gay— cre-a-tive—and well ad-just-ed.

VERSE 1.

we don't need the men, We don't need the men, We don't need to have them 'round, ex-cept for now and then. They can come to

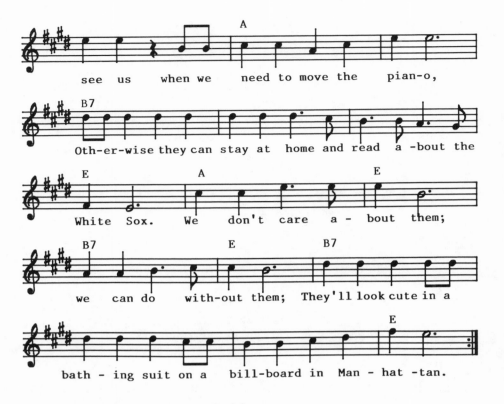

see us when we need to move the pian-o,

Oth-er-wise they can stay at home and read a -bout the White Sox. We don't care a - bout them; we can do with-out them; They'll look cute in a bath - ing suit on a bill-board in Man - hat -tan.

2. We don't need the men, we don't need the men,
   We don't need to have them 'round, except for now and then.
   They can come to see us when they have tickets for the symphony,
   Otherwise they can stay at home and play a game of pinochle.
   We don't care about them; we can do without them;
   They'll look cute in a bathing suit on a billboard in Wisconsin.

3. We don't need the men, we don't need the men,
   We don't need to have them 'round, except for now and then.
   They can come to see us when they're feeling pleasant and agreeable,
   Otherwise they can stay at home and holler at the T.V. programs.
   We don't care about them; we can do without them;
   They'll look cute in a bathing suit on a billboard in Madagascar.

4. We don't need the men, we don't need the men,
   We don't need to have them 'round, except for now and then.
   They can come to see us when they're all dressed up with a suit on,
   Otherwise they can stay at home (spoken) and drop towels in their *own* bathroom.
   We don't care about them; we can do without them;
   They'll look cute in a bathing suit on a billboard in Tierra del Fuego.

## 16. IF YOU LOVE ME

Malvina Reynolds's songs and her singing influenced many other performers and songwriters. She wrote "Little Boxes" and "Turn Around" in the sixties, but she also composed love songs, political songs, songs about the special concerns of women, such as birth control and raising children. She made albums for children and gave concerts for political, environmental, and social causes. We included "If You Love Me" as one of several gender-free and victimless love songs.

### If You Love Me

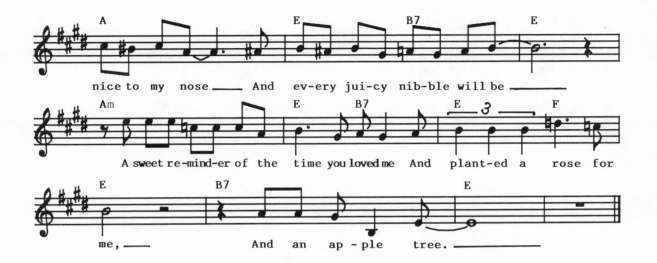

nice to my nose____ And ev-ery jui-cy nib-ble will be ____

A sweet re-mind-er of the time you loved me And plant-ed a rose for

me, ____ And an ap-ple tree. ____

## 17. KEEP IN MIND (THAT I LOVE YOU)

Few are untouched by this song written by Jane Voss, who also penned "Standing Behind a Man" (p. 274). She writes and sings what Holly Near has called "responsible love songs," those that stress equality in relationships.

We have especially enjoyed researching songs about friendship. As Jane says, "Lovers may come lovers may go ... Sometimes the only thing that keeps us going is our friends." (Her biography is also on p. 274.)

Jane Voss. Photograph by Elizabeth Emery

### Keep in Mind (That I Love You)

What are friends for, but to let you know you're

shove, —— Don't be dis - cour - aged, keep in

mind that you are loved. ——

shove, May it ev - er be a bless-ing, keep in

mind that you are loved. ——

2. We'll be parting in a day or so
        to go our separate ways,
   And I don't expect we'll meet again
        for many's the sad long day;
   But I hope you won't be lonely,
        and you'll never lack for friends,
   And may each and every one of them
        be true as I have been.
   *Chorus*

3. Sometimes this crazy world
        can make you feel you have no place,
   As if there's no one on this earth
        who's glad to see your face;
   But those who do not know you well
        are the poorer by far,
   So remember there are those of us
        who know how good you are.
   *Last chorus*

        Keep in mind that I love you,
            keep in mind that I care,
        Though the world that's moving 'round you
            may bring grief and despair.
        When you find yourself alone
            amidst the city's push and shove,
        May it ever be a blessing,
            keep in mind that you are loved.

FRIENDS AND LOVERS    39

# Activism

I Sell the Shadow to Support the Substance.
SOJOURNER TRUTH.

Sojourner Truth. National Portrait Gallery, Smithsonian Institution, Washington, D.C.

### 18. BUTTERMILK HILL (JOHNNY HAS GONE FOR A SOLDIER)

"Buttermilk Hill" is a love song about war. The words of the originally Irish chorus have been so corrupted by time and by its many singers that it has the approximate meaning of "tra, la, la." The line "If I should die for Sally Bobolink" has many variants as well.

"Buttermilk Hill" refers to a location near the Hudson River, and this version dates to Washington's Continental Army. Other versions have been found in many areas of the United States.

The words of the verses themselves remain in virtually the same form in each of the published versions we have found in the differing locations, with the following exception. This is a version we heard from a local folksinger, which shows the influence of the peace movement on the folk process.

> Oh my baby, oh my love,
> Gone a rainbow, gone a dove,
> Your father was my only love,
> Johnny has gone for a soldier.

> —Peter, Paul and Mary*

**Buttermilk Hill (Johnny Has Gone for a Soldier)**

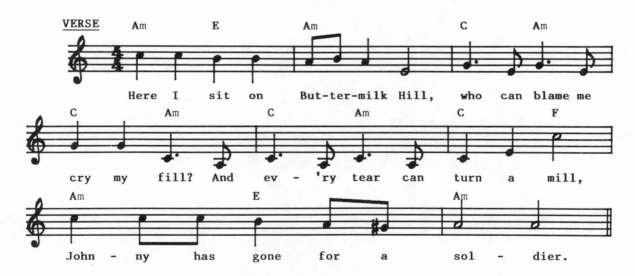

Traditional

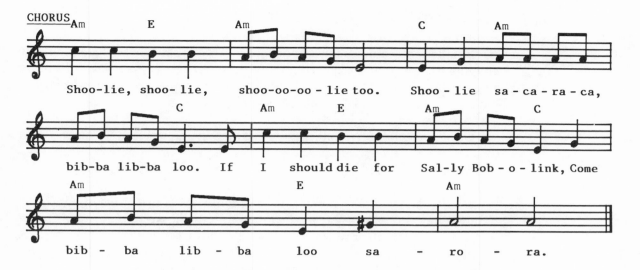

**CHORUS**

Shoo-lie, shoo-lie, shoo-oo-oo-lie too. Shoo-lie sa-ca-ra-ca,

bib-ba lib-ba loo. If I should die for Sal-ly Bob-o-link, Come

bib - ba lib - ba loo sa - ro - ra.

2. I sold my rack and sold my reel, I even sold my spinning wheel
   To buy my love a sword of steel, Johnny has gone for a soldier.
   *Chorus*

3. Me, oh my, I loved him so, broke my heart to see him go;
   And only time will heal my woe, Johnny has gone for a soldier.
   *Chorus*

## 19. TO THE LADIES

In the 1600s women had many opportunities to participate in the life of the developing nation. It was not uncommon for women to operate sawmills and slaughterhouses, to run blacksmith shops, print shops and newspapers, schools and inns, to supervise plantations, practice medicine, and even to speak out in courts of law.

As the conflict between the colonists and England worsened, women took an active part in the rebellion. When, in 1768, a boycott of British goods was organized, women refused to use British cloth on which a tax had been imposed.

*To the Ladies*, a very popular song published as a broadside in approximately thirty versions, influenced women to wear homespun garments as a practical symbol of their resistance to British injustice.

The tune is reminiscent of the British Isles music performed in many folk circles today. The song was recorded during the nation's bicentennial celebration.

### To the Ladies

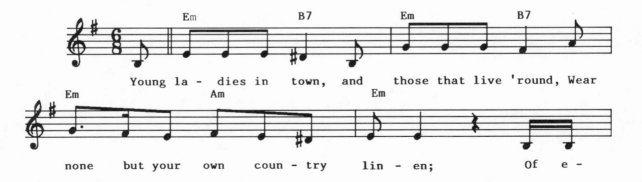

Young la - dies in town, and those that live 'round, Wear none but your own coun - try lin - en; Of e -

Traditional

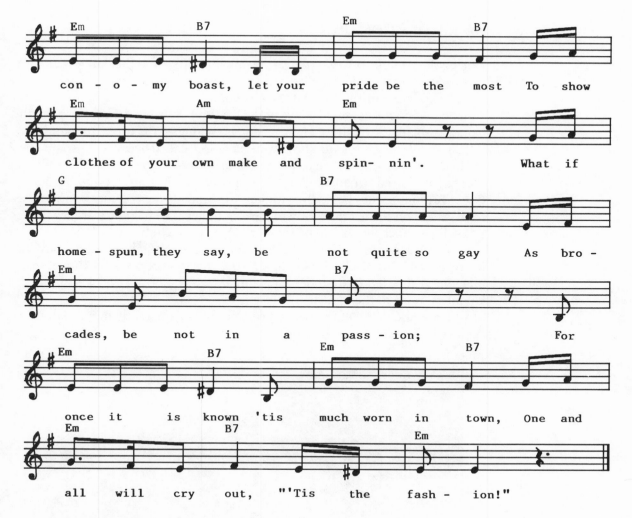

con - o - my boast, let your pride be the most To show
clothes of your own make and spin- nin'. What if
home - spun, they say, be not quite so gay As bro -
cades, be not in a pass - ion; For
once it is known 'tis much worn in town, One and
all will cry out, "'Tis the fash - ion!"

2. And as one all agree, that you'll not married be
   To such as will wear London factory,
   But at first sight refuse, tell 'em such you will choose
   As encourage our own manufactory.
   So no more ribbons wear, nor in rich silks appear,
   Love your country much better than fine things;
   Begin without passion, 'twill soon be the fashion
   To grace your smooth locks with a twine string.

3. These do without fear, and to all you'll appear
   Fair, charming, true, lovely and clever;
   Though the times remain darkish, young men will be sparkish,
   And love you much better than ever.
   What if homespun, they say, be not quite so gay
   As brocades, be not in a passion;
   For once it is known 'tis much worn in town,
   One and all will cry out, " 'Tis the fashion!"

## 20. REVOLUTIONARY TEA

During the American Revolution women willingly shared the dangers and privations in the colonial struggle for independence from England.

By the time of the Revolution, the colonists had a repertory of lyrics by American composers, set to tunes of the traditional British Isles folk songs and ballads. Amateurs are more likely to sing new songs if the tunes are familiar.

This allegory is told in a broadside ballad, so called because the songs were printed on paper longer than it was wide and because they often made a political statement ("fired broadside" at the opposition). A domineering "Queen," Great Britain, argues heatedly with her "daughter," the colonies, who refuses to pay a tax on the tea the mother is selling to her. The daughter argues that as a family member she should be required to do no such thing.

The Tea Act of 1773, taxing colonial tea, was passed in order to save the nearly defunct East India Tea Company (the Queen's "servant" of the song), by allowing it the chance to undersell colonial tea. The Boston Tea Party was the colonists' reply to the tax.

This tune is one of many for the same song. Apparently more than thirty verses to "Revolutionary Tea" exist.

A Thetfort, Vermont, frontierswoman farming the land while her husband is fighting during the American Revolution. Courtesy of National Life Insurance Company, Montpelier, Vermont

# Revolutionary Tea

There was an old la-dy liv'd o-ver the sea, And
she was an Is - land Queen. ___ Her
daugh-ter liv'd off in a new ___ coun-trie, With an
o - cean of wa - ter be - tween. ___ The
old la -dy's pock-ets were full ___ of gold, But
nev -er con -tent -ed was she, ___ So she
called on her daugh-ter to pay her a tax Of
three pence a pound on her tea, Of
three pence a pound on her tea. ___

Traditional

2. "Now mother, dear mother," the daughter replied,
   "I shan't do the thing you ax.
   I'm willing to pay a fair price for the tea,
   But never the three-penny tax."
   "You shall," quoth the mother, and reddened with rage,
   "For you're my own daughter, you see,
   And sure 'tis quite proper the daughter should pay
   Her mother a tax on her tea,
   Her mother a tax on her tea."

3. And so the old lady her servant called up
   And packed off a budget of tea;
   And eager for three pence a pound, she put in
   Enough for a large familie.
   She ordered her servants to bring home the tax,
   Declaring her child should obey,
   Or old as she was, and almost woman grown,
   She'd half whip her life away,
   She'd half whip her life away.

4. The tea was conveyed to the daughter's door,
   All down by the ocean's side;
   And the bouncing girl pour'd out every pound
   In the dark and boiling tide;
   And then she called out to the Island Queen,
   "Oh, mother, dear mother," quoth she,
   "Your tea you may have when 'tis steep'd quite enough
   But never a tax from me,
   But never a tax from me."

## 21. MY COUNTRY

This early antislavery song is set to the tune of "America," which was also the tune to "God Save the King." As is common, political songwriters often chose a familiar tune for their new words.

The ideals inspired by the French Revolution, especially concepts of human equality and of individual freedom, still inspired Americans of the 1830s. American abolitionists saw the plight of the slaves as a terrible blot upon the nation which possessed a greatly admired Constitution and a Declaration of Independence pronouncing *all* men to be created equal. Beginning in 1833, the American Anti-Slavery Society set up a network of speakers to appear in halls and churches all over the Northern states to influence the public against the evils of slavery.

Two young women, Angelina and Sarah Grimké, daughters of a wealthy North Carolina judge who was also a slave-owning planter, left their home and moved North in order to live away from the slave system. They soon became part of the group of abolitionists writing and speaking before "promiscuous" audiences—that is, blacks and whites and men and women together. This was the very first time in America that women had been allowed to be the featured speakers in front of men, since audiences of that time had always been separated by sex, as well, except in a few religious organizations, like the Quakers. Thousands came to hear the eloquent Grimké women, who maintained great calm and poise wherever they went.

"Women's rights" as the issue it is today did not exist, although fledgling ideas about the subject had been around since the publication of a book by Mary Wollstonecraft, an Englishwoman, in 1792. Called *A Vindication of the Rights of Women,* it was the first volume that championed women's causes, and the same one that would also influence Lucretia Mott, Elizabeth Cady Stanton, Susan B. Anthony, and others in the years of the Women's Rights Conventions from 1848 onward. But in the 1830s, activists were simply questioning the authority men had over women, as those fond of quoting scripture had not done. These women also asked for recognition from their husbands, acknowledging women's contributions to the partnership of marriage. They believed that women should have custody of their children in cases of divorce or widowhood, and they believed it their right to own property. This is why Angelina Grimké (Weld) would say, at one point, "I want to be identified with the negro; until he gets his rights, we shall never have ours."

In 1840, the huge membership of the American Antislavery Society was split in two by a deep philosophical schism. The followers of the militant William Lloyd Garrison demanded that women be included in the workings of the Society, and that "moral influence," but *not political action,* should be used in the battle against slavery. But a second faction, which walked out to form its own society, ran a presidential candidate, an abolitionist named James Birney, under the banner of the new Liberty Party. That group limited its membership in the antislavery society to *men only.*

In 1840, when Lucretia Mott and Elizabeth Cady Stanton attended the World Anti-Slavery Convention in London, they found that no women's credentials would be accepted. They agreed that they would have to work for their own emancipation, as well as the negroes'.

## My Country

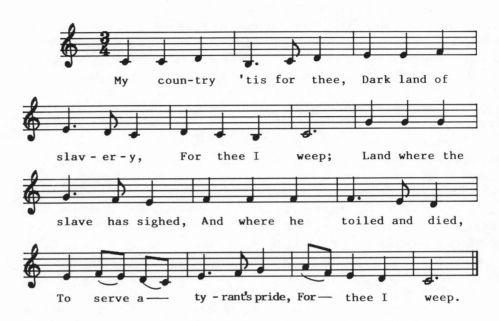

My coun-try 'tis for thee, Dark land of

slav - er - y, For thee I weep; Land where the

slave has sighed, And where he toiled and died,

To serve a—— ty - rant's pride, For—— thee I weep.

2. From every mountain side,
   Upon the ocean's tide,
   They call on thee;
   Amid thy rocks and rills,
   Thy woods and templed hills,
   I hear a voice which trills—
   Let all go free.

3. Our fathers' God, to Thee,
   Author of liberty,
   To Thee we pray;
   Soon may our land be pure,
   Let freedom's light endure,
   And liberty secure,
   Beneath Thy sway.

Traditional. Tune is "America."

## 22. THE DRINKING GOURD

"The Drinking Gourd," while not truly a "woman's song," was the favorite of Harriet Tubman, who sang it while she and the slaves traveled on the route northward known as the Underground Railroad. They were helped along by friends called "conductors." Harriet Tubman was the most important of these, but "conductors" also referred to the residents along the route north who would shelter the escaping slaves on their way.

The Drinking Gourd is the Big Dipper—a constellation in which a line through the dipper's two outside edge stars points to the North Star. The lyrics refer to "the old man ... a-waitin' for to carry you to freedom"—a conductor, some say, with a price on his head for helping slaves to escape. Legend has it that his foot became caught in a bear trap while being chased by a bounty hunter. Forced to part with either his foot or his life, he had a peg foot the next time he met a group of escaping slaves, thus the reference, "The left foot, the peg foot, traveling on." Many of these slave songs were "code songs": they had secret meanings and contained hidden directions.

For many years this song has been a favorite among folksingers, and new recordings of it continue to appear. For more about Harriet Tubman, see the song by Walter Robinson, p. 226.

### The Drinking Gourd

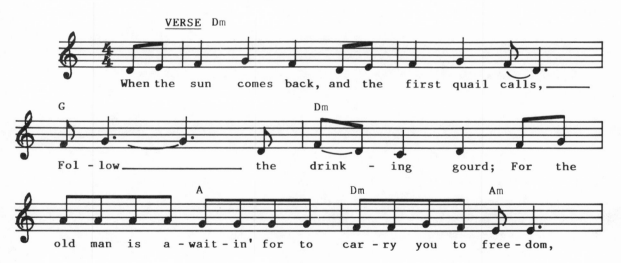

VERSE Dm
When the sun comes back, and the first quail calls, ___

G / Dm
Fol-low ___ the drink - ing gourd; For the

A / Dm / Am
old man is a - wait - in' for to car - ry you to free - dom,

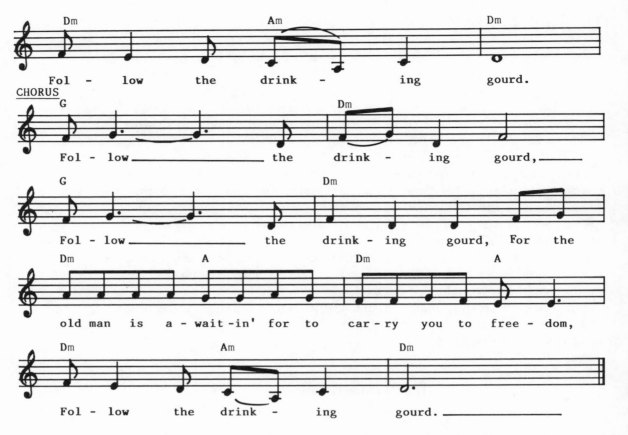

2. The river bank will make a mighty good road,
The dead tree will show you the way.
The left foot, the peg foot, travelin' on,
Follow the drinking gourd.
*Chorus*

3. The river ends between two hills,
Follow the drinking gourd,
The road to freedom's on the other side,
Follow the drinking gourd.
*Chorus*

## 23., 24.  VOTE FOR PROHIBITION and GOING DRY

The Woman's Christian Temperance Union, or WCTU, was a formidable foe of the liquor industry. Organized in 1874, its second president was the noted educator and reformer, Frances Willard. By 1911, it had 225,000 members.

The WCTU was active until the enactment of prohibition in 1920, and still exists, although prohibition was repealed in 1933. Today the organization focuses on changing the social structure which it believes contributes to alcoholism and drug abuse.

Alcoholism was a major problem in the nineteenth century, especially in the industrial communities where men working as many as sixty hours per week could not support a family. Women could not sue for divorce against drunken or cruel husbands, and a man who did not support his family could leave it to starve. Prohibition was one of the reforms temperance women promised to advocate if they won the right to vote. For this reason the liquor industry's money fought women's suffrage.

Carrie Nation. The Kansas State Historical Society, Topeka, Kansas

The WCTU songbook sold for a nickel, and twenty-five copies for a dollar, a bargain at twice the price. This, one of about sixty songs, was sung to the tune of the "Battle Hymn of the Republic":

Then no more the drunkard's hand shall smite the one he loves the best,
Then no more the babe shall die of want upon the mother's breast,
Then no more the drunkard, trembling, stands a murderer confessed,
Saloons shall be no more.

The excesses of the drunken man could only be excelled by that of the rhetoric of the songs. When our local choir tried out the WCTU *Campaign Songbook* in preparation for this book, it found that the temperance hymns go best with an old parlor organ and just a touch of the grape. Old habits die hard.

The Anti-Saloon League was very effective in getting cities, townships, and counties to "go dry." Fill in the blanks of "Going Dry" (at the asterisk) with the name of any two-syllable town, county, or state. Your refreshments will assure good harmonies (the tunes are probably familiar).

## Vote for Prohibition

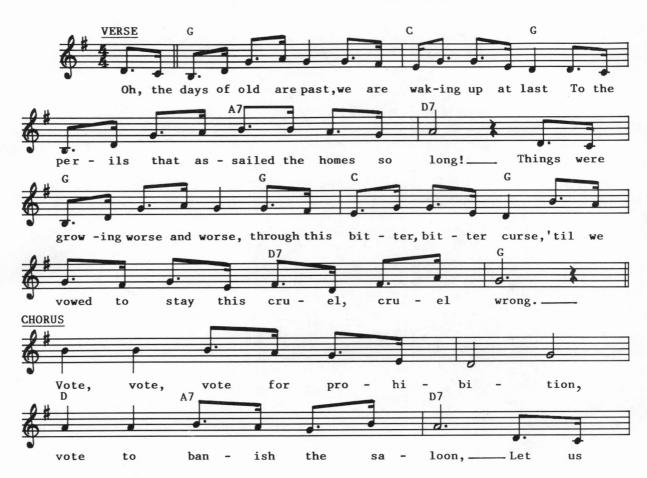

Words by Elisha E. Hoffman.
Tune by George F. Root ("Tramp, Tramp, Tramp").

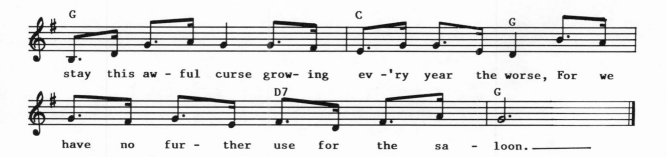

stay this aw - ful curse grow- ing ev -'ry year the worse, For we

have no fur - ther use for the sa - loon. _____

2. The saloon men stand aghast while our ranks are filling fast,
   And they see the dread handwriting on the wall;
   Let us push the work along, fight with steady heart and strong,
   And the evil traffic very soon must fall.
   *Chorus*

3. Float your banners in the breeze over lands and over seas,
   And let "Home and Native Land" your motto be;
   Sing to God a triumph song, and the battle push along,
   And the fight will issue soon in victory.
   *Chorus*

# Going Dry

*Boston's or New York's or Lompoc's, etc. Fill in your favorite state, county, or town.

Words by Elisha E. Hoffman.
Tune by George A. Minor ("Bringing In the Sheaves").

2. To the front, crusaders, where the fight is waging,
   For the liquor traffic has been doomed to die;
   Gird you on the armor; and the foe engaging,
   Pass along the watchword, _____ 's going dry.
   *Chorus*

3. God's strong arm of justice is reached forth to save us,
   And unto the fight he summons from on high;
   Banish the saloons from the good land he gave us,
   And be this our watchword: _____ 's going dry.
   *Chorus*

4. Forth, O men of faith! and be ye full of courage,
   And the hosts of evil in His strength defy,
   For the Lord Jehovah pledges glorious vict'ry;
   Rally to the watchword, _____ 's going dry.
   *Chorus*

## 25., 26. FEMALE SUFFRAGE and I AM A SUFFRAGETTE

Here are two songs from the era when men considered it immodest for women to speak in public or to participate in politics. Supposedly these activities would make women unfeminine, hard, crude, and vulgar. Men might not treat them as gallantly as before, they said. If women voted, many believed, the consequence could be the breakdown of the home. Voting might even have an effect on unborn fetuses! It would certainly lead to female supremacy and a matriarchal society (see "Female Suffrage"). These "period pieces" then, date from 1867 ("Female Suffrage") and 1912 ("I Am A Suffragette").

The early nineteenth century was an age of reform. The earliest of our women's rights advocates came directly out of their abolition work, where they proved themselves fully capable leaders: hardworking and intelligent organizers, with stamina and strength. During those years it became apparent to them that, in order to participate fully in the workings of the nation, they would have to turn their attention to promoting equality of the sexes, along with equality of the races.

This idea was verbalized by two great leaders of the antislavery movement, Elizabeth Cady Stanton and Lucretia Mott (see the song about Mott, p. 230, and commentary to "My Country," p. 49). Meeting for the first time at the World Antislavery Convention in London in 1840, they became friends and talked seriously about holding the first Woman's Rights Convention in the United States in the near future. Little did they realize that it would be eight years until they would both be free enough from their family obligations to organize it. But in 1848 they finally brought it about in Seneca Falls, New York.

At this convention first a "Declaration of Sentiments" was read, a kind of woman's version of the Declaration of Independence; it was debated and adopted. Resolutions that objected to "the monopoly of the pulpit," and those promoting equal access to education, the trades, and the professions passed easily. However, "the sacred right of elective franchise," or the vote, passed by only a narrow margin! It was considered radical to want to vote, even by these women particularly interested in their rights.

While the press ridiculed the Seneca Falls Women's Rights Convention and its leaders, calling the meeting "a petticoat rebellion," it was to be the first of a series of such conventions which would have an ever-increasing attendance and become more militant. Other important leaders would join: Susan B. Anthony in 1851, for example, and Lucy Stone, an educator and abolition speaker who had expressed her views on women's rights in her antislavery lectures.

In 1869, Stanton and Anthony organized the National Woman Suffrage Association. This group opposed the 15th Amendment, since it gave only the black man the vote, but no women, black or white. These two leaders also published the first women's periodical, called *Revolution*, which supported the idea of "educated suffrage" for women and blacks. Their elitist view was abhorrent to the members of the American Woman Suffrage Association, their opposition, who were also angry with Stanton and Anthony for allowing the radical paper to be financed by a reputed racist. The split in the women's rights movement was deep, for the latter (conservative) wing did not wish to deny the black man his voting rights and was interested in persuading the *states* to give women the vote, thus avoiding another long wait for a U.S. Constitutional amendment. The two suffrage organizations united in 1890, an entire generation later. The new organization, called the National American Woman Suffrage Association, had as its long-time leader a second-generation suffragist, Carrie Chapman Catt, who managed to keep the goal of the vote clearly in front of the women until its passage. (Catt went on to organize the League of Women Voters afterward.)

While several individual states eventually did give the women the franchise (Wyoming first), it was not until 1920 that the 19th Amendment giving *all* U.S. women the vote was signed into law, after more than fifty years of struggle.

Elizabeth Cady Stanton and Susan B. Anthony. Smithsonian Institution, Washington, D.C.

### Female Suffrage

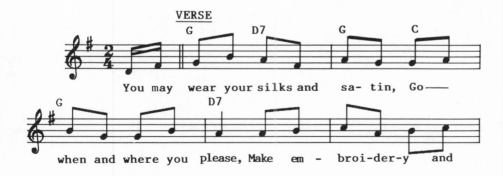

Words by R. A. Cohen.
Music by A. J. Phelps (from 1867).

tat -tin', And—— live quite at your ease. You may go to ball and con-cert, In gau- dy hat and coat, In fact, my charm-ing crea - tures, Do ev-'ry-thing but vote.

**CHORUS**

You may vis-it ball and con-cert In gau -dy hat and coat, In fact, my charm-ing crea - tures, Do ev - 'ry-thing but vote.

2. You may seek for health and riches,
   And marry at your will,
   But man must wear the breeches,
   And rule the household still;
   For nature so designed it,
   And so our fathers wrote,
   And clearly they defined it,
   That man, alone, should vote.
   *Chorus*

3. You wish to be our equal,
   We prize you something more,
   And proudly look upon you
   Than angels little lower.
   We would not have you equal,
   But superior to us;
   A something we can idolize,
   Though fashioned out of dust.
   *Chorus*

4. But when from her position,
   A careless woman's hurled,
   She's the loathing of our manhood,
   The scorn of all the world;
   She loses her identity,
   With all that's noble, then,
   And seeks the common level
   Of the commonest of men.
   *Chorus*

5. I have given my opinion
   And I hold that it is true—
   What would strengthen politicians
   Would tend to weaken you.
   It would bring you to its level,
   In spite of all that's said,
   And political corruption
   Would show its hydra-head.
   *Chorus*

6. Then mothers, wives and sisters,
   I beg you keep your place;
   And remain what nature made you—
   The help-meets of our race.
   Let no temptation lead you,
   Nor any wily fox,
   To descend unto the level
   Of the nation's ballot box.
   *Chorus*

"The first picket line, College Day in the picket line—Feb. 1917." Smithsonian Institution, Washington, D.C.

### I Am a Suffragette

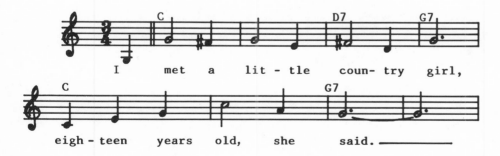

I met a lit-tle coun-try girl,
eigh-teen years old, she said. —

Words by M. Olive Drennen.
Music by M. C. Hanford (from 1912).

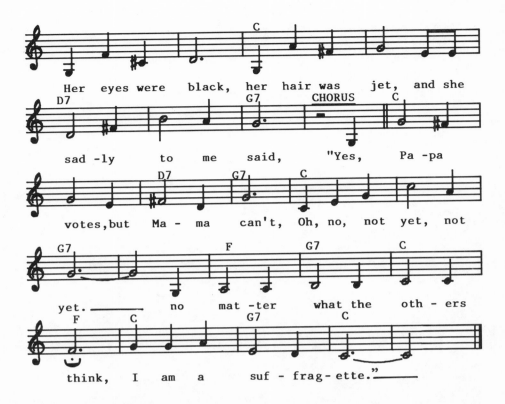

Her eyes were black, her hair was jet, and she
sadly to me said, "Yes, Pa-pa
votes, but Ma-ma can't, Oh, no, not yet, not
yet. _____ no mat-ter what the oth-ers
think, I am a suf-frag-ette." _____

2. Oh, all the men make all the laws, which makes the women fret,
   But wait and see those laws when we at last our suffrage get.
   *Chorus*

3. I have a dandy little beau, he lives down in the town,
   And when he asks me to "be his," I'll look at him and frown.
   *Last chorus*

> "Yes, Papa votes, but Mama can't, Oh, no, not yet, not yet.
> And I'll not marry any man, 'til I my suffrage get."

## 27. GIVE YOUR HANDS TO STRUGGLE

The second black freedom movement was the Civil Rights struggle in the 1950s, with its massive voter registration drive and "sit-ins" on buses, at lunch counters, in public swimming pools—everywhere that racial segregation had been in effect in the deep South.

Bernice Johnson Reagon was one of the Freedom Singers of the Student Non-Violent Coordinating Committee (SNCC) during her college years, beginning in 1961. "My education and training continued through my participation in the Civil Rights Movement as a singer, field researcher, and organizer," she writes.

In 1975 Reagon received a Ph.D. in history from Howard University, Washington, D.C., and since 1974 she has been the Program Director and Culture Historian for the Program in Black American Culture at the Smithsonian Institution's Museum of American History.

Her extensive research on the music and culture of the African Diaspora has taken Reagon to Haiti, Guyana in South America, and to a number of African countries. Her work has included teaching, research, writing, singing, songwriting, lecturing, and program development and implementation. She has also developed and coordinated festivals in black oral tradition and music, and has published works on black music and culture, including *Black People and Their Culture: Selected Writing From the African Diaspora* (Washington, D.C.: Smithsonian Institution Press, 1976), and "The Songs of the Civil Rights

Bernice Johnson Reagon. Smithsonian Institution, Washington, D.C.

Movement, 1955–65, A Study in Culture History" (Washington, D.C.: Howard University Press, 1975).

Reagon has performed internationally as a solo singer since 1962, and was a leading member of The Freedom Singers and The Haramboo Singers before forming the renowned ensemble, Sweet Honey in the Rock (see Bernice Johnson Reagon's second song in this collection, "Oughta Be a Woman," p. 120).

"Give Your Hands to Struggle" was inspired by the example of Civil Rights activist Septima Clark. Reagon says: "Septima Clark told me that black people had survived because we understood the relationship between survival and struggle, that no matter how dark things seemed, if we continued to fight for what was believed we would survive. She said that there was no life where there was no struggle.

"Septima Clark began teaching in the nineteen-teens, on the islands just off Charleston, South Carolina. She worked there because of racial discrimination in the Charleston school system. She joined the NAACP in its struggle against lynching and in a suit brought by black teachers against the Charleston system for unequal pay and working conditions. During the fifties, after having won the suit and getting a job in Charleston, Septima Clark began to teach school at night on the islands, so that people would learn to read and write to be able to vote. The Charleston School Board fired her from her teaching job. Through Highlander Folk School and the Southern Christian Leadership Conference, she continued this work, organizing a training center for teachers, who set up citizenship schools throughout the South during the 1960s. When she was seventy-five, she resigned from the SCLC, and ran for the School Board of Charleston. At eighty-five, she still sits on that board. I wrote 'Give Your Hands to Struggle' because of what she taught me."

## Give Your Hands to Struggle

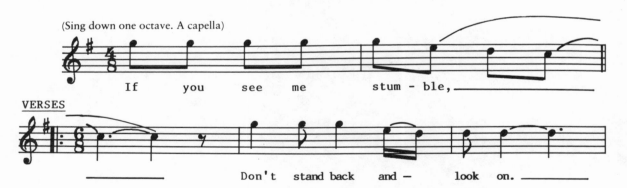

Reach out now, brother,
Give your hands to struggle.

**CHORUS**

Give your hands to struggle.
Give your hands to struggle.
Give your hands to struggle.
(All but the last chorus)
Give your hands to struggle.
(Last chorus only)
2. If you feel my heart -gle.

2. If you feel my heart break,
   Don't just count the soundwaves,
   Hold me close now, baby,
   Give your arms to struggle.
   *Chorus*

3. If you see me crying,
   Don't just pat my shoulder.
   Help me go on, right on.
   Give me your strength to struggle.
   *Chorus*

4. If you hear my lovesong,
   Don't stand back and listen.
   Help me sing it right now.
   Give your voice to struggle.
   *Chorus*

5. Then we'll be moving,
   We'll be really moving,
   Building up our union,
   If we give our all to struggle.
   *Chorus*

## 28. THE ERA OF THE ERA

"Equality of rights under the law shall not be denied or abridged by the United States or by any State on account of sex."

The wording of the famous proposed Equal Rights Amendment (ERA) is slightly changed from its original version as it was drafted in 1923 by women's rights activist, Alice Paul. The ERA was introduced into every Congress for forty-nine years, and was just three states short of national ratification in 1982. The thirty-five states that ratified comprised 72 percent of the U.S. population.

Phyllis Unger Hiller's satirical song gives nearly all the arguments we have heard against the ERA. (The suffragists had a counterpart to the unisex bathroom argument: on the front of a piece of old sheet music is an illustration of two long lines in front of separate voting booths—one for men, and one for women!)

Hiller owns her own music company, writes, composes, teaches, and performs. She has degrees from the University of California at Berkeley and from Vanderbilt University in Nashville, Tennessee, and is a teacher and marriage and family counselor.

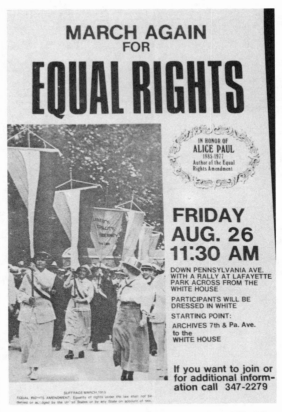

Poster for an ERA march. Smithsonian Institution, Washington, D.C.

# The Era of the ERA

(Lively tempo)

VERSE

The E-qual Rights A-mend-ment__ came up in Ten-nes-see;__ The leg-is-la-ture vo-ted "Yes," thought best for you and me.__ Ten-nes-see__ came on strong to have it rat-i-fied;__ It looked like jus-tice had pre-vailed, and

1. all were sat-is-fied.__
2. signs on rest-room doors. Re-

CHORUS

scind! Re-scind! Don't let this thing be-gin!__ Free-dom of this kind af-fects a wo-man's mind.__ Re-scind! Re-

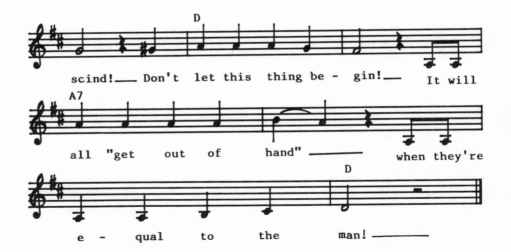

scind!__ Don't let this thing be - gin!__ It will all "get out of hand" _____ when they're e - qual to the man! _____

Once it was all ratified, Tennessee had done its part,
But no, that wasn't right enough, someone made another start.
Should have heard one senator, debating on the floor,
Equating equal rights with the signs on restroom doors.
*Chorus*

2. Isaiah and Peter were quoted left and right.
Pro and con, rescind or not, became the issued fight.
"They want to draft your mother, kids, and send her off to war,
Then you won't have a mommy to love you anymore.
And what about drafting women? Be glad for what they've got.
Protect the family unit and destroy this Commie plot.
Women are the weaker sex and belong at home at night,
Not in an army barracks with soldiers left and right."
*Chorus*

3. Some fine words were spoken in behalf of equality.
When senators prepared their talks—not afraid of bein' free.
"There's nothing wrong with this amendment, I recommend vote 'aye';
We can pass it once again, and I recommend we try."
The people in the gallery were told to hold their cheers.
There were mostly women there in a variety of years.
To some the thoughts of freedom were the thoughts of doom,
Others couldn't believe their ears, the senators wouldn't make room.
*Chorus*

4. "Pass the buck," it's easier (and) more familiar to the ear,
   Changes make life difficult and the whole thing gets unclear;
   I guess it's hard to hear the truth when you've got to get re-elected
   And you're so afraid to go against whatever is expected.
   This world needs all the talent that we could ever find
   To discover the solutions that give us peace of mind;
   Somehow we'll muddle through it, somehow we always do—
   Women seeking freedom—so the men can find theirs, too!
   *Last chorus*

   Alas, alas! This too will pass;
   It's not a "Commie plot" to use the best you've got.
   Alas, alas—some day we'll all be free,
   If it's good enough for the men-folk, it's good enough for me!

## 29. STILL AIN'T SATISFIED

Token measure won't make it. Bonnie Lockhart, a California feminist singer/songwriter, wrote another song we have included. See her biography with "The Witch Song," p. 202.

### Still Ain't Satisfied

(Usually sung a capella)

VERSES 1. - 5.

Dm
Well, they got wo - men on T. V. but I

A7      Dm
still ain't sat - is - fied. 'Cause co - op - ta - tion's

A7      Dm
all I see, and I still ain't sat - is - fied. They call me

A7      Dm
"Ms.," they sell me blue___ jeans,___

A7
Call it "Wo - men's Lib," they make___ it sound

Dm      CHORUS 1. - 5.
ob - scene. And I still ain't, woa they

G      Dm      G
lied, And I still ain't, woa they lied, And I still ain't

woa they lied, _____ And I still ain't sat - is -

**1.-5.**
fied.                                        2.Well,

**6.**
fied. I've got some

pride,                I won't be lied _____ to.

I did de - cide              that half - way

(LAST CHORUS)
won't ___ do.      And I still ain't,      woa they

lied, And I still ain't,      woa they lied, And I still ain't,

woa they lied, _____      I still ain't sat - is -

fied. _____

2. Well, they got women prison guards,
   but I still ain't satisfied.
   With so many still behind bars,
   and I still ain't satisfied.
   I don't plead guilt, I don't want no bum deal.
   I ain't askin' for crumbs, I want the whole meal.
   *Chorus*

3. They liberalized abortion,
   but I still ain't satisfied,
   'Cause it still costs a fortune,
   and I still ain't satisfied.
   I'm singin' about control of my own womb,
   and no reform is gonna change my tune.
   *Chorus*

4. They give out pennies here and there,
   but I still ain't satisfied,
   To set up centers for child care,
   and I still ain't satisfied.
   And while we work at slave wages,
   They brainwash our kids at tender ages.
   *Chorus*

5. Well, this world sure don't look my way,
   and I still ain't satisfied.
   'Cause women get raped every day,
   and I still ain't satisfied.
   They say, "OK, we'll give you a street light,"
   But they get uptight when we learn how to street fight.
   *Chorus*

6. I've got some pride, I won't be lied to.
   I did decide that halfway won't do.
   *Last chorus*

## 30. HAY UNA MUJER

"The candle burns not for us, but for all those whom we failed to rescue from prison, who were shot on the way to prison, who were tortured, who were kidnapped, who 'disappeared' ... "

—Peter Benenson, 1951
(Founder of Amnesty International)

This song calls out the names of eight real women, missing in Chile. They symbolize thousands of prisoners and other people who have "disappeared" into the hands of dictatorships around the world.

"Hay Una Mujer" was originally on the Holly Near album, *Imagine My Surprise,* as was the song, "Old Time Woman" (p. 156). In 1983 "Mujer" was recorded again, this time with Ronnie Gilbert, formerly of the Weavers. That album, *Lifeline,* presents the new ending written for the song, as it appears here.

"Hay Una Mujer" is a highly dramatic piece. Holly Near's music bridges several styles of music: folk, pop, rock, and even cabaret and light opera forms. Once she said, "I've always felt closer to Kurt Weill [than to folk music]. I've never learned to play the guitar." The dramatic influence of Weill is indeed apparent in the song. See Holly Near's biography, also on p. 156.

### Hay Una Mujer

Words and music by Holly Near.
© 1978 Hereford Music. New ending added 1983.
All rights reserved. Used by permission.

u - na mu - jer des - a - pa - re - ci - da, Hay

u - na mu - jer des - a - pa - re - ci - da En

CHORUS 2.

Chi - le en Chi - le, en Chi - le. ____ And the

jun - ta, _____ and the jun - ta knows ____ And the

jun - ta knows where she is _____ And the

jun - ta knows where they are Hi - ding her, she's dy - ing. Hay

u - na mu - jer des - a - pa - re - ci - da. Hay

u - na mu - jer des - a - pa - re - ci - da En

DA CAPO

Chi - le, en Chi - le, en Chi - le. ____

NEW ENDING
(Freely)

Miss - ing _____ in Bra - zil _____

Miss - ing _____ in U - ru - guay _____

Miss-ing in Gua - te -ma - la _____ Miss-ing _____ in

El Sal - va - dor _____ (Hay) un hom - bre _____

(Sorrowfully rit.)

_____ Hay un ni - ño _____ O los

ni - ños _____ Hay u - na mu -

jer de - sa - pa - re - ci - da. _____

spir - it _____ lives _____ in Chi - le New

lives, _____ new songs _____ A

spir - it _____ grows _____ in Chi - le _____ New

lives, _____ new songs are ris - ing up A

spir - it sings in Chi-_____ le _____ New

lives, _____ new songs are ris - ing up A

spir - it lives in Chi - le New

lives, _____ new songs _____ In Chi - le!

2. Clara Elena Cantero
   Elisa del Carmen Escobar
   Eliana Maria Espinosa
   Rosa Elena Morales
   *Chorus 1 and 2, repeat Chorus 1*

## 31. THE UNIVERSAL SOLDIER

"The Universal Soldier," now more than a quarter of a century old, was one of the anthems of the anti-Vietnam War movement, and it made Buffy Sainte-Marie famous.

"Now That the Buffalo's Gone," p. 170, followed. Those and many others of her songs have been recorded in sixteen languages by more than two hundred different performers: Elvis Presley, Barbra Streisand, the Boston Pops Orchestra—not to mention the recordings by many folksingers.

Concert tours and benefits have brought Buffy Sainte-Marie to every corner of the world. She has given a Royal Command Performance for Queen Elizabeth II on one day and appeared at a benefit concert on an Indian reservation the next. In two decades she has never ceased to pour time, energy, and foundation money into Indian rights.

Buffy says "The Universal Soldier" did what she wanted it to do: "It got people out of their classrooms and onto their feet."

### The Universal Soldier

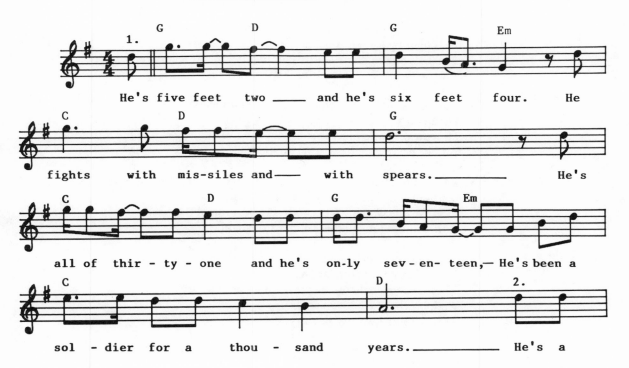

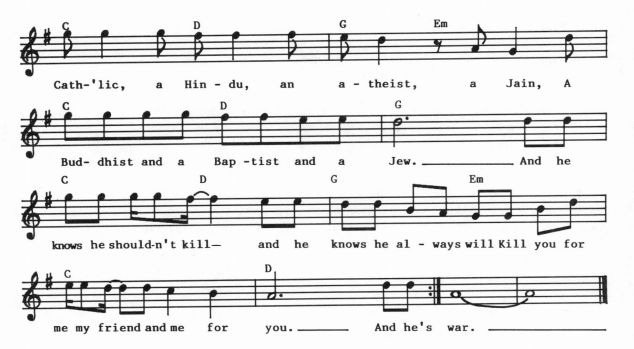

Cath-'lic, a Hin-du, an a-theist, a Jain, A Bud-dhist and a Bap-tist and a Jew. _____ And he knows he should-n't kill— and he knows he al-ways will Kill you for me my friend and me for you. _____ And he's war. _____

3. And he's fighting for Canada, he's fighting for France,
   He's fighting for the U.S.A.
   And he's fighting for the Russians and he's fighting for Japan
   And he thinks we'll put an end to war this way.

4. And he's fighting for democracy, he's fighting for the Reds.
   He says it's for the peace of all.
   He's the one who must decide who's to live and who's to die
   And he never sees the writing on the wall.

5. But without him how would Hitler have condemned him at Dachau,
   Without him Caesar would've stood alone.
   He's the one who gives his body as a weapon of the war,
   And without him all this killin' can't go on.

6. He's the universal soldier and he really is to blame.
   His orders come from far away no more.
   They come from here-and-there and-you-and-me,
   And, brothers, can't you see,
   This is not the way we put an end to war.

## 32. MOTHERS, DAUGHTERS, WIVES

Because this is the best antiwar song of the 1980s, to date, we include "Mothers, Daughters, Wives" in this volume, although the writer is not American. Judy Small's lyrics seem to begin where those of "The Universal Soldier" leave off; they indicate that, historically, women have played an unwitting part in men's soldiering.

An Australian born in New South Wales, Small grew up listening to 1960s folk music, and at the age of fourteen had saved enough money to buy her first guitar. Later at the University in Sydney, she sang occasionally in the folk clubs, but it was not until 1982 that she left her job and began to devote herself to full-time performing and songwriting. In her first three years of performing, Small has released three albums. *Mothers, Daughters, Wives* is the title of the second.

Judy Small tours regularly in Australia as a solo performer, sometimes sharing the stage with other leading Australian performers. In 1982 and again in 1985 she toured the United States and Canada.

"Anything for me, if you please." Post office of the Brooklyn Fair in Aid of the Sanitary Commission during the Civil War, by Winslow Homer. *Harper's Weekly,* March 5, 1864

# Mothers, Daughters, Wives

The first time it was fa-thers The last time it was sons And in be-tween, your hus-bands marched a-way with drums and guns. And you nev-er thought to ques-tion You just went on with your lives 'Cause all they'd taught you who to be was moth-ers, daugh-ters, wives. And you can

on-ly just re-mem-ber The tears your moth-er shed As they sat and read their pa-pers Through the lists and lists of dead And the gold frames held the pho-to-graphs That moth-ers kissed each night And the door-frames held the shocked And si-lent stran-gers from the fight.

moth-ers daugh-ters wives. And you be-lieved them.*

*But we are changing.

Words and music by Judy Small.
© 1984 by Hereford Music.
All rights reserved. Used by permission.

2. It was twenty-one years later
   With children of your own
   The trumpet sounded once again
   And the soldier boys were gone
   And you drove their trucks and made their guns
   And tended to their wounds
   And at night you kissed their photographs
   And prayed for safe returns
   And after it was over
   You had to learn again
   To be just wives and mothers
   When you'd done the work of men
   So you worked to help the needy
   And you never trod on toes
   And the photos on the pianos struck
   A happy family pose.
   *Chorus*

3. Then your daughters grew to women
   And your little boys to men
   And you prayed that you were dreaming
   When the call-up came again
   But you proudly smiled and held your tears
   As they bravely waved goodbye
   And the photos on the mantlepieces
   Always made you cry
   And now you're getting older
   And in time the photos fade
   And in widowhood you sit back
   And reflect on the parade
   Of the passing of your memories
   As your daughters change their lives
   Seeing more to our existence
   Than just mothers, daughters, wives.
   *Tag:* And you believed them.
     or: But we are changing.

## 33. BOMBS AWAY!

Written in 1975, Joanna Cazden's "Bombs Away!" emphasizes strongly that the citizens of the United States have the right to make decisions concerning their future.

Her arguments against the B-1 bomber center around the cost and destructiveness of the weapon. The military and industry in alliance profit enormously from taxpayers' dollars that are no longer available to fund those services vital to the people. The needed foreign resources are often tapped, as well, and ideology is the pretext for ensuing wars.

Cazden's solution is peace conversion: using a bomber factory to manufacture mass transportation equipment, for example. Studies show that *nondefense* industry is considered labor-intensive, rather than cost-intensive, she told us. It employs more people and will cost the nation less. She argues in her song that our money should be used for life-enhancing projects.

Joanna Cazden's biography follows her second song in the collection, "The Left-Handed Song for Human Rights," p. 163.

### Bombs Away!

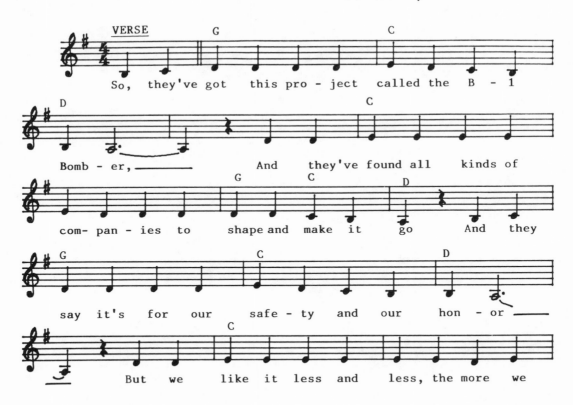

2. With the money that it takes to build a bomber
   We could be raising hospitals and co-ops and schools
   But the profits can't compare with those monsters of the air
   And "if you don't like war you're a sissy or a fool"

   So the contractors are eager
   While wages stay meager
   We murder to earn a poor week's pay—
   *Chorus*

3. All the metal that it takes to build a bomber
   Comes from countries we therefore have to keep for our "friends"
   All the tungsten and the chrome come from other people's homes
   Which we invade—then find we must defend—

   > So the generals get securer
   > But our neighbors just get poorer
   > Danger grows;
   > War is surer every day—
   > *Chorus*

4. It just takes too much of life to build a bomber
   All that thinking about death isn't good for human souls
   All the slick, expensive lies and the pessimistic sighs
   Make it feel like our own lives are full of holes

   > Things are bad and getting worse
   > But we can put it in reverse
   > Work for Peace Conversion
   > That's the only way—
   > *Chorus*

## 34. NO PLACE TO HIDE

"I can't think of anything more painful than surviving a nuclear war and wondering how it was that we didn't see it coming..."

—Norman Cousins

"It's the most important part of parenting to make sure your children grow up and live a normal lifespan. I see no point in making them clean their teeth, giving them good food or a good education, or having a good stable family life, if they're not going to survive."

—Helen Caldicott

Australian pediatrician Helen Caldicott considers the planet to be "terminally ill." As founder of Physicians for Social Responsibility in 1961, she exemplifies what one person can do to combat the nuclear threat; as a mother, she views children to be at the heart of her crusade to stop the arms race. Practicing what she calls, "the ultimate form of preventive medicine," she speaks all over the world presenting factual information about weapons in an effort to ward off nuclear holocaust.

As a mother, Linda Arnold is also especially interested in the arms race as it applies to the future's children. The much-acclaimed documentary, *The Last Epidemic: Medical Consequences of Nuclear Weapons and Nuclear War,* employs the title song from her second record, *Sweet Mother Earth,* from which we present this song. "It was written to help people to confront fear, facing the nightmare, and take responsibility for our lives. Overcoming denial is the first step in the process," she says. (This is also the message of the Cathy Winter song, "Sure Is Good to Know," p. 184.)

Disarmament rally, Union Square, San Francisco, California, May 1978. Photograph by E. Salkind, courtesy East Bay Women for Peace

# No Place to Hide

Words and music by Linda Arnold.
© 1982 Arnold Music Company.
All rights reserved. Used by permission.

2. I'm grieving for the children
   And the innocence I once knew
   Before I finally realized
   This nightmare can come true
   Standing at the crossroads
   Of humanity's last hour
   My rage is mounting
   And it's filling me with power.
   *Chorus*

3. Now I'm raising my voice
   To make my anguish known
   The future will not hear us
   If we tremble all alone
   Courage will guide us
   In this struggle to survive
   And strengthen us to build a world
   Where no one needs to hide.
   *Chorus*

## 35. SOMEONE ELSE'S COUNTRY

"I was a troublemaker from an early age," Leslie Fish writes. "I organized and led a brief revolt against an ill-liked teacher in first grade. By junior high school I was preaching in favor of civil rights to anyone who'd listen.

"When I was little, my mom sent me to a dance class that was taught by Marjorie Mazia. She often brought a man with her who had silver eyes, played the guitar, and sang wonderful kids' songs in a twangy voice. I didn't remember his name, but I remembered the songs."

The man with the "silver eyes" was Woody Guthrie. At sixteen, when Leslie learned to play the guitar, she found a book of Woody Guthrie's songs and got in touch with Marjorie to find out where he was. She found him in a hospital in New York, where he was dying of Huntington's chorea. For months she visited him whenever she could to play his songs for him.

In high school Leslie Fish was active in the Civil Rights movement, and at the University of Michigan she became an antiwar activist and feminist. After college she moved to Chicago to become a member of the "Wobblies" (the Industrial Workers of the World), as her grandfather had been. She worked as a writer, cartoonist, and editor on the I.W.W. paper, *Industrial Worker,* and became a counselor and mimeograph operator for the Vietnam Veterans Against the War. Changing jobs many times, she nonetheless formed a band with other I.W.W. musicians and continued her singing and writing.

*Star Trek* inspired her to write science fiction songs, and as a following developed, she was hired by Off Centaur Publications in El Cerrito, California, to write science fiction material full-time. She lives there, when she is not traveling for Off Centaur, "attending WesterCon, WorldCon, Mile-HighCon ... "

"Someone Else's Country" was written during the final days of the Vietnam War. But the country in question bears some resemblances to ancient Rome, and should probably be taken as an allegory about imperialism.

### Someone Else's Country

Once there was a raw new land — where
out-laws went to make a stand, When their moth-er

coun-tries would as soon have seen them dead. They

had no oth - er place to go, __ but here they stayed to

build and sow, __ And when the old -er na-tions came to

**CHORUS**

take them back they said: __ This is

some - one el - se's coun - try,

land that you had bet -ter leave __ a - lone. __

__ Keep your hands off oth - er peo -ple's

coun - try __ Or who knows what might

hap - pen to your own? __

2. By craftsman's shop and family farm, love of freedom and strength of arm,
   They built a mighty nation—sometimes cruel and sometimes blind,
   But still the rights outweighed the wrong. The land grew wealthy, vast and strong,
   So long as all its people kept their founding dream in mind.
   *Chorus*

3. An ancient empire built on slaves came a-conquering across the waves.
   The new land and the empire met head-on in bloody war.
   The younger nation won the day, but with their victory took away
   Too much of empire manners, not what they'd been fighting for.
   *Chorus*

4. They made new gods of Luxury, of Power and Efficiency.
   Plantations took the countryside. The factory took the town.
   The farmer lost his land again, and had to go work for other men
   Who looked on other countries as just jewels for their crown.
   *Chorus*

5. Then one tiny country said: "We'll fight until we're free or dead."
   The new-grown empire smashed them down and killed their man of peace.
   So the last respect its people had went down the drain and left them madly
   Wondering why corruption grew and riots wouldn't cease.
   *Chorus*

6. So they lost belief in right and wrong. They only lived to get along,
   And people raised on narrow causes don't defend you well.
   So when the savages stormed the wall, the people shrugged and let it fall.
   No one cared to save it, so the Roman Empire fell.
   *Last chorus*

   > They put their hands to other people's country,
   > Land that they'd have better left alone.
   > They tried to master soneone else's country,
   > And all they really did was lose their own.

# Labor

Mechanic Myrtle Hand assembles an engine at Douglas Aircraft, Santa Monica, California, during World War II. The Schlesinger Library, Radcliffe College

## 36. BABIES IN THE MILL

In 1791, the first textile mill, Slater's Mill, was built in Rhode Island. The workers in it were nine children, all under the age of twelve. They worked fourteen hours a day, six days a week.

By 1832, two-fifths of the workers in the textile industry were children. Many of these "mill mites," as they were called, were worked literally to death, dying after a few years spent in the cold, dank, air-polluted mills.

By the end of that century, women and men sought to end child labor. Journalists, social reformers, preachers, and labor organizers began to call attention to the use of children in factories and coal mines. The struggle went on for many years, because big business spent large sums to hamper the work of these reformers.

In 1938, the Fair Labor Standards Act was finally passed. The minimum age for children's employment was set at sixteen, unless the work did not involve mining or manufacturing or where it did not interfere with health and education.

We still have problems with labor laws concerning young people, however. During conservative administrations legislators attempt to lower the minimum wage for teenagers, who have the highest rate of unemployment in the nation. Proponents claim that employers will hire a greater number of young people if labor is cheap. This is, ironically, the same argument used in the early days of industrialization.

"Babies In The Mill" is a composed folk song written in the old style. Dorsey Dixon, like his father before him, worked in the cotton mills of Carolina from the age of twelve, with only brief forays into other jobs during World War I. His sister, Nancy, also a singer of old traditional songs, worked as a spinner in the cotton mills from the age of eight, when she received only eight cents a day. Their brother, Howard Dixon, who sang duets with Dorsey on radio and records, was stricken at work in a mill in 1961.

The two men recorded sixty songs; Dorsey himself sang thirty-eight songs for the Library of Congress.

Dorsey Dixon earned very little of his money by way of music, and never copyrighted any. Nor did he consider himself a mill bard; he was dedicated to sacred songs, and the fact that he had a first-hand knowledge of industrial life was apparently more interesting to collectors of labor songs than to him. A number of folksingers perform this song, including Hedy West (see the Discography).

The song tells a remarkable story—and very much from a woman's perspective: the first industrial workers in this nation were women and children. We find the fourth verse rather syrupy, and tend to leave it out in performance.

# Babies in the Mill

I used to be a fac-tory hand when things _____ were mov-in' slow, _____ When chil-dren worked in cot-ton mills, each morn-ing had to go. _____ Ev-ery morn-ing jest at five, the whis-tle _____ blew _____ on time, _____ And called them ba-bies out of bed at the age of eight and nine. _____ Come out of bed, lit-tle

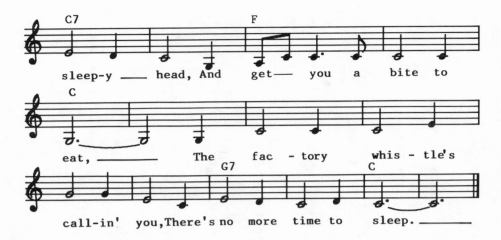

sleep-y ____ head, And get ____ you a bite to

eat, ____ The fac - tory whis - tle's

call-in' you, There's no more time to sleep. ____

2. The children all grew up unlearned, they never went to school,
   They never learned to read or write, but they learned to spin and spool.
   Every time I close my eyes, I see that picture still,
   When textile work was carried on with babies in the mill.
   *Chorus*

3. To their jobs those little ones were strictly forced to go,
   Those babies had to be on time through rain and sleet and snow,
   Many times when things went wrong their bosses often frowned,
   Many times those little ones was kicked and shoved around.
   *Chorus*

4. Old timer, can't you see that scene, that through the years go by,
   Those babies all went on the job, the same as you and I,
   I know you're glad that things have changed, and we have lots of fun,
   As we go in and do the jobs that babies used to run.
   *Chorus*

## 37. THE FACTORY GIRL'S COME ALL YE

In the first decades of the nineteenth century, the factory girls, from New England farms, had the opportunity to earn an independent income. Rising before dawn to face a fourteen-hour day, they often saved enough for a dowry, or to help pay the mortgage on the family farm, or even to send a brother to college.

As more and more mills were built, competition grew, and conditions at the mills deteriorated. Increased workloads and reduced wages finally caused the factory girls to "turn out," or strike. In 1836, fifteen hundred women marched in Lowell, Massachusetts.

By an unknown composer, "The Lewiston Factory Girl," as this song is also called, describes life in the textile mills of that century. Various versions, some of which may date to the 1830s, have been heard as far west as Texas, and more recently in North Carolina. This version is similar to that of Hedy West.

"Bell-Time" by Winslow Homer. *Harper's Weekly,* July 25, 1868

### The Factory Girl's Come All Ye

Come all ye Lew-is-ton Fac-tory girls, I

Traditional

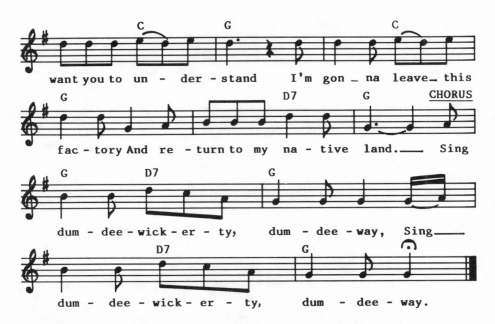

want you to un - der - stand    I'm gon _ na leave _ this
fac - tory And re - turn to my na - tive land. _ Sing
dum - dee - wick - er - ty,    dum - dee - way, Sing _
dum - dee - wick - er - ty,    dum - dee - way.

2. No more I'll take my shaker and shawl
   And hurry to the mill.
   No more I'll work so pesky hard
   To earn a dollar bill!
   *Chorus*

3. No more will I take the towel and soap
   And go to the sink to wash.
   No more will the overseer say,
   "You're making a terrible splosh!"
   *Chorus*

4. No more I'll take my bobbins out.
   No more I'll put them in.
   No more the overseer'll say,
   "You're weaving your cloth too thin."
   *Chorus*

5. No more I'll eat cold pudding,
   And no more I'll eat hard bread.
   No more I'll eat them half-baked beans.
   I vow they're killing me dead.
   *Chorus*

6. I'm going back to Boston town,
   I'll live on Tremont Street
   And I want all you factory girls
   To come to my house and eat.
   *Chorus*

## 38. BREAD AND ROSES

This song, loved and sung today, was inspired by a strike banner of 1912, whose slogan read: "We want bread and roses, too!"

In Lawrence, Massachusetts, half the workers in the woolen mills had been women and children. When a state law in 1911 reduced the work week for children under eighteen from fifty-six to fifty-four hours, the company retaliated by reducing *all* workers' hours to fifty-four, increasing their workload, but at the same time, refusing to increase their wages. The workers responded with a massive strike on New Year's Day, 1912. Encouraged and aided by the Industrial Workers of the World (the "Wobblies"), more than twenty thousand men, women, and children stayed out of work for ten weeks, finally winning concessions from the company.

**Bread and Roses**

As we come marching, marching, in the beau-ty of the day, A mil-lion dark-ened kitch - ens, a thou-sand mill lofts gray, Are touched with all the ra - diance that a sud - den sun dis - clo - ses, For the peo-ple hear us sing-ing: "Bread and ros - es! Bread and ros - es!"

Words and music traditional.
(Both Caroline Kohlsaat and Martha Coleman are credited for the tune.
James Oppenheim wrote the words.

2. As we come marching, marching, we battle too for men,
   For they are women's children, and we mother them again.
   Our lives shall not be sweated from birth until life closes;
   Hearts starve as well as bodies; give us bread, but give us roses!

3. As we come marching, marching, unnumbered women dead
   Go crying through our singing their ancient cry for bread.
   Small art and love and beauty their drudging spirits knew.
   Yes, it is bread we fight for—but we fight for roses, too!

4. As we come marching, marching, we bring the greater days.
   The rising of the women means the rising of the race.
   No more the drudge and idler—ten that toil where one reposes,
   But a sharing of life's glories: Bread and roses! Bread and roses!

## 39. THE MILL MOTHER'S LAMENT

By 1920, most of the cotton mills were located in the South, where there was a surplus of cheap labor. There the women and men struggled against the companies exploiting them.

Like the miners' bards—Aunt Molly Jackson, Sarah Ogan Gunning, and Florence Reese—Ella Mae Wiggins wrote songs while coping with poverty, starvation, and tragedy. Her life was typical of most of the women from the back country of the Great Smokies. Poverty, undernourishment, and unceasing toil and tragedy aged her prematurely. She had nine children, four of whom died of whooping cough because she had no money for medicine. Her salary in the cotton mills was never more than nine dollars a week. When the National Textile Worker's Union sent organizers down to the mills of Gastonia, North Carolina, they were received with open arms by the workers. The resentment of the mill people, buried during the years of destitution and economic slavery, erupted into militancy. In 1929, the police, deputy sheriffs, and mobs of townspeople, incited to violence, descended upon the strikers. Ella Mae Wiggins, whose songs told true stories and kept the workers' spirits high, was a definite threat to the bosses. She was shot in the back by hired thugs on her way to a union rally.

Strike sympathizers. Courtesy of the Library of Congress

# The Mill Mother's Lament

We leave our homes in the morn-ing, we kiss our child-ren good-bye, —— While we slave for the boss-es, our child-ren scream and cry. And here.

2. And when we drew our money, our grocery bills to pay,
   Not a cent to spend for clothing, not a cent to lay away.

3. And on that very evening, our little son will say,
   "I need some shoes, mother, and so does sister May."

4. How it grieves the heart of a mother, you everyone must know.
   But we can't buy for our children, our wages are too low.

5. It is for our little children, that seem to us so dear,
   But for us, nor them, dear workers, the bosses do not care.

6. But understand, all workers, our union they do fear;
   Let's stand together, workers, and have a union here.

Song by Ella Mae Wiggins.

## 40. COTTON MILL GIRLS

In the 1920s and 30s the men, women, and children ("hillbillies") who came down from the hills to work in the Southern cotton factories found their new destinies a bare improvement over their impoverished farm lives. As mill workers they were kept at a subsistence level, earning as little as twelve cents an hour for a fourteen-hour day, while paying exorbitantly high prices in the company-owned stores.

Malnutrition and physically unhealthy conditions in the factories caused 36 percent of the mill workers to die before the age of twenty-five, usually from "brown lung," a disease caused by breathing lint-laden air.

Although workers in most manufacturing industries in the Northeast are now organized and today have improved living standards, the textile workers in the South are still subject to intimidation, coercion, and threats of retaliation and dismissal which keep them from joining unions. In some locations only one mill worker in ten is unionized.

Many of the textile mills in the Northeast have shut down due to non-union competition from overseas and the American South.

**Cotton Mill Girls**

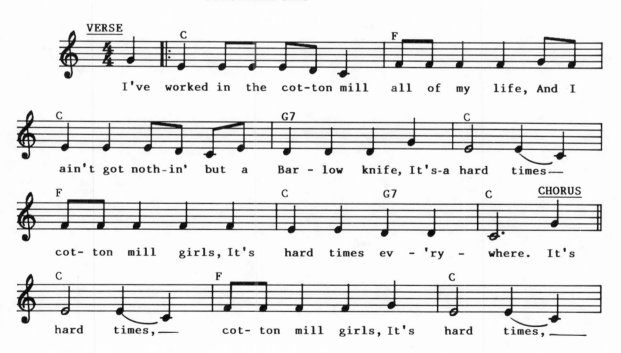

VERSE
I've worked in the cot-ton mill all of my life, And I ain't got noth-in' but a Bar-low knife, It's-a hard times cot-ton mill girls, It's hard times ev-'ry-where. It's CHORUS hard times,—— cot-ton mill girls, It's hard times,——

Traditional

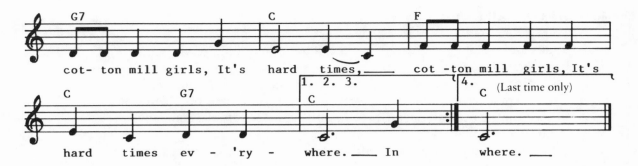

cot- ton mill girls, It's hard times,____ cot -ton mill girls, It's

hard times ev - 'ry - where. ____ In where. ____

2. In nineteen fifteen we heard it said,
   "Move to cotton country and get ahead,"
   But it's hard times, cotton mill girls,
   It's hard times everywhere.
   *Chorus*

3. Us kids worked twelve hours a day
   For fourteen cents of measly pay.
   It's hard times, cotton mill girls,
   It's hard times everywhere.
   *Chorus*

4. When I die don't bury me at all,
   Just hang me up on the spinning room wall,
   Pickle my bones in alkyhol—
   It's hard times everywhere.
   *Chorus*

## 41., 42.  I AM A UNION WOMAN and I AM A GIRL OF CONSTANT SORROW

In the early part of the century, Oliver Perry Garland was a young farmer and part-time minister in Harlan County, Kentucky, one of many who found himself making the transition from agriculture to mining. His daughter, Sarah, recounted often the days of his organizing activities, starting with the meetings with the Knights of Labor, in their coal camp home. Not long afterward, the United Mine Workers sent their organizers into the region.

When Garland's wife died, leaving him with four children, he remarried and presented his second wife with eleven more; thus another famous "miners' bard" was born into the family. Molly (Jackson) and Sarah's (Ogan Gunning) lives were parallel during their youth: the half-sisters were raised in the coal camps as daughters of a miner, and at the age of fourteen and fifteen they became wives of miners. (The mountains also produced two other singers of mill-and-mine protest music, Florence Reese, composer of "Which Side Are You On?" p. 106, and Ella Mae Wiggins, whose "Mill Mother's Lament" appears on p. 99.)

It was a life of assured poverty and even starvation for some of their children and many of their friends. The miners themselves faced a daily threat of mine explosions or cave-ins, and they often died of "black lung" disease, as the coal dust, over a period of time, filled their lungs and caused slow death by suffocation. The families of the miners, especially the organizers, were exposed to extraordinary violence from the hired company thugs. The owners and operators of the mines were determined that unions would not be brought into company towns. Legal justice is hardly possible when the judges and the sheriffs are also the mine operators.

Aunt Molly Jackson once said: "I reached under my arm and I pulled out my pistol, and I walked out backwards. And I said, 'Martin, if you try to take this grub away from me, if they electrocute me for it, I'll shoot you six times in a minute. I've got to feed some children; they're hungry and they can't wait'" [Kathy Kahn, *Hillbilly Women* (New York: Doubleday, 1972)].

The songs of Sarah Ogan Gunning and Aunt Molly Jackson come from an alliance of their conservative religious tradition, expressed in the old hymn tunes, and the most radical activism, written into their lyrics. The songs provide a vivid picture of the era and the people.

From the late thirties until the post—World War II years, both women were "lost." The folk revivalists recovered both their music and the women themselves, many years after they had moved North.

# I Am a Union Woman

(Unaccompanied)

I am a un - ion wo - man, just as brave as I can be. ___ I do not like the boss - es, ___ and the boss - es don't like me. ___ Join the N. M. U.,* Come join the N. M. U. ___

2. I was raised in old Kentucky, in Kentucky borned and bred,
   And when I joined the union, they called me a Rooshian Red.
   Join the N.M.U., Come join the N.M.U.

3. This is the worst time on earth that I have ever saw,
   To get killed out by gun thugs, and framed up by the law.
   Join the N.M.U., Come join the N.M.U.

*National Miners Union. (This song later was sung, "Come join the C.I.O.")

Song by Aunt Molly Jackson.
© 1966 by Stormking Music Inc.
All rights reserved. Used by permission.

# I Am a Girl of Constant Sorrow

(Unaccompanied)

I am a girl ____ of con - stant sor-row, ____ I've seen trou - ble ____ all my days. ____ I bid fare - well ____ to old Ken- tuck - y ____ The state where I ____ ____ was ____ born and raised. ____

2. My mother, how I hated to leave her,
   Mother dear, who now is dead;
   But I had to go and leave her
   So my children could have bread.

3. Perhaps, dear friends, you are wondering
   What the miners eat and wear;
   This question I will try to answer,
   For I'm sure that it is fair.

4. For breakfast we had bulldog gravy
   For supper we had beans and bread;
   The miners don't have any dinner,
   And a tick of straw they call a bed.

5. Well, we call this Hell on earth, friends,
   I must tell you all good-bye.
   Oh, I know you all are hungry,
   Oh, my darling friends, don't cry.

Words by Sarah Ogan Gunning.
Traditional tune.
© Folk Legacy Records (1965).

## 43. WHICH SIDE ARE YOU ON?

"Which Side Are You On?" was penned in 1931 by one of the miner's bards of Harlan County, Kentucky, during a strike by the United Mine Workers. Sheriff J. H. Blair led his gun thugs to beat up and murder the union leaders. One day the thugs came to the door of Florence and Sam Reese when Mrs. Reese and her seven children were home alone.

Asking them, "What are you here for? You know there's nothing but a lot of little hungry children here," she managed to get word to her husband not to return. The men ransacked the house looking for her union-leader husband, then kept watch outside in case of his return, ready to shoot him down.

The song she wrote on an old wall calendar has been used during other strikes, with new words fitted in: "My daddy was a miner / And I'm a miner's son / And I'll stick with the union / 'Til every battle's won," can now be sung " ... And I'm a miner, too / And I'll stick with the union / To see the battle through." In one version of the song (for Guy and Candie Carawan) she sang the line: "My daddy was a miner / He's now in the air and sun, / He'll be with you fellow workers / 'Til every battle's won."

Blue-Collar Asian Women. Photograph © JEB (Joan E. Biren) 1985

# Which Side Are You On?

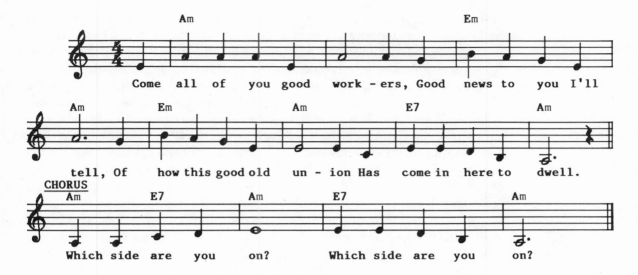

Come all of you good work-ers, Good news to you I'll
tell, Of how this good old un-ion Has come in here to dwell.

**CHORUS**

Which side are you on? Which side are you on?

2. Don't scab for the bosses,
   Don't listen to their lies.
   Us poor folks haven't got a chance
   Unless we organize.
   *Chorus*

3. We're starting our good battle,
   We know we're sure to win,
   Because we've got the gun thugs
   Lookin' very thin.
   *Chorus*

4. You go to Harlan County,
   There is no neutral there.
   You'll either be a union man
   Or a thug for J. H. Blair.
   *Chorus*

5. Oh, workers, can you stand it?
   Oh, tell me how you can—
   Will you be a lousy scab (or "a gun thug")
   Or will you be a man?
   *Chorus*

6. My daddy was a miner
   And I'm a miner's son
   (or "He's now in the air and sun")
   And I'll stick with the union
   (or "He'll be with you fellow workers")
   'Til every battle's won.
   *Chorus*

LABOR   107

## 44. GEORGIA COTTON MILL WOMAN

"Georgia Cotton Mill Woman" tells a true story about Nannie Washburn, a mill labor organizer now in her eighties, living in Atlanta. It is a recent cotton mill song by the co-founder of the Southern Folk Culture Revival Project, Anne Romaine, who started the Project in 1966 with Bernice Johnson Reagon.

The Southern Folk Culture Revival Project tours the country keeping alive the traditional music, black and white, of the region. They play mountain ballads, hoedown tunes, blues and slave songs—Southern music of all kinds, with varied programs and with both black and white performers on each tour. The organization seeks to develop an understanding of the cultural roots of the grassroots South, thereby helping to break down the social and racial divisions of the area.

Anne Romaine and the Southern Grassroots Music Tour have been "shot at, picketed, and thrown out of a million restaurants," she writes. This Nashville singer/songwriter grew up in the mill town of Gastonia, North Carolina, a daughter of a lawyer and the granddaughter of a cotton mill weaver. She is working on a Ph.D. at Vanderbilt University in Nashville, and plays autoharp, guitar, and piano in her own band. She has produced a thirteen-part television series for PBS titled *Carry It On* about traditional music of the South. This song is on the album, *Gettin' on Country* (see the Discography).

### Georgia Cotton Mill Woman

Words and music by Anne Romaine.
© 1976 by Cedarwood Publishing Co., Nashville, TN.
All rights reserved. Used by permission.
Copyright secured.

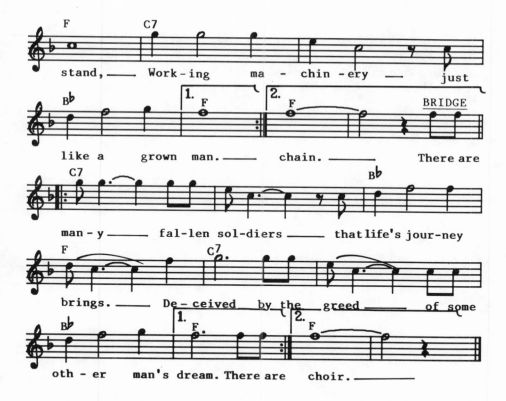

stand, \_\_\_ Work‑ing ma‑chin‑ery \_\_\_ just like a grown man. \_\_\_ chain. \_\_\_ There are man‑y \_\_\_ fal‑len sol‑diers \_\_\_ that life's jour‑ney brings. \_\_\_ De‑ceived by the greed \_\_\_ of some oth‑er man's dream. There are choir. \_\_\_

2. Others around her in sorrow and despair,
   They were working like dogs for that rich man up there.
   And the cruel sounds of lynch mobs that the bosses maintained
   They kept workers so separate—broken links on a chain.

   *Bridge*
   There are many fallen soldiers that life's journey brings,
   Deceived by the greed of some other man's dream.
   There are many fallen soldiers so hungry and so tired,
   Their cries pierce the darkness like Death's angel choir.

   *(Recited)*
   She decided there must be some other way,
   She went on down to the cotton mill that day.
   She said, "Listen, workers, I'm a worker like you,
   And there's way too much power in the hands of the few!
   The cotton mill owner, let *him* weave and spin,
   'Cause we're gonna be out on that picket line
        . . . 'til the day that we win!"
   They carried her into Atlanta to the Big Rock County Jail,
   Told her she's gonna be electrocuted and sent down into Hell.

*Bridge*

There are many fallen soldiers that life's journey brings,
Deceived by the greed of some other man's dream.
But that cotton mill woman, she said the fight had begun—
There'd be no more fallen soldiers when the workers' world is won!

## 45. THE BALLAD OF THE TRIANGLE FIRE

Many young immigrant women, largely Russian Jewish and Italian, worked in the garment industry in New York City at the turn of the century. They displaced men in the factories because they accepted lower wages. They planned to work only until they married. The fact that they were not, as a whole, militant about pay issues made it difficult to organize them and made them unpopular with the all-male unions.

Garment work was done in sweatshops in two ways. In the tenement buildings crowded with immigrants entire families did piecework. They sewed together the cut-out garment pieces from the factories and returned them finished, often working as many as eighty-four hours a week. Women's shirtwaists, popular in 1880 and for several decades thereafter, were made entirely in the factory. Workers, busy for as many as fifty-nine hours per week, were often required to pay for their own needles, thread, and other equipment used in their work. Low pay, speed-ups, long hours, and unhealthful working conditions were the norm.

Sweat-shop in Ludlow Street Tenement, ca. 1889. Photograph by Jacob A. Riis, Jacob A. Riis Collection, Museum of the City of New York

The Women's Trade Union League (WTUL), a federation of native-born, well-off American women, fostered solidarity between these wealthy women and the female workers themselves. The League sponsored protective legislation for women (laws for better working conditions, hours, and wages) and vocational training for women. Most of all the League encouraged the workers to join unions and assisted them when they went out on strike.

On the morning of November 24, 1909, garment workers, newly recruited members of the International Ladies Garment Workers Union (ILGWU), struck at 500 of New York City's shirtwaist shops. Thousands of women joined by men, came out to fill the streets. This was the culmination of six weeks of lock-outs in various shops. Public sympathy was with the strikers and the manufacturers were forced to make concessions. The strikers, who had previously worked fifty-six to fifty-nine hours, won a fifty-two-hour week, plus wage increases.

On March 25, 1911, in the Asch Building, not far from Washington Square in New York City, a fire broke out on the tenth floor lofts of the Triangle Shirtwaist Factory. In the absence of any kind of safety exits or fire extinguishers, approximately 146 young girls perished in that fire.

All events and conditions described in the ballad are true.

Ruth Rubin is an author, editor, performer, songwriter, and compiler of Jewish folksongs, both Yiddish and Israeli. Her prodigious work is listed in the Bibliography. Renowned for her interpretations of Yiddish folksongs, she is a self-taught musician, born and educated in Montreal, Canada. Rubin has a Ph.D. in Humanities (1975–76) from Union Graduate School (without walls), formerly in Yellow Springs, now located in Cincinnati, Ohio. As a lecturer and recitalist, she has appeared at New York's Town Hall, Cooper Union, and Carnegie Hall. She attends many conferences and folk festivals in this country and Canada, Europe, and Israel. Rubin has participated on television and radio programs and has designed tapes and manuals. Many recordings and books of her work have been issued (see Songbooks listing).

## The Ballad of the Triangle Fire

(A capella)

In the heart of New York Ci-ty near Wash-ing-ton Square, In nine - teen-e - lev - en, March winds were cold and bare. A

Words and music by Ruth Rubin.
© 1968 by Ruth Rubin.
All rights reserved. Used by permission.

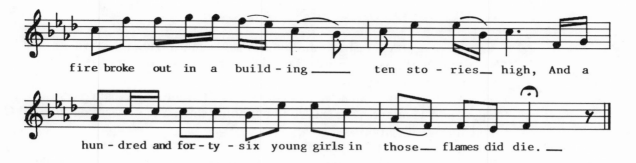

fire broke out in a build - ing ___ ten sto - ries ___ high, And a hun - dred and for - ty - six young girls in those ___ flames did die. ___

2. On the top floor of that building, ten stories in the air,
   Those young girls were working in an old sweatshop there.
   They were sewing shirtwaists for a very low wage,
   So tired and pale and wornout they were at a tender age.

3. The sweatshop was a stuffy room with but a single door.
   The windows they were gray with lint from off that dusty floor.
   There were no comforts, no fresh air, no light to sew thereby,
   And the girls they toiled from early morn 'til darkness filled the sky.

4. Then on that fateful day, dear God, most terrible of days!
   When that big fire broke out, it grew into a mighty blaze!
   In that firetrap away up there, with but a single door
   So many innocent working girls burned, to live no more.

5. A hundred thousand mourners, they followed those sad biers,
   The streets were filled with people, weeping bitter tears.
   Poets, writers everywhere, described that awful pyre—
   When those young girls were trapped to die in the Triangle Fire.

## 46. HERE'S TO THE WOMEN

A native of Seattle, Washington, Linda Allen began singing for a living in the late sixties in the San Francisco Bay area, as did many other singers. She was a friend of Malvina Reynolds.

After traveling extensively (including a USO tour of Vietnam, Australia, Japan, and Thailand), she settled in her home state, and now resides in Bellingham, Washington.

Allen wrote "Here's to the Women" for the Washington State Women's History Project, funded by the National Endowment for the Humanities. Her music supplemented a collection of oral histories, photographs, journals, and letters documenting Washington pioneer women. The exhibit toured the state.

Allen is married, with two children. Her music often concerns motherhood. She writes issue-oriented music, as well, on the subjects of aging, incest, and spouse abuse; happier songs of love and friendship; and those with a historical approach to women's lives. Her strong, unsentimental, yet touching performances are a reflection of her ideas about women's music: "The songs of women, songs lovingly memorized and passed down from mother to daughter, are the strongest cultural links I know to connect us to the lives, thoughts, and feelings of the women who have come before. And the cycle continues as we create new ones out of our current struggles."

Linda Allen also compiled *The Rainy Day Songbook,* a collection of Northwest songs (see Songbooks listing), and founded two folk centers in Washington: Applejam, in Olympia, and The Sunny Side, in Chehalis.

In performances Linda Allen accompanies herself on guitar, autoharp, and dulcimer, and she has shared the stage with many of the great women singers including Margie Adam, Malvina Reynolds, and Joan Baez.

Linda Allen. Photograph by David Scherrer

# Here's to the Women

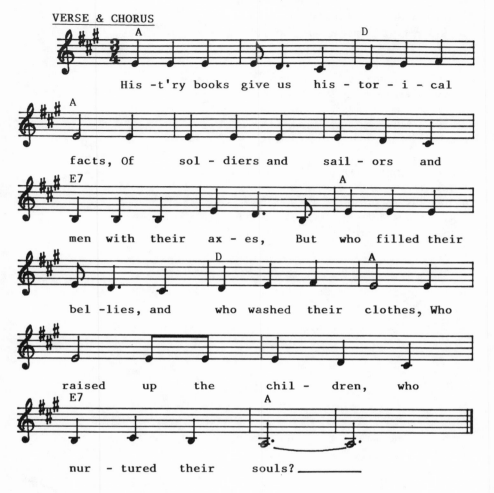

**VERSE & CHORUS**

His -t'ry books give us his - tor - i - cal facts, Of sol - diers and sail - ors and men with their ax - es, But who filled their bel -lies, and who washed their clothes, Who raised up the chil - dren, who nur - tured their souls? _____

*Chorus*

    Without all the women, now, where would we be?
    Working and caring throughout history—
    Their hands on the plow, but their stories untold,
    So here's to the women, who shouldered the load!

2. The wilderness held you in the palm of her hand,
   It took more than muscle to settle this land,
   Women together went straight to the task,
   With schools and libraries—a city at last.
   *Chorus*

3. It's down at the fact'ry, it's out on the line,
   A woman is working from morning 'til night,
   Her mind on the children, her hand on the frame,
   If the kids get in trouble, it's she who is blamed.
   *Chorus*

4. Then it's back home again to do supper and chores,
   Canning and mending and scrubbing the floors,
   Scarce see the children before they're in bed,
   Hard life to follow for beans and fried bread.
   *Chorus*

5. In hard times and good times the women would share
   Their songs and their stories, their loves and their fears,
   And their history's recorded, the song never ends,
   In the mem'ries of mothers and sisters and friends.
   *Chorus. The last chorus repeats its last line.*

## 47. THE HOUSEWIFE'S LAMENT

Housekeeping as unpaid labor is associated with economic dependence on another person and is still largely allocated to women.

Before industrialization the entire family shared work in the house and the farm, although there was a division of labor between the sexes. Roles changed for the middle-class women when men became salary earners in industry outside the home. While those women stayed at home as nonemployed housewives, poorer white women of every kind—immigrants, farm women, minority women—supplemented the family income. Widows were often the sole support of their families: taking in boarders, doing the laundry of others, sewing for others, or, in many cases, working as domestics in other peoples' houses. Women also taught school, became factory hands, shop girls and seamstresses in sweatshops. After industrialization, the women's work force in industry steadily increased. Women took on the dual roles of worker and housewife.

For the farm housewife of the early days, work was endless. Carl N. Degler in his book, *At Odds* (p. 362 ff.) quotes a traveler in eighteenth-century Carolina who reported that "the ordinary women take care of Cows, Hogs, and other small Cattle, make butter and Cheese, spin cotton and flax, help to sow and reap corn, wind silk from the worms, gather Fruit and look after the House." In addition to bearing and rearing large families, the women did the cooking, baking, canning, cleaning, and made soap, candles, and most of the medicines for the family. At peak planting and harvesting days they also assisted the men in the fields.

In the house women battled dirt and dust endlessly. The words of "The Housewife's Lament" were found in the diary of a Mrs. Sara Price, who, it is said, lost seven sons in the Civil War. The words are as meaningful today as they were a hundred years ago.

### The Housewife's Lament

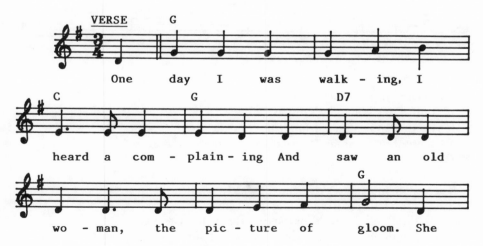

One day I was walk-ing, I heard a com-plain-ing And saw an old wo-man, the pic-ture of gloom. She

Traditional

gazed at the mud on her door - step, ('twas
rain -ing,) And this was her song as she
wield - ed her broom. —— Oh,
life is a toil, —— and love is a
trou - ble, Beau - ty will fade —— and
rich - es will flee, Plea - sures, they
dwin-dle, And pri - ces they dou - ble, and
no-thing is as I would wish it to be. ———

2. "It's sweeping at six and it's dusting at seven;
   It's dinner at eight and it's dishes at nine.
   It's potting and panning from ten to eleven,
   We scarce break our fast 'til we plan how to dine.
   *Chorus*

3. There's too much of worriment goes into a bonnet;
   There's too much of ironing goes into a shirt.
   There's nothing that pays for the time that you waste on it;
   There's nothing that lasts us but trouble and dirt.
   *Chorus*

4. Last night in my dreams I was stationed forever
   On a far little isle in the midst of the sea.
   My one chance for life was a ceaseless endeavor
   To sweep off the waves 'ere they swept over me.
   *Chorus*

5. Alas, t'was no dream, for ahead I behold it;
   I know I am helpless my fate to avert."
   She put down her broom and her apron she folded,
   Then lay down and died, and was buried in dirt.
   *Chorus*

## 48. OUGHTA BE A WOMAN

Bernice Reagon told us the history of this song: "June Jordan wrote the words to 'Oughta Be a Woman' after I talked about my mother. (The poem itself was titled, 'A Way Out of No Way.') The first long working title was 'There oughta be a woman who's not a people.' For me, the song speaks so strongly to the way in which each generation of Black women has to find what they have to do in order to continue the job of being Black women. The lyrics lay out the phenomenon of a woman who is a people-woman, whose life is lived for the continuance of her people. Many times she is severely overextended, and though surrounded by children, husband, and boss ladies, alone with her exhaustion. The song says that 'a way out of no way' is not romantic and it is not noble. It is suicide. We need to end this state where we spend so much energy with work and responsibilities to the ones we love that we have nothing left to connect with other women doing the same thing. That's too much."

An award-winning poet and an essayist, teacher and activist, June Jordan is the author of fourteen books and numerous articles on themes that concern her: the welfare of black people in third world countries and South Africa, oppression of women, black literature, child welfare, street violence, education. Her articles and poetry have appeared in a number of quality journals and periodicals.

Born in Harlem and raised in the Bedford-Stuyvesant section of Brooklyn, Jordan studied at Barnard College in New York City, and at the University of Chicago. At this writing, she is a professor of English at the State University of New York at Stony Brook.

"Oughta Be a Woman" is from Sweet Honey in the Rock's album, *Good News* (see the Discography), and is arranged here from black quartet singing. The background is repeated softly and continuously, as the solo voice flows around it. Each verse is ornamented differently from the previous ones.

Bernice Reagon, the leading member of Sweet Honey, writes music drawn from her cultural roots of black gospel, work songs and blues. Her song, "Give Your Hands to Struggle," p. 63, is also included in this collection. Her biography is on p. 63–64.

### Oughta Be a Woman

(Background acc. voice)

Doo  Doo  Doo  Doo    Doo  Doo  Doo

way out— of no _____ way _____ is flesh out— of flesh,

_____ Is brav -er - y kept _____ out of sight.

_____ way _____ A way out — of no —

_____ way _____ is too much— to ask,

Too much of a task _____ for an - y one —

wo - man. _____

2. Biting her lips and lowering her eyes
   To make sure there's food on the table.
   What do you think would be her surprise
   If the world was as willing as she's able?

3. Hugging herself in an old kitchen chair
   She listens to your hurt and your rage.
   What do you think she knows of despair?
   What do you think is the aching of age?

### 49. PLEASE TIP YOUR WAITRESS

Willie Sordill was inspired to write this song when a waitress friend told him the following story. She had been annoyed by a certain man who came in to eat every night, enjoyed service with a smile and, following the meal, never left a tip.

One night this customer brought a date with him, and to show off how well-known he was in the restaurant, he said to the waitress, "I'll have the usual—you know—right?"

The waitress was ready for him. "Well of course," she replied, "Medium well-done steak, mashed potatoes, and the vegetable of the day, and *no tip, right?*"

She always received a tip after that, says Willie.

Willie Sordill grew up in New Jersey. His goals are modest. He simply wants "to change the world" with his music and "have a good time in the process." A former teacher in a small alternative school, he left for Cambridge, Massachusetts in 1977 to join the folk circuit with his songs and guitar. Within a year of the time he began his new career, he produced an album for Folkways, *Walls to Roses: Songs of Changing Men.* This is the first known recording by a group of men to actively support the women's movement and its goals. His solo album, *Please Tip Your Waitress,* followed, then *Silent Highways* (see the Discography).

Sordill has also composed songs for a children's theater production and for the documentary film, *Men In Early Childhood Education.* Currently he performs both solo and as a member of a six-piece Latin American New Song ensemble, Flor de Caña.

## Please Tip Your Waitress

some jerk o-ver there — says she's too slow — Please tip your
wait-ress, she's work-in' hard for you — She'll
walk a few miles more be-fore she's through She's got
bills to pay and food to buy like you — Please tip your
wait-ress 'cause she's work-in' hard for you. —

2. It's "honey" this and "dear" that all the time
   But that's not half as bad as all those lines
   She's a strong woman and her temper's gonna perk
   If one more guy asks when she gets off work
   *Chorus*

3. When she gets home from work she still can't rest
   'Cause tomorrow at the college there's a test
   She's up early in the morning as a rule
   Makin' sure the kids get off to school
   *Chorus*

4. Her paycheck's low, she does the work of two
   When something's wrong, folks blame you-know-who
   And then they say, Come on now, where's your smile?
   While the owner's gettin' richer all the while
   *Chorus*

## 50. THE TEACHER'S LAMENT

An Arkansas teacher, name unknown, wrote these words to the tune of "Sixteen Tons," Merle Travis's much-parodied song about laboring in the mines.

The serious point, however, is that education is a major issue in the United States. White collar workers, traditionally among the last to organize, now turn to trade unions and use collective bargaining procedures to improve their economic futures and to build more solid careers. Teachers among them, they negotiate for better working conditions, more equitable salaries, and even more preparation time.

Striking teachers emphasize that they are not interested only in their own welfare, but in the quality of American education generally. To attract and keep quality people in the teaching profession, adequate state and federal funding is needed to pay them.

### The Teacher's Lament

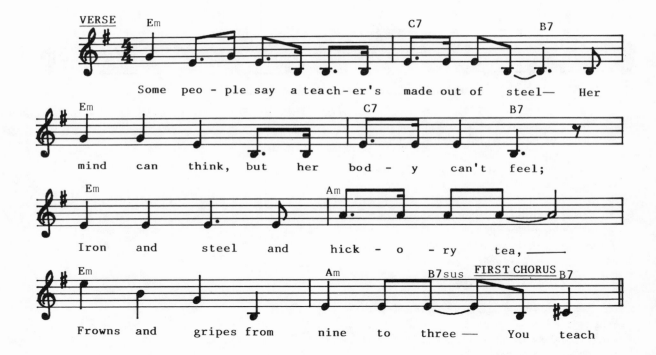

Some peo-ple say a teach-er's made out of steel— Her mind can think, but her bod-y can't feel; Iron and steel and hick-o-ry tea,— Frowns and gripes from nine to three — You teach

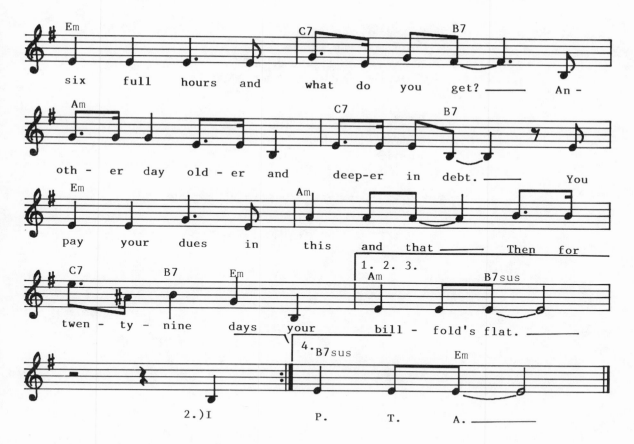

six full hours and what do you get? ____ An-
oth-er day old-er and deep-er in debt. ____ You
pay your dues in this and that ____ Then for
twen-ty-nine days your bill-fold's flat. ____

1. 2. 3.
2.) I P. T. A. ____

2. I woke one morning, it was cloudy and cool
   I picked up my register and started for school,
   I wrote eighty-four names on the home room roll
   And the principal said, "Well, bless my soul."
   *Second chorus*

> You teach six full hours and what do you get?
> Cuts and bruises and dirt and sweat.
> I got two black eyes and can hardly walk.
> When I turned my back, then came the chalk.

3. I got eighty-four kids and forty-two seats—
   Sixty are talking, while twenty-four sleep.
   I can hardly get 'em all through the classroom door
   And if I don't watch out they'll give me twenty-four more.
   *Third chorus*

> You teach six full hours to eighty-four brats
> And all of them yelling like dogs and cats.
> They're cutting on the seats and writing on the walls,
> Hugging and kissing in the upstairs halls.

4. The last bell rings and I start for the door,
   My head is ringing and my feet are sore.
   I taught six full hours—my day is made
   But I still have three hundred papers to grade.
   *Last chorus*

   You teach six full hours and what do you get?
   Another day older and deeper in debt.
   I'll go to St. Peter, but I can't stay—
   I gotta come back to the P.T.A.

## 51. FARMER

Kristin Lems, activist and singer/songwriter from Illinois, first came to the attention of the nation in 1976 when she wrote and performed "The Ballad of the ERA," unofficially adopted as the anthem of the National Organization for Women (NOW).

Born in Evanston and educated at the University of Michigan, Lems also holds two masters degrees from the University of Illinois, one in Middle Eastern studies and another in teaching English as a second language. Her articles, poetry, and music have been published in a number of journals and songbooks (see the Bibliography).

After being the semi-official bard of NOW, Kristin Lems received a Fulbright Scholarship and Lectureship in Algeria, North Africa, where she traveled as a consultant to teachers of English. ("Teaching English to English teachers" is her own description of the job.)

Upon her return to the United States, she released her fourth album, and with a collaborator, Karma Ibsen-Riley, wrote the music and lyrics for a "herstoric" musical, based on a period in the life of Jane Addams of Hull House, titled *Saint Jane and the Devil Baby.*

Becker sisters on their family ranch in San Luis Valley. Courtesy of Colorado Historical Society

"Farmer" is the song Lems most wanted represented in this collection. The lyrics explain the plight of many farm women who face the inheritance taxes on the family farm after their husbands' deaths. In most states husbands are considered the sole owners of farm property, even though the couple together contribute to the business. This ballad tells the entire story through the eyes of a determined woman farmer—not a "farmer's wife."

In a single year not long ago, three movies were made on this subject. Kristin Lems shows her strong concern for women struggling alone. Her own mother raised her two children by herself.

**Farmer**

Words and music by Kristin Lems.
© 1978 by Kleine Ding Music.
All rights reserved. Used by permission.

This is ___ my ___ land. _____

2. We raised two children, they are farmers too
   A crop and garden every year we grew
   Two hundred acres ain't no easy haul,
   But it's a good life, no regrets at all.

3. When Joe turned fifty, his back was actin' up
   We three took over, so's he could rest up;
   My Joe was buried where his Daddy lies,
   And soon some men came askin' for my price.

4. I said, I live here, and here I'm gonna stay;
   What makes you think I wanna move away?
   They smiled real sly, said, now your farmer's dead,
   The farm ain't yours 'til you pay the overhead.

5. I know we women, we ain't been in the know,
   But we're no fools as far as farming goes;
   The crop don't know no woman's work or man's
   There ain't no law can take me from my land;

6. Cause I'm a farmer, I been one all my life
   Call me a farmer, not a farmer's wife;
   The plough and hoe left their patterns on my hand;
   No one can tell me this is not my land,
   This is my land.

## 52. WHAT SHE AIMS TO BE

In the early 1970s, women began to apply for underground jobs in the coal mines. Traditionally, American women did not work in the mines, although women do in Great Britain. During World War II, women here were recruited to work on the surface sorting coal.

There is a great deal of prejudice against women working in mining; a certain amount of superstition is connected with the job. It was (and is) believed to bring bad luck to have women down in the mines—accidents or tragedies might occur. To keep them out of mining, women were told that the work was too dirty and too arduous for them.

Finally in the seventies, largely through the efforts of the Coal Employment Project in Tennessee, women successfully challenged discrimination in hiring practices. Women have now begun to enter the mining workforce in moderate numbers; there are about four thousand women miners nationwide.

Sue Massek of the Reel World String Band was born in Topeka, Kansas, and comes from a long line of fiddlers and banjo players. She started learning the guitar at nine, and played professionally in high school.

The Reel World String Band. Photograph by Barbara Dumesnil

Hitching rides to Pipestem, West Virginia, she stayed at Don West's Appalachian South Folklife Center. The center teaches underprivileged children skills and crafts, as well as pride in their mountain heritage. Old-time musicians are part of the program, and there Massek learned the banjo and taught guitar.

She and the other members of the Reel World String Band live in central Kentucky. They write and perform songs of coal miners and other working people, many of which focus around women's rights. The Reel World String Band is dedicated to the preservation and continuation of their Appalachian heritage, and it performs the music of Si Kahn, Mary Lou Layne, Malvina Reynolds, Woody Guthrie, Aunt Molly Jackson, Holly Near, and others.

## What She Aims to Be

Words and Music by Sue Massek.
© 1981 by Sue Massek.
All rights reserved. Used by permission.

what she wants to be, —— She breathes that black and
dus - ty air, —— wears pads up - on her knees, She's
proud to be —— a wo - man, and she's work - ing to —— be
free, She's a coal min - ing wo - man and that's
(to be a)
what she aims to be. ——————

2. Robin's learned it's hard to find a job that satisfies,
   A woman's need to use the strength that in her body lies;
   It's a rough and rocky journey from the kitchen to the mine,
   But strength is gained from struggle and now Robin's doin' fine.
   *Chorus*

3. It's dark and cold and dangerous down in that dusty mine,
   And the fear of fire and cave-in are hard to leave behind;
   But the life that woman faces down in that lonely hole
   Would be brighter now if you'd respect that woman loadin' coal.
   *Chorus*

## 53. TRUCK DRIVING WOMAN

Si Kahn is one of the outstanding writers of topical and work songs in the United States today. He came to both music and organizing through his work in the Southern Civil Rights Movement in the sixties. After that time he worked with the Brookside strikers in the coal mining camps in Harlan County, Kentucky, and the J. P. Stevens Campaign (mill workers) in the Carolinas. Kahn is especially interested in building coalitions between blacks and whites, women and men, rural and urban people of the South.

Grassroots Leadership, Inc., which Si Kahn directs, provides people at the local level with the organizing assistance they need to deal with such issues as voting rights, health care and disability rights, welfare, discrimination, and environmental problems, from toxic waste to strip mining.

Kahn's first book, *How People Get Power* (McGraw-Hill, 1971), is a standard text in undergraduate courses. His second, *Organizing: A Guide for Grassroots Leaders* (McGraw-Hill, 1982) is also a tool for organizers and activists.

Kahn himself records extensively, and his songs have also been recorded by the Red Clay Ramblers, the Reel World String Band, Hazel Dickens, and many others (see the Discography for his albums).

He was raised in rural Pennsylvania, where his father was a rabbi and his mother an artist.

Ellen Hickey. Photograph by Susan Jørgensen

# Truck Driving Woman

Words and music by Si Kahn.
© 1973 by Joe Hill Music (ASCAP).
Transcribed from the singing of Si Kahn.
All rights reserved. Used by permission.

2. When you see me in the truck stop
   And my long hair hangs in curls
   Don't you try to buy my coffee
   'Cause I ain't no good time girl.

   > No, I'm a truck drivin' momma
   > Five children waiting when I end my run
   > And I got to get movin'
   > Got to be in Georgia with the rising sun.

3. So when you see me on the highway
   And you hear my diesel moan
   Don't you whistle at me buddy
   'Cause you know I'm not alone.

   > I got my good friend* beside me
   > Working together, it's the way we feel
   > Yeah I'm a truck drivin' woman
   > Night haul from Pittsburgh with a load of steel.

*Repeat first verse*

*or "my old man," "my woman"

## 54. TALKING WANT AD

A Bay area Californian originally from Dallas, Janet Smith attended the University of California at Berkeley for two years and graduated from Oberlin.

She played in coffee houses and folk festivals before traveling to Europe in the sixties, where she lived in Rome and managed a folk club. Returning to the United States in the seventies, she started writing her own songs and accompanying Malvina Reynolds; "Talking Want Ad" was Malvina's favorite song of Smith's. Both Smith and Peggy Seeger have recorded it, and it has been published in Sweden, as well.

Smith makes her living making music transcriptions and calligraphy for many clients, including Country Joe MacDonald, Taj Mahal, and others. She has transcribed classical and serious music as well, both from abroad and in the United States. Janet Smith is also a part-time illustrator for the Biochemistry Department at Berkeley, and in her spare time she continues to write songs.

Janet Smith. Photograph by Barbara Renan, Frog Photo Company

## Talking Want Ad

(Spoken) 1. Oh, I'm look-in' for a man to wash my clothes,

Iron my shirts and blow my nose, Sweep the floor and

wax the kitch-en While I sit a-round play-in' gui-tar an' bitch-in'!

Mud all o - ver my boots,

Feet up - on the ta-ble, - Just do-in' my

1. (All but the last time)

thing.                                        2. Oh, I'm

2. (Last time only)

(Guitar acc.)

Words and music by Janet Smith.
© 1973 by Bella Roma Music.
International copyright secured.
All rights reserved. Used by permission.

2. I'm lookin' for a man to cook my meals,
   Wash the dishes and take the peels
   Off my bananas with a grin,
   And ask me how my work day's been—
   *In*sufferable, as usual,
   Playing music is such a struggle.

3. Well, I'm lookin' for a guy with curly hair
   And great big muscles and a nice derrière
   Who'll get up nights and feed the baby
   An' bring my coffee when I'm ready—
   I gotta feel good in the morning—
   That's when I make my best music.

4. So if you feel you'd like to apply,
   Just send a photo or drop on by,
   And I'll let you shine my shoes today,
   'N if you do that good, I'll let you stay
   And cook my dinner
   And after you've cleaned up after yourself
   (If you're lucky—)
   I *might* let you listen to me practice my guitar!

# Contemporary Issues

From "The Spirit of Houston," the First National Women's Conference in observance of International Women's Year, November 1977. Courtesy of Women Strike for Peace

## 55. THE LITTLE ORPHAN GIRL

A traditional song of poverty and inequality, "The Little Orphan Girl" has been sung for generations in our Southern mountains. Printed as a broadside in America, it is typical of the turn-of-the-century sentimental ballads that were so popular in the United States. It is included here because of our current interest in the rights of children; in any civilized society every child has the right to a home.

Unlike the last century, today our interest in child welfare includes prenatal care for low income families, school lunch programs, child support by absent or divorced parents; programs like Head Start, and childcare for working mothers; family and child counseling; foster home regulation and just adoption laws. Feminists believe that government has a responsibility to aid those unable to help themselves, and these essential programs must be maintained, since it is estimated that by the year 2000, almost all poor people will be women and children.

### The Little Orphan Girl

"No home, no home," cried a lit-tle girl, At the door of a rich man's home As she trem-bling stood on the mar-ble steps, "A home and a piece of bread."

Traditional

2. "My father, alas, I never knew,"
   And the tears did fall so fast,
   "My mother sleeps in a new-made grave,
   'Tis an orphan who begs tonight."

3. The night was dark and the snow fell down,
   But the rich man closed his door,
   He proudly said, as he turned away,
   "No home, no bread for the poor."

4. The rich man slept on his velvet couch,
   And he dreamed of his silver and gold,
   While the poor little girl made her bed on the snow
   And murmured, "So cold, so cold."

5. The morning dawned, and the little girl
   Still lay at the rich man's door,
   But her soul had fled to the world above,
   Where there's room and bread for the poor.

## 56. BRIGHAM, BRIGHAM YOUNG

Brigham Young was much-ridiculed in his day, and this song may have originated on the minstrel stage. It found its way into books of Mormon folk songs over the years; the church appears to view its radical departures from other sects with good humor. It occurred to us that interest in limiting the size of families goes back many generations.

    We sing it unaccompanied. Rosalie Sorrels, a collector of Mormon songs of the West, sings a version of it accompanied with her guitar.

### Brigham, Brigham Young

Old Brig-ham Young was a Mor-mon bold, And a lead-er of the roar-ing rams, And a shep-herd of a heap of pret-ty lit-tle sheep, And a nice fold of pret-ty lit-tle lambs. And he lived with five and for-ty wives In the ci-ty of Great Salt Lake, Where they woo and they coo as pret-ty doves do And cac-kle like ducks to a drake.

Traditional

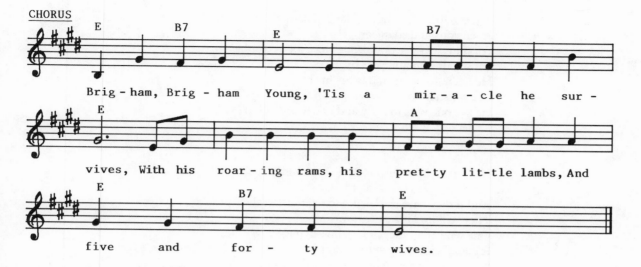

Brig - ham, Brig - ham Young, 'Tis a mir - a - cle he sur -
vives, With his roar - ing rams, his pret - ty lit - tle lambs, And
five and for - ty wives.

2. Number forty-five was about sixteen,
   Number one was sixty-three,
   And among such a riot how he ever keeps 'em quiet
   Is a right-down mystery to me.
   For they clatter and they claw, and they jaw, jaw, jaw,
   Each one has a different desire;
   It would aid the renown of the best shop in town
   To supply them with half what they require.
   *Chorus*

3. Old Brigham Young was a stout man once
   But now he is thin and old,
   And I love to state, there's no hair on his pate
   Which once had a covering of gold.
   For his youngest wives won't have white wool
   And his old ones won't take red,
   So in tearing it out they have taken turn about
   'Til they've pulled all the wool from his head.
   *Chorus*

4. Now his boys sing songs all day,
   And his girls they all sing psalms;
   And among such a crowd he has it pretty loud
   For they're as musical as Chinese gongs.
   And when they advance for a Mormon dance,
   He is filled with great surprise,
   For they're sure to end the night with a tabernacle fight
   And scratch out one another's eyes.
   *Chorus*

5. There never was a home like Brigham Young's,
   So curious and so queer,
   For if his joys are double, he has a lot of trouble,
   For it gains on him year by year.
   He sits in his state and bears his fate
   In a satisfied sort of way;
   He has one wife to bury and one wife to marry
   And a new kid born every day.
   *Chorus*

6. Now if anybody envies Brigham Young,
   Let them go to Great Salt Lake,
   And if they have the leisure to examine at their pleasure
   They will find it's a great mistake.
   One wife at a time, so says my rhyme,
   Is enough for the proudest don,
   So e'er you strive to live lord of forty-five,
   Live happy if you can with one.
   *Chorus*

## 57. THE PILL

We heard this song on a now-rare record called *Dangerous Songs* (Columbia CS9303). The singer was Pete Seeger, the composer, Matt McGinn of Scotland. Pete says, "McGinn just accepts the natural Laws of the Three C's: Continence, Contraceptives, or Chaos."

Although the safety of the pill is once again under question, it was the first method of birth control to provide easy-to-use and nearly perfect protection against unwanted pregnancy. To counter the chaos, activist women now advocate working for those candidates who support planned parenthood for all women.

We broke the rules when we included a British Isles singer, but we could not resist this particular "pill" song. (There are now quite a few.) Matt McGinn was born in the slums of Glasgow in 1928, and spent his thirteenth and fourteenth birthdays in an "approved (reform) school." However, he gained a trade union scholarship to Oxford University at the age of thirty, and became a teacher before becoming a professional folksinger. His first professional appearance was at Carnegie Hall in 1962, and Pete Seeger and Bob Dylan were on the bill with him.

The composer of more than a thousand songs, McGinn also wrote a novel based on his approved school experiences. Then, as an actor, he played in Shakespeare's *Macbeth* at the Edinburgh Festival. His success led to future television appearances. He died in 1977.

### The Pill

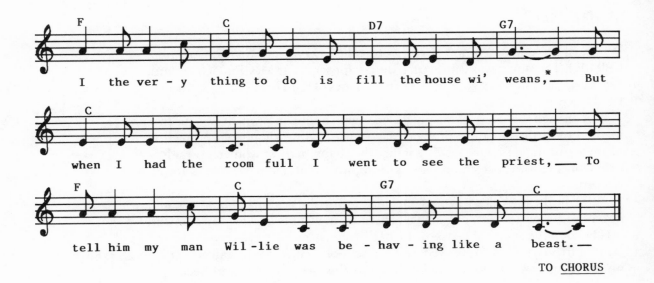

I the ver-y thing to do is fill the house wi' weans,* —— But when I had the room full I went to see the priest, —— To tell him my man Wil-lie was be-hav-ing like a beast. ——

TO <u>CHORUS</u>

2. He gave me such a terrible row, my eyes were filled with tears,
   How long have you been wed, says he, says I, these seven years;
   Says he, you'd better give over all your evil sinful tricks;
   You've been married seven years and you've only got the six.
   *Chorus*

3. Now I'm coming up for forty, in my faith I've aye been true;
   The very last time I tallied them I counted twenty-two;
   But now I've lost the notion for we're running short o' names,
   Though Willie he would welcome more—he's fond o' having weans.
   *Chorus*

4. Now they're talking o' the pill, they've filled my heart wi' hope;
   I'm sitting here and waiting on a signal frae the Pope;
   I went along to buy some at fifteen bob a tin,
   I hope we hae the Pope's O.K. before my man comes in.
   *Chorus*

*babies

## 58. SOMETHING I'VE BEEN MEANING TO TELL YOU

"I wanted to write a song in country-and-western style ... so many are about divorce, broken love affairs, that sort of thing. But I'd never heard one about abortion, though I think it's very much on the minds of the women who listen to those songs."

—Lyn Hardy

Born in Michigan and raised in New York, Lyn Hardy wrote this song as a member of the Putnam String County Band in the early seventies. She now lives in Massachusetts, and plays in a band called Rude Girls.

The 1973 Supreme Court decision giving women the right to safe and legal abortion is again a political football. Opponents of abortion feel that the fetus is already a defenseless human being, with rights of its own. Abortion has been termed "feticide" by some, with the mother described as the "murderer." The fact remains, however, that unwanted pregnancies have been ended by abortion throughout human history, among both married and single women. Regardless of legislation to the contrary, women will persist in maintaining control over their own bodies.

When the practice goes underground, well-to-do women will go out of state or out of the country to obtain a safe, clean, and inexpensive abortion with a doctor in attendance. Poorer women will again be subject to procedures that can leave them sterile or otherwise permanently injured—or even dead.

### Something I've Been Meaning to Tell You

Words and music by Lyndon Hardy.
© 1973 by Lyndon Hardy.
All rights reserved. Used by permission.

all star-ted off \_\_\_ so hap-py,      just

you and\_\_ me \_\_\_ and a dream \_\_\_      Then you

said that\_\_ you wan-ted a fam - 'ly,      and we

star-ted los-in' steam \_\_\_ Well, first came Joe and then

Ma - ry,      now an-oth-er one is on the way, \_\_\_\_\_ I don't

won-der why you're gone all night, I on-ly won-der why I stay.\_\_\_\_\_

**TO CHORUS**

2. They say two point five's the limit, and I see the reason why
Well, I hear it's legal in New York now, and I think I'll give it a try
Well, you can leave me if you want to, take your lady and give her your all,
And when you've had enough of her, well, don't bother to give me a call.
*Chorus*

## 59. BALLAD OF THE WELFARE MOTHER

Linda Allen's unaccompanied dramatic ballad should be sung freely. It tells an important story and makes a strong statement about the plight of the nation's poorest families, two-thirds of which are women and children.

Myths about the women who receive Aid to Families With Dependent Children abound, but the truth is quite different, as this song says. Actually, children and parents are being cheated out of more than $4 billion in private funds per year because of the refusal of many absent parents to make child support payments to their families. Currently strong efforts are being made to enforce child support and expedite the collection of these funds.

Pesha Gertler is the Seattle poet who wrote these words. The mother of five children, she raised them alone, while putting herself through college, living on school loans, and taking odd jobs. She also had to deal with the stigma of being a "welfare bum." When she read a newspaper account of a jailed welfare mother who pitched a rock through the local welfare office window, Pesha wrote this poem, which Linda Allen later put to music. Pesha filled in the details as she thought they might very well be, for her own ex-husband also had a high-paying job which enabled him to pay costly lawyers' fees in order to avoid paying child support.

Both this song and "Here's to the Women" are on Linda Allen's first album, *Mama Wanted to Be a Rainbow Dancer* (see the Discography). Her biography appears on page 114.

### Ballad of the Welfare Mother

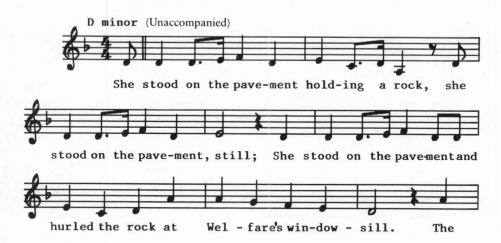

She stood on the pave-ment hold-ing a rock, she stood on the pave-ment, still; She stood on the pave-ment and hurled the rock at Wel-fare's win-dow - sill. The

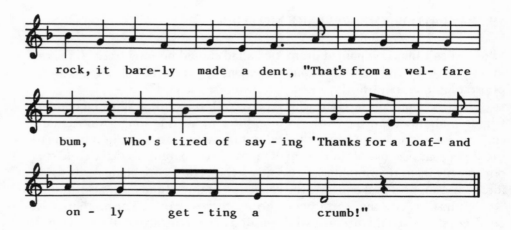

rock, it bare-ly made a dent, "That's from a wel-fare

bum, Who's tired of say-ing 'Thanks for a loaf-' and

on-ly get-ting a crumb!"

2. She stood on the pavement holding a rock, she stood like one harassed;
   She stood on the pavement and hurled the rock—it bounced off the window glass.
   "You hold up my check again and again, and you don't give a damn
   If me and my kids are hungry and broke, while it's steak for my ex-old man!"

3. She paced on the pavement, holding a rock, she paced like one attacked;
   She stopped, took aim, and hurled the rock, and watched the window crack.
   "You sneer at me, sneer at my kids, when we buy food with stamps,
   But you never sneer at him each night when he goes out to dance."

4. She paced on the pavement, holding a rock, while her sweat poured like rain;
   She stopped, took aim, and hurled the rock—it shattered the windowpane.
   "The judge awarded the kids to me, my man was to pay support,
   But you protect the men who run, and the children are victims in court."

5. A crowd rushed out on the pavement, backing off as she took aim:
   One brick in each hand and she hurled them right through the windowpane.
   "You sneer at the holes in our shoes and clothes, and rip off each dime I make,
   And shut the doors of school in my face, then tell me to like my fate."

6. "How's it feel to have holes in *you* for a change?" she shouted through the broken glass;
   And the crowd on the pavement yelled with her: "Up your bureaucratic ass!"
   The sirens in the distance came closer; two cops shoved her aside—
   "What have ya done?" they snarled at her. "A moral act!" she cried.

7. They say she laughed in the jailhouse, and sang the whole night long,
   While the people gathered outside and recalled the day in song:
   How she'd paced on the pavement, holding a rock, while her sweat poured like rain,
   Then stopped, took aim, and hurled the rock—and shattered the windowpane.

## 60. TAKE BACK THE NIGHT

Myths about rape abound, but understanding the facts about rape is the first step toward reducing sexual assault. Most sexual assaults are planned in advance, and the majority of victims are acquainted with their assailants. Rape affects not only the victim, but friends, family, partners, roommates, and coworkers. Most of the victims' primary relationships break up within a year of a rape, including their marriages.

The tendency of both the public and law-enforcement to blame the victim is a major obstacle to apprehending and convicting the rapist, according to rape crisis counselors. We also need to look at the behavior that perpetuates and creates the atmosphere in which rape exists. It will take united action, not the cloistering of women, to eventually set women free from the worry of sexual assault.

Sue Fink is an accomplished keyboard player, and co-founder with Joelyn Grippo of the Women's Chorus in Los Angeles, where Fink is the conductor. Together they toured extensively with comedy and music. Both are active in theater production, and co-wrote the L.A. musical, *Workshop*. Fink writes and arranges for recording artists and recently released the album, *The Big Promise*.

Joelyn Grippo, born and educated in Pennsylvania, attended a two-year writers' program at the University of California at Los Angeles. She develops pilots for television and movies-of-the-week, and is a member of the improvisational group, Off The Wall. She has written material for many stand-up comics and situation comedy shows. Four of her songs are on Sue Fink's album (see the Discography).

### Take Back the Night

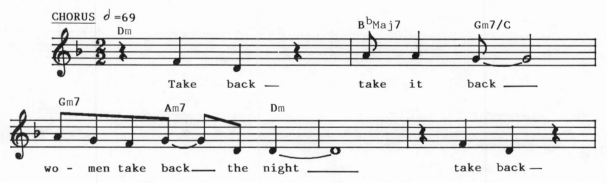

Words by Joelyn Grippo.
Music by Susan Jane Fink.
© 1978 by Susan Jane Fink and Joelyn Grippo.
Used by permission.

take it back ____ wo-men take back ___ the night! _____ She
wore tight clothes your hon — or _____ how
could she want ____ re-spect? _____ She
drew at - ten - tion to ____ her self, ____ now
what did she ____ ex - pect? _____
Now the wo - man is ___ con - vict - ed, the ra - pist is ___ set free ___
____ While de - sign - ers of ____ her clothes ___
rake in a high - er fee _____ While de - sign - ers of ___
____ her clothes ___ rake in a high - er fee. _____

GO BACK TO <u>CHORUS</u>

2. *Chorus*
   She's waiting for the bus to come
   on an empty street.
   She knows that it's a risk to take
   working while others sleep.
   But when a woman heads a family
   with children home to feed,
   She can't wait for laws from Congress
   to satisfy her needs.

3. *Chorus*
   They tell her that she's too old
   to be out all alone.
   A woman in her helpless state
   should stay locked in her home.
   So she wraps her house around her
   pretending she is safe,
   Until women fight together
   no doors will stop the rape.

## 61. OLD-TIME WOMAN

Holly Near, like Pete Seeger, has successfully blended music and politics. A "folk-to-Broadway" performer, Near is almost a household name in music. She never harangues an audience but projects charismatic warmth and humor. The diverse subjects of her songs make her listeners eager to become involved, whether she sings about nuclear power, war, aging, gay rights, or repressive governments. She sings a lot of *responsible* love songs—nonvictimizing, free from dependency. Her thoughtful lesbian lyrics do not offend the crowds of straight men and women in her audiences; she is a woman for all reasons.

Growing up in a rural community outside of Ukiah, California, she began entertaining at gatherings around her town at the age of seven. At eighteen she enrolled in UCLA to study drama, but after just one year she acquired roles in major television shows and in movies, then went to New York to take a major part in the Broadway cast of *Hair.*

Holly Near toured Vietnam during the heat of the war and, with a focused political consciousness, she became eager to bring her songs to the public; immediately after returning home she started her own record company (Redwood) with Jeff Langley, her oft-times accompanist and co-writer of many of her songs. Her first album, *Hang In There,* was a musical tribute to the courage of the Vietnamese people. It sold forty thousand copies.

We have included two songs by Holly Near in this songbook. "Old Time Woman" is one of three about aging in the volume. (See "Maggie Kuhn" and "Coming into My Years," also about growing older.) Our country has paid scant attention to the welfare of the elderly, which is the fastest growing group in the country. (The baby-boomers are rapidly growing older and will soon have to look to their future, social historians tell us.)

Holly Near, singer/songwriter—social activist. Photograph by Irene Young

## Old-Time Woman

INTRO. (Ad lib)

I just found out this af-ter-noon, I've been car-ry-ing life for two, ___ Need-ed con-ver-sa-tion ___ to know what I should do, I was walk-ing down a lone-ly street when I heard this talk-ing chair, ___ So I climbed up on the moon-lit porch ___ to see what was there. ___

VERSE

She was propped up on a pil-low ___ and rock-ing in a rock-ing chair, ___ She looked like she might be lone-ly, like she

Words by Jeff Langley and Holly Near.
Music by Jeff Langley.
© 1973 by Hereford Music.
All rights reserved. Used by permission.

may-be had some words to share, ____ So I pulled up close and

asked her name ____ and this was her ex-act re-ply, ____ "I am an

old - time wo - man, ____ a - wait - ting to

**1.** die." ____ **2.** Well good. ____ She

told me ____ she'd nev-er had a man ____ 'til she was firm-ly wed,

____ Nev - er un - der - stood ____ her ma ____ un -

til her pa ____ was dead, ____ But still her man came first and

then her thir-teen sons, ____ It was-n't 'til they had all gone

____ a - way ____ That she star-ted to have an - y kind of fun at all. I

un - til I _____ die. _____

When I _____ left her house that night my prob-lems seemed so

small, If I grow _____ to be like her _____ soon I

won't have ma- ny prob-lems at all, _____ I know _____ I'm go - ing

back a - gain _____ to rock with my fin- est friend, I'll love that

old time wo-man _____ un - til the end. _____

2. Well we got to talking and soon we were the best of friends,
   I told her about my problems, she told me how it was back then,
   We talked about a lot of things I never thought she would have understood,
   But that old time woman, she did me good.
   *Bridge*

3. I wanted to make her young again but all I could do was cry,
   She took my swollen cheeks in hand and made me look her in the eye,
   She said, "If I had not suffered, you wouldn't be wearing those jeans
   Being an old time woman ain't as bad as it seems."

4. She was propped up on a pillow, rocking in her rocking chair,
   I'd never had such good talking, I knew that she really cared,
   I'm glad I couldn't make her young again, this moment might have passed us by,
   I'll love that old time woman until I die.
   *Coda*

## 62.  COMING INTO MY YEARS

This powerful song is an anthem for today's older women. "Coming into My Years," with its upbeat view of aging, was published by the Gray Panthers in their *National Newsletter.*

Betsy Rose writes songs on the subjects of racism, sexual harassment, the rights of minorities, growing up and living in the nuclear age, and growing old in our society.

Besides performing at folk festivals around the country and in Canada, Rose appears at conferences held on the issues of women's rights, world peace in the nuclear age, and racial equality. She has participated in workshops and residencies in songwriting and also in music and social issues.

She has shared the stage with Sweet Honey in the Rock, Pete Seeger, Odetta, Holly Near, the Paul Winter Consort, Meg Christian, Taj Mahal, Bright Morning Star, Ginni Clemmens, Utah Phillips, Tom Paxton, Rosalie Sorrels, Fred Small, Casselberry and Dupree, Ronnie Gilbert, and others. Her songs have been recorded by Ronnie Gilbert, Meg Christian, Peggy Seeger and Ewan MacColl, and Judy Gorman-Jacobs.

Betsy Rose. Photograph by Susan Fleischmann

## Coming into My Years

I'm a gray-haired wo-man and I'm com-ing in—— to my years ———— I'm a wea-thered wo-man and I'm com-ing in - to my years———— No more hold - ing back, —— no more trying to please—— I got the will and the pow - er to get off my knees—— I'm an ag - ing wo - man and I'm com - ing in—— to my years ————

but
I'm a streetwise woman and I'm coming into my pride
I'm a fight back woman and I'm coming into my pride
No more shrinking with fear when they whistle and jeer
I got a fist that's hard and a mind that's clear
I'm a nightwalk woman and I'm coming into my pride.

Words and music by Betsy Rose.
© 1980 by Betsy Rose.

I'm a loudmouth woman and I'm coming into my voice
I'm a talk back woman and I'm coming into my voice
There's an ocean of words that got caught in my throat
I'm gonna let loose the waters gonna learn how to float
I'm a sing out woman and I'm coming into my voice.

I'm a fighting woman and I'm coming into my strength
I'm a make change woman and I'm coming into my strength
I won't save the world I won't drain my song
But I'll fight any battle that'll move us along
I'm a far-sighted woman and I'm coming into my strength.

I'm a loving woman and I'm coming into my own
I'm a heartbeat woman and I'm coming into my own
I'll go for passion, I'll go for strength
I'll go for the moment and I'll go for the length
I'm a give-take woman and I'm coming into my own.

## 63. THE LEFT-HANDED SONG FOR HUMAN RIGHTS

This song was a semi-finalist in Dr. Demento's 1982 Bizarre and Topical Song Contest. It was written to counter Anita Bryant's anti-gay rights rhetoric of the late seventies.

Joanna Cazden was born in Champaign, Illinois, but the pressures of the McCarthy era soon forced her family to relocate in the East. She grew up in Bridgeport, Connecticut, and Lexington, Massachusetts. In addition to the influence of her father, composer and musicologist Norman Cazden, she learned to appreciate "the social and political side of songmaking" at the progressive Camp Woodland in New York State, where artists ("like Pete Seeger") visited every summer.

Cazden studied music and drama from childhood, but it was not until the seventies and the discovery of the women's movement that she began to take her writing seriously and to seek an audience. Since that time she has performed at folk festivals and at many peace, human rights, and feminist events around the country. She records and writes articles for music journals, where her songs also appear. One of her songs was published in *All Our Lives*, a woman's songbook of the seventies (see the Bibliography and the Discography).

Joanna Cazden. Photography by Larry Coleman

# The Left-Handed Song for Human Rights

VERSE

Come ___ ga-ther 'round good peo-ple, and you must lis-ten well There's a dan-ger in our coun-try as you will hear me tell It be-gins with bang-ing el-bows as peace-ful-ly you dine It will end with the de-struc-tion of all that's good and fine.

CHORUS (Becoming faster)

So ___ pass the laws, pass the laws, make it clear in ev-ery clause Left hand-eds are hu-man-oid, we've got to keep them un-em-ployed South-paw lib-er-a-tion is the ru-in of our

(Slow)

na-tion Make it for-mal, make 'em nor-mal, pass the laws! ___

( D7 )

Words and music by Joanna Cazden.
© 1977 by Joanna Cazden.

2. We can't have them in the army or teaching in our schools
   Their minds are backward-sinister, they'll undermine the rules
   And they're stubborn as the devil though we lecture every night
   That the Bible cautions us to follow all that's good and Right
   *Chorus*

3. We have tested them and twisted them and taunted them with rocks
   Tried Thorazine and Freud, behavior-mod, electric shocks
   We've erased from all our history books this mutant ten-percent
   We have robbed them of their children and still they won't repent
   *(Chorus, or spoken break)*

   "But you must understand I carry no personal bitterness against these unfortunate people," she
   said, "As a matter of fact it's at a great personal sacrifice that I have undertaken this cause.")

4. I can no longer hire to babysit the young girl living next t' us
   For I heard her tell the children that she is Ambidextrous
   Worst of all: she had the nerve to say that anyone can learn
   The "fulfilling, conscious joy" of using either hand by turn!
   No!
   *Chorus*

5. There's left and right, and white and black, short ones below, tall ones above
   Many ways we choose to live, ways we look and ways we love
   And though differences are scary, I declare the bigger fright
   Is in bigotry legitimized: the danger's on the Right!
   *Last chorus*

   So pass the laws, pass the laws, make it clear in every clause
   People are created free: you're a perfect you, I'm a perfect me
   Human liberation is our only salvation
   Make it formal; not abnormal; pass the laws!!!!

## 64. TALKING WHEELCHAIR BLUES

In 1980, Fred Small gave up his environmental law practice to devote his energies to writing and singing songs for social change.

A native of Plainfield, New Jersey, he earned a B.A. from Yale, and an environmental law degree from the University of Michigan. He gave up his job as an attorney for the Conservation Law Foundation of New England in Boston to become a full-time songwriter and performer.

Small has been active in support of the women's movement since the early 1970s, and in the antisexist men's movement shortly thereafter. He has performed with Betsy Rose in their "Building Bridges" concert and workshop program, and Small also conducts workshops on men's music and changing men. He has performed for the National Organization for Women, 9 to 5, the National Network for Reproductive Rights, Supporters of Silkwood, Working Women for Labor Law Reform, the National Organization for Changing Men, and Men for Nonviolence. He participates nationally at folk showcases, schools, benefit concerts, and rallies for peace, justice, and safe energy.

"Talking Wheelchair Blues" is recorded on *The Heart of the Appaloosa.* *Breaking From the Line,* a book of Fred Small's songs, was published by Yellow Moon Press in 1985 (see Songbooks listing and the Discography).

### Talking Wheelchair Blues

("Talking Blues" guitar style)

```
     G                       C
I went for a jog in the city air
     D
I met a woman in a wheelchair
               G                    C
I said, "I'm sorry to see you're handicapped."
               D                              G
She says, "What makes you think a thing like that?"


         G                           C
         And she looks at me real steady
                 D                         G      (C)  (D)  (G)
             And she says—"Do you want to drag?"
```

Traditional tune.
Words by Fred Small.
© 1983 by Pine Barrens Music (BMI).
All rights reserved. Used by permission.

```
        G                      C
So she starts to roll and I start to run
              D
And she beats the pants off my aching buns
              G            C
You know going uphill I'd hit my stride
        D                        G
But coming down she'd sail on by!


            G
    When I finally caught up with her
                     C                           D
    She says, "Not bad for somebody able-bodied.
              G
    You know, with adequate care and supervision
      C                      D
    You could be taught simple tasks.
                             G
    So how about something to eat?"


              C
I said that'd suit me fine
        D
"We're near a favorite place of mine."
      G              C
So we mosied on over there
        D                        G
But the only way in was up a flight of stairs.


          G
    "Gee, I never noticed that," says I.
                C
    "No problem," the maitre d' replies.
                    D                      G
    "There's a service elevator around the back."


          G                      C
So we made it upstairs on the elevator
            D
With the garbage, flies, and last week's potatoes
      G                      C
I said, "I'd like a table for my friend and me."
      D                                  G
He says, "I'll try to find one out of the way."
              G                      C
Then he whispers, "Uh, is she gonna be sick,
        D
I mean,  pee on the floor or throw some kind of fit?"
      G                  C
I said, "No, I don't think so,
        D
I think she once had polio."
```

          G              C  
But that was twenty years ago.  
        D  
You see, the fact of the matter is,

If the truth be told (pause)—  
        G  
She can't walk." (in hushed tones)


        G                C  
So he points to a table, she wheels her chair  
     D  
Some people look down and others stare  
        G         C  
And a mother grabs her little girl  
       D                  G  
Says, "Keep away, honey, that woman's ill."


We felt right welcome.


        G                C  
Then a fella walks up and starts to babble  
      D  
About the devil and the holy Bible  
       G                C  
Says, "Woman, though marked with flesh's sin,  
 D                     G  
Pray to Jesus, you'll walk again."


        G                C  
Then the waiter says, "What can I get for you?"  
        D  
I said, "I'll have your best imported brew."  
        G         C  
And he says, "What about her?"  
 D                 G  
I say, "Who?" He says, "Her."


        G                C  
"Oh, you mean my friend here."  
       D          G  
He says, "Yeah." I say, "What *about* her?"  
       C            D  
"Well, what does she want?"  
           G  
"Well, why don't you *ask* her?"


           C  
Then he apologizes.  
     D                                  G  
Says he never waited on a cripple before.

```
           G                          C
Well, she talks to the manager when we were through
              D
She says, "There's something you could do
           G                    C
To make it easier for folks in wheelchairs."
           D            G              (C)  (D)
He says, "Oh, it's not necessary.


              D                              G
         Handicapped never come here anyway."


G                                 C
Well, I said goodnight to my newfound friend,
     D
I said, "I'm beginning to understand
     G            C
A little bit of how it feels
     D                        G
To roll through life on a set of wheels."


                           C
She says, "Don't feel sorry, don't feel sad,
   D
I take the good along with the bad
     G                  C
I was arrested once at a protest demo
        D                   G
And the police had to let me go.


         See, we were protesting the fact
                 C                                        D
         That public buildings weren't wheelchair accessible.
         D                              G
         Turned out the jail was the same way.


              G                        C
         Anyway, I look at it this way—
              D
         In fifty years you'll be in worse shape than I am now.
              G                C
         See, we're all the same, this human race.
              D
         Some of us are called disabled. And the rest—
                                        G
         Well, the rest of you are just temporarily able-bodied."
```

## 65. NOW THAT THE BUFFALO'S GONE

Historically, the Indians have been allocated the poorest land. Now, as precious resources are discovered on their land, the people are moved away so that the profits can accrue to the powerful. Singer and songwriter Buffy Sainte-Marie is sensitive to this past and present treatment of her people. "First it was the Gold Rush, then oil was discovered on Indian land. Now it's uranium," she says. "For a long time America was not ready to look at the American Indian except as a victim. For two years I couldn't sing 'Now That the Buffalo's Gone' on television. Then two years later everyone wanted to be an Indian."

"Some Indians went to college," she says. "Some of us became lawyers. . . . I went to *Sesame Street* for nearly five years. Children are important. They watch a lot of television, and *Sesame Street* is on three times a day. When a little kid in South Dakota hears another one say, 'Indians are no good,' that little kid watching T.V. sees Indians, and knows we're here—we have families, we have a language, we're not stuffed in a museum someplace—and he says, 'I know some Indians, and they're O.K.' He knows my little boy, Dakota, and his dad, Sheldon Wolfchild, and he knows *me*. Children [who watch the program] know what's going on in contemporary Indian life." Buffy has also published a book, *Nokosis and the Magic Hat,* a children's adventure story set on an Indian Reservation.

Buffy Sainte-Marie.

Cree Indian Buffy Sainte-Marie was born in the Pay-e-pot reserve in the Qu'Appelle Valley of Saskatchewan. She lost her parents early, was adopted, and grew up in a New England town "where people didn't believe in Indians." She was readopted into Cree at eighteen and graduated from college in Oriental philosophy and religion. She writes songs in French, Cree, and English.

Buffy Sainte-Marie appears at many Indian benefits, and funds the Nihewan Foundation, which has educated scores of Native Americans in virtually every profession and field. She also founded the Native American Women's Association to strengthen the role of native women, and to show them how to supplement their children's education. To nourish the creative arts among Native Americans she established Creative Native Inc.

Two of her most famous songs are included in this collection (see "The Universal Soldier," p. 77).

### Now That the Buffalo's Gone

Can you re-mem-ber the times

That you have held your head high And

told all your friends of your In-di-an claim,

Proud, good la-dy, and proud, good man? Your

great, great, grand-fa-ther from In-dian blood sprang And you

feel in your heart for these ones. Oh, it's

Words and music by Buffy Sainte-Marie.
© 1965 Gypsy Boy Music.

Now that the buf - fa - lo's —— gone. ——

2. Oh, it's written in books and in songs
   That we've been mistreated and wronged.
   Well, over and over I hear the same words
   From you, good lady, and you, good man.
   Well, listen to me if you care where we stand,
   And you feel you're a part of these ones.

3. When a war between nations is lost,
   The loser we know pays the cost,
   But when Germany fell to your hands,
   Consider, dear lady, consider, dear man,
   You left them their pride and you left them their land,
   And what have you done to these ones?

4. Has a change come about Uncle Sam,
   Or are you still taking our lands?
   A treaty forever George Washington signed,
   He did, dear lady, he did, dear man,
   And the treaty's being broken by Kinzua Dam,
   And what will you do for these ones?

5. Oh, it's all in the past, you can say,
   But it's still going on here today.
   The government now wants the Iroquois land,
   That of the Seneca and the Cheyenne.
   It's here and it's now you must help us, dear man,
   Now that the buffalo's gone.

## 66. BLACK WATERS

Jean Ritchie was born and raised in Viper, Kentucky, in "the heart of the Southern Appalachian Mountains" (the Cumberlands), the youngest of fourteen children born to Balis and Abigail Ritchie. Their ancestors were among the first to settle the region in 1768.

Her father taught Jean, at the age of five, to play the mountain dulcimer, and through the years she has continued to play the traditional old ballads, play-party songs, and love songs handed down from their Scottish, Irish, and English ancestors. "Changing times are catching up with the mountains, but folks still love the old songs," she says. Their favorites were "Barbry Ellen," "Over the River, Charlie," "Sourwood Mountain," and "Lord Randall."

"Hillbilly music and tin-pan alley songs were never very popular," she tells us. "They made up a lot of new songs, often based on news accounts of local events—hangings, elections, ground-hog hunts, elopements, feuds—each a living part of the growth of the region." We have included a "folksong" composed by Jean Ritchie. "Black Waters" tells of the destruction of nature by strip mining. People of the United States are becoming aware of the hazards faced when giant corporations are allowed to create irreversible ecological damage.

Jean Ritchie. Photograph by George Pickow

Ritchie was graduated from local schools, then the University of Kentucky with a Phi Beta Kappa key. With her bachelor's degree in social work, she took her first job at the famous Henry Street Settlement in New York City, where she often entertained children with her dulcimer and songs. Alan Lomax recorded her songs for the Library of Congress Folksong Archives and introduced her at Oxford Press. Her first book, *Singing Family of the Cumberlands*, published in 1955, was widely reviewed as an American classic and is still in print today (see the Bibliography). Many books have followed; *Celebration of Life* won a national prize upon its publication.

Jean Ritchie is frequently consulted as a folklorist. She often sings at folk festivals and was one of the seven original directors of the Newport Folk Festival. She served a term on the first folklore panel of the National Endowment for the Arts. She has made many television appearances. Her album, *None But One*, won the Rolling Stone Critics' Award as Best Folk Album of the Year in 1977.

## Black Waters

Words and music by Jean Ritchie.
© 1967, 1971 Geordie Music Publishing.
All rights reserved. Used by permission.

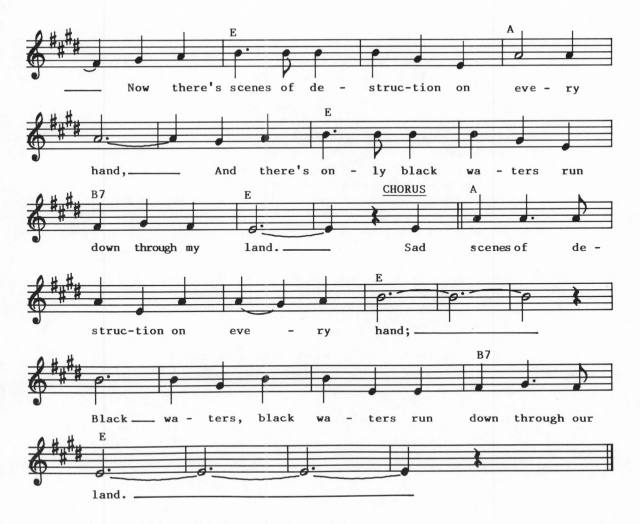

Now there's scenes of de - struc-tion on eve - ry
hand,_____ And there's on - ly black wa - ters run
down through my land._____ Sad scenes of de -
struc-tion on eve - ry hand;_____
Black _ wa - ters, black wa - ters run down through our
land._____

2. O the quail, she's a pretty bird, she sings a sweet tongue;
   In the roots of tall timbers she nests with her young.
   But the hillside explodes with the dynamite's roar,
   And the voices of the small birds will sound there no more;
   And the hillsides come a-sliding so awful and grand,
   And the flooding black waters rise over my land.
   *Chorus*

   Sad scenes of destruction on every hand;
   Black waters, black waters run down through the land.

3. In the rising of the springtime we planted our corn,
   In the ending of the springtime we buried a son,
   In summer come a nice man, said, "Everything's fine—
   My employer just requires a way to his mine"—
   Then they threw down my mountain and covered my corn,
   And the grave on the hillside's a mile deeper down,
   And the man stands and talks with his hat in his hand
   As the poisonous water spreads over my land.
   *Chorus*

   > Sad scenes of destruction on every hand;
   > Black waters, black waters run down through the land.

4. Well, I ain't got no money and not much of a home;
   I own my own land, but my land's not my own.
   But if I had ten million—somewheres thereabouts
   I would buy Perry County and I'd run 'em all out!
   Set down on the bank with my bait in my can,
   And just watch the clear waters run down through my land!
   *Last chorus*

   > Well, wouldn't that be like the old Promised Land?
   > Black waters, black waters no more in my land!

## 67. WHAT HAVE THEY DONE TO THE RAIN?

The first book that was a best seller on the subject of endangering the environment with chemical pollutants was Rachel Carson's *Silent Spring,* first published in 1962. Since then environmental pollution has become a national concern in this country, while at the same time a government scandal. This song was originally about nuclear fallout. It applies as well to acid rain: "Just a little breeze with smoke in its eye...."

Malvina Reynolds was one of the best contemporary writers of topical material until her death in 1978. Besides "What Have They Done to the Rain?," three other songs of Malvina Reynolds appear in this collection: "We Don't Need the Men," "If You Love Me," and "Mario's Duck."

When Malvina Reynolds came in contact with Pete Seeger, Woody Guthrie, and Alan Lomax, she wrote songs which she gave to them to sing, being too timid to sing them herself. "We were just a few people getting together to make up some songs," says Pete. "Here was a woman of forty-five or so, with white hair—she seemed real ancient to me then. I was about twenty-seven...."

**What Have They Done to the Rain?**

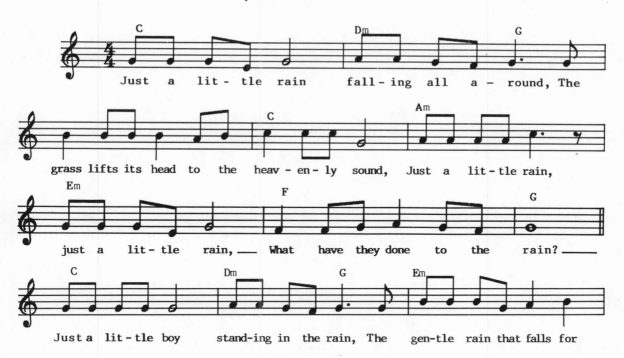

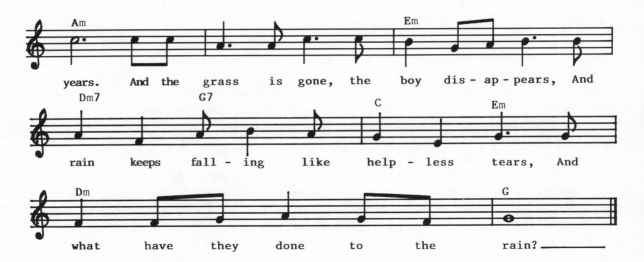

years. And the grass is gone, the boy dis - ap - pears, And

rain keeps fall - ing like help - less tears, And

what have they done to the rain? _____

Just a little breeze out of the sky,
The leaves pat their hands as the breeze blows by,
Just a little breeze with smoke in its eye,
What have they done to the rain?
*(Second part again)*

## 68. ORGANIC

"Organic" was first published in a 1972 folio of twenty compositions, entitled *Growin' Songs,* by Patty Hall (see Songbooks listing and the Discography). It seems to be a particularly appropriate song for today, when the country is obsessively exercise-and-health conscious. However, it does appear that heart disease is decreasing as a result of our fanaticism—one good result.

Patty Hall was born in Berkeley, California. She says that it was a set of tickets to the Berkeley Folk Festival, won from a radio station when she was fifteen years old, that began her love affair with folk music. "That festival opened up a new world for me; a world of Cajun, salsa, topical, stringband, and contemporary music. I immediately taught myself the rudiments of five-string banjo and started a folksinging group called the Song Spinners. We wore black tights, played two banjos, one guitar and four ukeleles, and sang our hearts out. For a high school band, we really *cooked.*" In 1971 she began to write and compose her own material, and in the next year she published her songbook (see Songbooks listing).

Patty Hall has been featured at a number of festivals. In 1975, after completing a master's degree in folklore at the University of California, she moved to Nashville to work at the Country Music Foundation, where she conducted oral histories of women in early country music. In 1977 she was hired for the American Association for State and Local History, developing education programs for staff working in museums throughout the country. She wrote articles for journals about historical country music and women's music, and co-produced an album for Rounder Records: *Banjo Pickin' Girl: Women in Early Country Music.* She has written the liner notes for both Time-Life and Franklin Mint albums.

### Organic

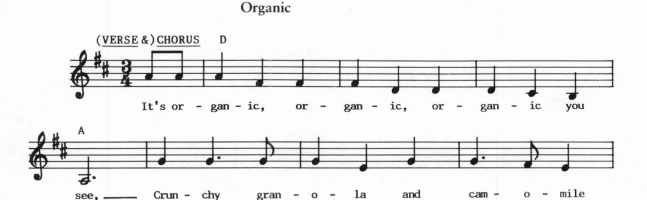

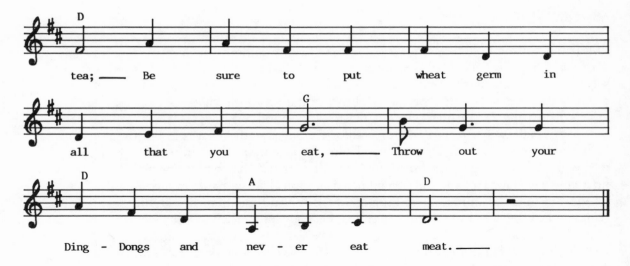

tea; — Be sure to put wheat germ in all that you eat, — Throw out your Ding - Dongs and nev - er eat meat. —

1. We used to all live in the city and feast
   On Big Macs and Ripple and Twinkies, at least,
   But now we've all moved to the country and say
   If you don't live organic, it just ain't the way.

2. We've broken old habits of unhealthy vice,
   We now eat fresh seaweed and short-grained brown rice;
   We've cleared out our cupboards, threw out those stale rolls,
   By planting a garden, we've cleaned up our souls.
   *Chorus*

3. Marty's our neighbor who lives up the hill,
   He gave up Hostess cupcakes and old Taco Bell;
   I went over to borrow some yogurt last night,
   Walked into his kitchen and met with this sight:

4. He was frying up catnip and grasshopper heads,
   While stirring his banquet he looked up and said,
   "I know it looks putrid, it tastes just like hell,
   But, man, it's organic, that makes it all swell."
   *Chorus*

5. Oh, Hillary lives upstairs, alone in her room,
   She reads Adele Davis and weaves on her loom;
   There's a rumor, though, that Hillary, despite what she said,
   Keeps a big box of Hershey bars stashed under her bed.

6. But we forgive these transgressions and don't say a word
   When one of us slips and eats something absurd;
   We all sneak our Fritos in moments of stress,
   But at least we're organic when there's friends to impress.
   *Chorus*

## 69.  TAKE THE CHILDREN AND RUN

The Harrisburg, Pennsylvania, Three-Mile Island Nuclear Power Plant sustained a near-meltdown on March 28, 1979, and radioactive gases poured into the air.

While many people made "NO NUKES" their slogan, the power companies announced to the press that the accident was only a temporary setback and claimed that nuclear energy could be made both safe and profitable.

Opponents of nuclear energy argue that it will never be either safe or profitable. Spokesmen for the industry have discussed standardizing atomic reactors in order to provide safer models. In this way they hope to restore public confidence in nuclear energy and to encourage a stable investment climate. Government decontrol of the industry, however, has allowed for the plant problems to exist, and now, from all indications, the cost of building, starting, maintaining, and dismantling nuclear plants is making this form of power even less feasible today.

The Big Four companies which supply this form of energy are giant conglomerates. Nuclear power accounts for about 10 percent of their total financial interests; of the six companies designing and building reactors, Bechtel controls 40 percent of the domestic market. While the companies say that fifteen orders are needed per year to sustain the industry, orders have stopped completely since 1977.

Citizen's groups, such as Mothers for Peace, say that it will take the public's involvement in order to promote the people's interests. In this song Don Lange lays the blame for this dangerous environmental situation on corporate greed and government's complicity.

A Midwesterner from Illinois, Don Lange has degrees in English and poetry (a master's degree in Fine Arts) from the University of Iowa, and has spent years teaching English, world literature and composition, creative writing, guitar, and songwriting.

He has toured as a performer and songwriter since 1974, and has recorded three albums for Flying Fish Records. His songs have also been recorded in Ireland, England, and Germany. Lange received a grant from the National Endowment for the Arts for songwriting and has been given the Songwriter's Guild Award. Besides performing at the major folk festivals, Lange has appeared on PBS-TV and National Public Radio. His songs have appeared in folk song magazines and recently in *New Folk Favorites*.

A number of singers have added "Take the Children and Run" to their repertoires. It has been recorded by Guy Carawan in this country and by Don Lange in Germany. A German singer has also translated and recorded the song.

# Take the Children and Run

Words and music by Don Lange.
© 1981 Barking Spider Music Company (BMI).
Administered worldwide by Bug Music Company.
All rights reserved. Used by permission.

3. Doctor Atomic lyin' through his teeth
   Says we've nothin' to fear except fear itself
   And he visits the plant in a lead-lined suit
   And he comes out lookin' like courage on the evenin' news

   > Take the children and run
   > Take the children and run
   > Take the children and run.

4. You're on the Commission and you're sixty years old
   You make a deal with the devil, and his profits unfold
   But twenty years down the line and that little girl
   Is in the prime of her life and her blood cells grow wild

   > Take the children and run
   > Take the children and run
   > Take the children and run.

5. I saw the reactor through an April haze
   It looked like a blunderbuss aimed at the sky
   It's your friendly atom ragin' out of control
   And your scientists are prayin' for Lady Luck's smile

   > Take the children and run
   > Take the children and run
   > Take the children and run.

## 70. SURE IS GOOD TO KNOW (WE'RE READY FOR A NUCLEAR WAR)

One of our government's ongoing projects over the years has been its plan to make "nuclear preparedness" a reasonable community concern. From zipcode and license plate evacuation plans to the commitments of hospital beds and personnel, there exists an effort to generate support for the concept of "limited" nuclear war as a viable U.S. tactic. Humor may seem a strange way to treat this most serious issue of our time, but officials in towns and cities all over the nation (as well as abroad) are openly challenging and even ridiculing these efforts, concerned that such "preparedness" might bring about a self-fulfilling prophecy.

Many of our communities are declaring themselves "nuclear free zones" in an effort to make the government rethink its position. "Sure Is Good to Know" reminds us of the power of laughter.

Cathy Winter presents images of strong, focused women in most of her songs. (The following song is a dreadful exception, but the woman with her credit cards has certainly focused on what is important to *her!*)

Winter often places women in a very clear historical setting, bringing alive women long gone whose contributions often remain unnoticed. Her contemporary women, too, are examples of strength and character. Like Malvina Reynolds, Cathy Winter speaks of specific events or eras, and the women she sings of might well be our grandmothers, sisters, daughters, or friends.

Born in Syracuse, New York, Winter graduated from Boston University with a degree in linguistics and French literature. She was a solo performer for six years before teaming with Betsy Rose, another fine songwriter included in this volume. Working together for seven years, they released four cassette tapes (one for children) and an album. This song is from Cathy Winter's recent solo album, *Breath On My Fire* (see the Discography).

### Sure Is Good to Know (We're Ready for a Nuclear War)

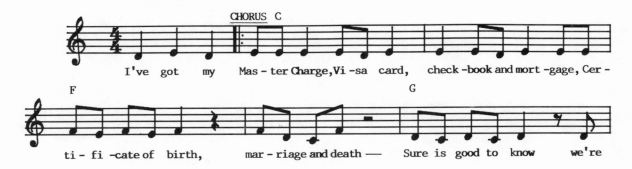

ready for a nu-cle-ar war. My ear is to the ra-di-o, my

feet are on the ground, I'm no fool, no, I'm get-ting it down;

Sure is good to know, we're read-y for a nu-cle-ar war. _____ 1. They

say it can't hap-pen, well, at least not here, It's just a pre-cau-tion, and we

need not fear; I trust those men 'cause I know they're real-ly high-

paid__ I've got the bus stops learned on the e-vac-u-a-tion plan, but they've

got no driv-ers and it seems to me I'd be stand-ing on the cor-ner

soak-ing up the nu-cle-ar rays. But I'd have my

CODA

war. _____ Sure is good to know when the

si - rens start to blow, we all know where we'll go ___

Sure is good to know we're rea-dy for a nu-cle-ar war! ___

2. They say to tell your kids about the siren sound
So if they ever hear it they can head right down
To the basement where they'll be safe 'til it blows away.
And in a few hours we can take a deep breath
Poke out our heads and just see what's left
Shake out our clothes and we can start all over again.
      It won't be hard, we'll have our Master Charge . . .

3. They say it can't happen, but they're training all the troops,
Equipping all the hospitals with medicine for nukes,
Checking out the maps to find out the best escape routes.
Now you can go north, east, or south
But if they blow it up, you know the only way out
Is a rocket ship—headed straight for Mars—
Where you'll need your Master Charge . . .
*Chorus then Coda*

# Growing Up

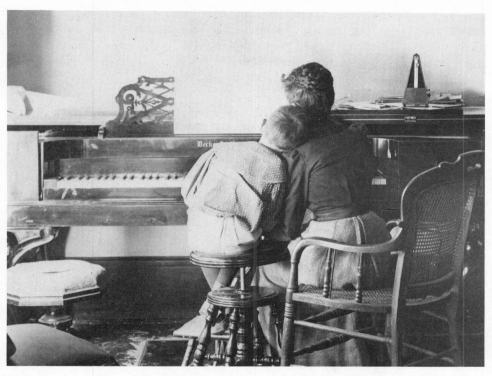

Teacher and pupil at the California School for the Deaf, Berkeley, California, from Mildren Albronda, *The Magic-Lantern Man: Theophilus Hope d'Estrella* (Fremont, CA: Graphic Arts Department, California School for the Deaf, 1985).

## 71. SLEEPYHEAD

Linda Arnold, born in New York City, moved to California at the age of eight. At the University of California at Santa Cruz she majored in dance, and during the Bicentennial she toured the country with the Baroque Dance Ensemble, as part of the Smithsonian Institution's *Dance and Music of the Age of Jefferson* program.

Arnold married soon after, and during her first pregnancy she found herself spending more and more time composing. Her birth class was deeply responsive to her songs, and its members encouraged her to record them.

*Songs of Pregnancy and Birth/Nine Months* is the result. Distributed through Folkways, it is a collection of songs about pregnancy and birth composed in a gentle folk-jazz idiom, reminiscent of the early music of Joni Mitchell. (At the end of the record there is a sound of a baby's first cry, and Linda's exclamation, " . . . a little girl! Oh, I knew it, I knew it!") Besides giving her listeners a positive visualization of labor, she feels that the songs point up important feminist issues concerning a woman's right to decide where she will give birth, who will be present, and how the baby will be delivered. The woman's right to control her own body, she believes, should extend to the birth process.

Linda Arnold. Photograph by Eric Thiermann

Linda Arnold now sings for birth-related organizations, in prenatal classes in hospitals, at La Leche League conferences, and for nurses and birth educators. Most recently, having lost a baby through miscarriage, she is connecting the experiences of dying and death with the birth process, envisioning the entire life process as a circle, something else she is now sharing with other women.

Her interest in the value of life and in providing a healthy environment has led her to songwriting on that subject, as well (see "No Place to Hide," p. 85).

## Sleepyhead

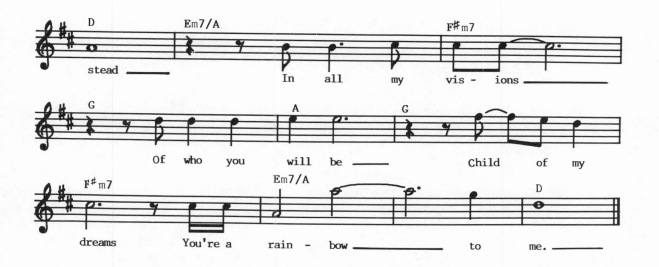

stead _____ In all my vis - ions _____

Of who you will be _____ Child of my

dreams You're a rain - bow _____ to me. _____

### 72., 73. IT'S ONLY A WEE-WEE and MY BODY

Peter Alsop is a unique performer and writer who holds a Ph.D. in educational psychology and has a background in music, theater, and teaching. Alsop has produced and recorded four solo albums, and his songs are part of three anthologies. Traveling worldwide, he has appeared with Elizabeth Kübler-Ross, Benjamin Spock, Masters and Johnson, Cesar Chavez, Barry Commoner, Pete Seeger, Holly Near, and Bruce "Utah" Phillips, among others. Alsop has been called "a psychological Woody Guthrie" and "a musical Mark Twain." Visiting in classrooms, Alsop regales children with upbeat songs and anecdotes, while generating serious discussion on the themes of aging, sex roles, family violence, and violence against women.

"It's Only a Wee-Wee" describes the stereotyping of male and female sex roles that usually takes place as soon as a child is born. "My Body" teaches children self-protection—the ability to say *no* rather than to submit to any physical act with which the child feels uncomfortable.

One in every four or five girls and one in every nine or ten boys are sexually abused before the age of eighteen, according to Margaret Heckler, secretary of Health and Human Services. While sexual abuse is now a widely discussed issue, only rarely is a child in a position to talk with someone to obtain help in extricating herself from an unwanted situation. More often than not the abuser is someone the child knows well—77 percent are parents. "My Body" is useful in opening communication on the topic.

*Wha'd Ya Wanna Do?*, the album on which "My Body" appears, was chosen as the Children's Album of the Year by the National Association of Independent Record Distributors and Manufacturers. "It's Only a Wee-Wee" appears on Alsop's record, *Uniforms* (not a children's album). (See the Discography.)

Peter Alsop lives in Topanga Canyon, California, with his family.

## It's Only a Wee-Wee

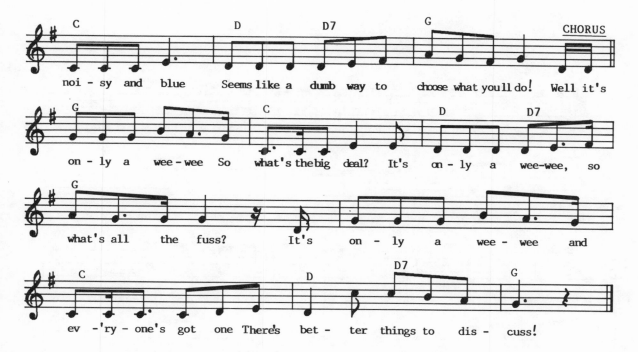

noi-sy and blue  Seems like a dumb way to  choose what you'll do!  Well it's

on-ly a  wee-wee  So  what's the big deal?  It's  on-ly a  wee-wee,  so

what's all  the  fuss?  It's  on-ly  a  wee-wee  and

ev-'ry-one's got  one  There's  bet-ter  things to  dis-cuss!

2. Now girls must use make-up, girls' names and girls' clothes
   And boys must use sneakers, but not pantyhose
   The grown-ups will teach you the rules to their dance
   And if you get confused, they'll say "Look in your pants!"
   *Chorus*

3. If I live to be nine, I won't understand
   Why grown-ups are totally obsessed with their glands
   If I touch myself, "Don't you do that!" I'm told
   And they treat me like I might explode!
   *Chorus*

4. Now grown-ups watch closely each move that we make
   Boys must not cry, and girls must make cake
   It's all very formal and I think it smells
   Let's all be abnormal and act like ourselves!
   *Chorus*

5. *Grown-up's verse:*
   She walked to the market past brave cavaliers
   She tried to avoid them, they whistled and jeered
   She gave them the finger, they gave her more noise
   So she stopped and she sang to those bright little boys!
   *Chorus*

# My Body

**CHORUS**

My bod - y's no - bod - y's bod - y but mine ——

You run —— your own bod - y, let me run mine!

**VERSE**

My nose —— was made —— to sniff and to sneeze —— To

smell what —— I want, and —— to pick when —— I please!

2. My lungs were made to hold air when I breathe
   I am in charge of just how much . . . I need!!!
   *Chorus*

3. My legs were made to dance me around
   To walk and to run, and to jump up and down
   And my mouth was made to blow up a balloon,
   I can eat, kiss and spit, I can whistle a tune!
   *Chorus*

4. No one knows my body better than me
   It tells me "Let's eat!" it tells me "Go pee!"
   *Chorus*

5. Don't hit me or kick me, don't push or shove
   Don't hug me too hard when you show me your love!
   *Chorus*

Words and music by Peter Alsop.
© 1980 by Moose School Music Company.
All rights reserved. Used by permission.

6. Sometimes it's hard to say "No!" and be strong
   When the "No!" feelings come, then I know something's wrong!
   'Cause my body's mine from my head to my toe
   Please leave it alone when you hear me say "No!"
   *Chorus*

7. Secrets are fun when they're filled with surprise
   But not when they hurt us with tricks, threats and lies.
   My body's mine, to be used as I choose,
   Not to be threatened, or forced or abused!
   *Chorus*

8. Our body's one body, one voice is heard
   We each sing for freedom, when we sing these words!
   *Chorus*

## 74. THE FAMILY SONG

Uncle Ruthie Buell, who since the early 1960s has hosted the award-winning children's Saturday morning radio show, *Halfway Down the Stairs* on KPFK in Los Angeles, wrote "The Family Song." We include it here in order to celebrate the many effective ways in which people live together today.

Buell often deals with controversial subjects on her show, knowing that children worry—as adults do—about issues that affect their lives: sexuality, divorce, nuclear war, death, anger, sibling problems. She covers these and many other topics in her sensitive, and often humorous, manner. We wish that her programs could reach children and adults all over the country.

Ruth Buell was born in Chicago. As a teenager, from ages seventeen to nineteen, she lived with the Dyer-Bennetts, then attended Bennington College and California State in Los Angeles.

In her late thirties, Buell went back to school and has been a teacher ever since. Uncle Ruthie has worked with autistic and with severely retarded children, and has made video documentaries about rare retardation syndromes. Currently she works with the orthopedically handicapped.

Besides giving workshops and concerts, she writes about her work, composes songs, and presents her radio show each week.

The traditional one-time-only marriage with two kids and a split-level house is becoming a thing of the past. By 1990, according to Carin Rubenstein, writing in *Psychology Today* (April 1983), more spouses will be part of a second marriage than a first, and one out of every five children may be living with a stepparent. In less than a decade we will be on our way to becoming a nation of stepfamilies. Many more women will be choosing to raise children without marrying; we are already seeing fathers who have sole custody or shared custody in cases where divorce has ended a marriage. Both lesbian and gay couples with children are unusual but are becoming more numerous.

### The Family Song

Bob - by and his sis - ter live with a Ms. and
Mis - ter Who vowed to love for bet - ter or for worse. ___ And

Bob - by real-ly loves his folks and does-n't un - der - stand the jokes, His mom's a doc - tor and his dad's a nurse. And they're a fam - ily, a re - al fam — - ily! There may be dust up - on the floor; the roof might leak a - bove, But they're a fam - ily, a re - al fam — - ily That's liv - ing in a house that's made of love. ——

2. Maya and her mother live alone, there are no other
   People in the house, but still they get along.
   And their laughing and their singing sound like fifty bells a-ringing
   So let's put them in the chorus of our song.
   *Chorus*

        'Cause they're a family, a little family ...

3. Susie and her brother live with their mother
   And someone whom their mother loves a lot.
   And they've got a cat named Rover, and a dog who won't roll over
   And I'll tell you something else that they have got—
   *Chorus*

        They've got a family, a real family ...

4. Now, all of you who hear this song, if there's a place where you belong
   I don't care if you're young or if you're grown,
   If there is someone special who will love you and be close to you,
   You never have to feel you're all alone.
   *Chorus*

   'Cause you're a family, you've got a family . . .

## 75. MARIO'S DUCK

Malvina Reynolds's songs all speak of the human condition; she sang about people in far-off countries; she sang of political problems, family relationships, and children's feelings; she sang about pets: "I have a doggie—his name is Dollaly, O Dally, Dolally, so faithful and true. He lives upon flip-floppers, golly-whoppers and soda poppers..." (from *Tweedles and Foodles For Young Noodles,* a fine collection of songs for young children).

The song we chose for this section has all of those elements. Adults may smile at the bitter ending. Children will undoubtedly feel the frustration and unhappiness of poor, helpless Mario, who lost his friend largely because of the poverty of his Chilean family.

Malvina Reynolds wrote a great many songs for children. They are available on three albums and in her three songbooks (see the Songbooks listing and the Discography).

One of the best contemporary writers of topical material, Malvina Reynolds was born in Berkeley, California, in 1900. As socialists, her parents were vocal critics of the United States' participation in World War I. The San Francisco High School administrators decided to make a public example of her by withholding her diploma; she therefore skipped the ceremony and entered Berkeley without it. She earned a Ph.D. in English literature, with plans to be a writer.

### Mario's Duck

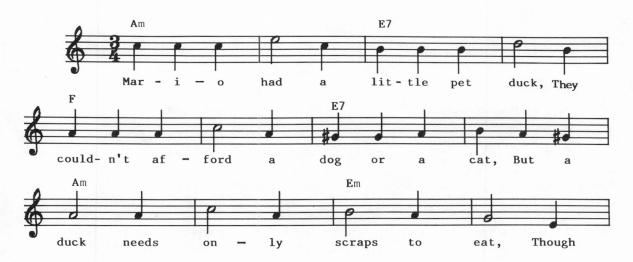

scraps were the fam - ily's prin - ci - pal meat._____
Mar - i - o's fa - ther was God knows where. _____ Af - ter a drunk he would stag - ger in, _____ Out of work and in des - pair, _____ To brood and curse and be gone a - gain. _____

2. Mother washed fine clothes every day
   For the rich people, for little pay,
   Seven kids she raised alone,
   And Mario was the youngest one.
   This was in Chile some years ago
   When the people were poor as they are now.
   Allende tried to change things around
   But the CIA's Junta shot him down.

3. The story that I am telling you
   Happened in Chile a while ago,
   Mario walking a dusty road
   Looking for rags or a scrap of food.
   But there as he walked along his way
   Somebody's duck that had gone astray
   Followed him down around the bend
   And took the boy for his brother and friend.

4. The farmer laughed and let him go,
   But Mario's mother said, "Oh no!
   We can't afford pets in the barrio."
   "I'll find him his food," said Mario.
   Everyone smiled at the funny two,
   The little duck went where the boy would go,
   They played all day by the cabin door
   And slept on the pallet on the floor.

5. As if there weren't troubles to spare,
   Alicia gets pregnant, Alicia the Fair,
   And how can they marry with no place to go?
   There are no more rooms in the barrio.
   But mama manages everything,
   A wedding dress and a wedding ring.
   Two satin sheets that got lost somehow
   In the washing, become the wedding gown.

6. The wedding ring is a silver band
   That once graced Mamacita's hand,
   And a room is made out of boards and tin
   Built onto the hut that they all lived in.
   The wedding bouquet was Mario's find,
   Field flowers of every kind.
   Pretty and bright and arranged with taste
   To hide Alicia's swelling waist.

7. And what did they have for the wedding feast,
   For the bride and the guests and the village priest?
   It was Mario's duck, with the feathers gone,
   Crowning the table, roasted brown!
   What a strange wedding they had that day,
   Eating and drinking and all so gay,
   And Mario, crying, up in the tree
   Throwing rocks at the company.

## 76. THE WITCH SONG

There was a time when witches were not always considered ugly, evil creatures. Before the days of Christianity they were respected as wise, capable women, familiar with herbal medicines. They attended mothers during childbirth, and, before the time of modern medicine, they were the only doctors. In some societies they are revered even today.

Some anthropologists believe witchcraft had its origins in pagan religious rites performed to insure fertility and the continuance of life. When the Church came into power in the Western world, witches were considered heretics and agents of the devil. During the Middle Ages witch hunts were rampant due to the superstition and ignorance of the times. Many women were unjustly persecuted and killed, as some were in the seventeenth century in our own country.

There has been a resurgence of interest in witchcraft today, especially among young people searching for a religion that gives them a bonding with nature, and among those searching for woman-centered ritual.

"The Witch Song" has been recorded by Kristin Lems and by Nancy Schimmel (see the Discography). Bonnie Lockhart is a Berkeley-area feminist and songwriter who compiled and edited *Out Loud!: A Collection of New Songs by Women* with Laurie Olsen (see the Bibliography). Her song, "Still Ain't Satisfied," is on p. 70.

Born a Californian, Lockhart's formal training has been in community college in the Bay area, in jazz workshops, and at Holy Names College in Oakland, where she studied the Kodaly music system. She teaches elementary-age children and performs with Nancy Schimmel and others in the song and story troupe, Plum City Players (see their recording, *Plum Pudding* in the Discography). Lockhart was also a member of Swingshift, a women's jazz group.

### The Witch Song

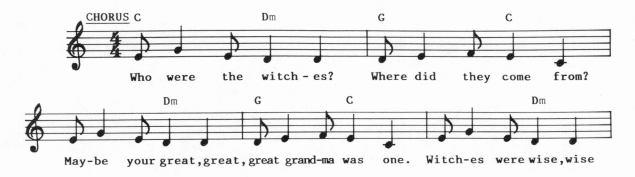

wo - men they say_____ And there's a lit - tle witch in ev- 'ry

**VERSE**

wo - man to - day._____ Witch-es knew all_____ a - bout

flow-ers and weeds, _____ How to use all their roots____ and their

leaves and their seeds._____ When peo - ple grew wear - ry from

hard workin' days, They made 'em feel bet- ter in so ma-ny ways.

2. When women had babies the witches were there
   To hold them and help them and give them care.
   Witches knew stories of how life began.
   Don't you wish you could be one? Well, maybe you can.
   *Chorus*

3. Some people thought that the witches were bad.
   Some people were scared of the power they had.
   But power to help and to heal and to care
   Isn't something to fear, it's a pleasure to share.
   *Chorus*

## 77. TURKEYS

Nancy Schimmel is the storytelling daughter of Malvina Reynolds. Her song, "Turkeys," was a hit on Uncle Ruthie Buell's concert for children in July of 1985, presented live on radio station KPFK in Los Angeles. We include it here.

Schimmel was born in Omaha, Nebraska, where her father was working as an organizer during the Depression, but she grew up in California and attended her mother's alma mater, the University of California at Berkeley, where she earned a master's degree in library science. After working as a librarian for ten years, she left her husband and her job in 1975 to become a freelance storyteller. She teaches storytelling in summer sessions at UCLA, and during the rest of the year she performs for adults and children and gives workshops around the country. Her presentation for teens and adults is called *A Heritage of Uppity Women: Folk Tales.*

Nancy Schimmel lives in Berkeley and performs in children's concerts in the San Francisco Bay area as part of The Plum City Players, with Bonnie Lockhart (also represented in this songbook) and others. Together the Players have made an album of stories and songs called *Plum Pudding* (see the Discography). Schimmel also has written a book, *Just Enough to Make a Story: A Sourcebook for Storytelling.*

Photo Booth. Photograph by Susan Jørgensen

## Turkeys

2. If your boss or teacher (*pause*) seems to put you down
   And you could get in trouble for a frown,
   Go (*razzberry*) in the bathroom mirror till you get it good and wet,
   Then sweetly tell your teacher you're "upset."

> And it's don't let the turkeys get you down,
> Don't let the turkeys get you down,
> When it isn't safe to sass, just let the moment pass,
> But don't let the turkeys get you down.

3. Some days I think that everyone is out to get me down,
   And I can't fight the whole darn town,
   But if I can let my steam off by running half a mile,
   Then I can suffer turkeys with a smile.

> And it's don't let the turkeys get you down,
> Don't let the turkeys get you down,
> If the turkeys are too numerous, remember, life is humorous.
> So don't let the turkeys get you down.

4. Now, if our leader hits the button, 'cause he is in a snit,
   Then going with the flow, it ain't worth a spit,
   So we've got to get together, to see what can be done
   To get the turkeys out of Washington.

> And we won't let the turkeys get us down,
> We won't let the turkeys get us down,
> We cannot turn the other cheek when that reactor starts to leak,
> And we won't let the turkeys get us down.

## 78. THE BALLAD OF ERICA LEVINE

Bob Blue wrote this song for a wedding, but we include it because it is a perceptive song about growing up.

"In real life," writes Blue, "I teach second grade. All the dumb males in my song represent me in various stages of my life. Society trained me how to behave in relationships with women, and somehow, with the help of smart women, I found myself able to begin to undo some of the training." (He adds that the singer should "pause pregnantly" after the italicized words.)

Born in New York City and now residing in the Boston area, Bob Blue is a political songwriter as well as a teacher. This song appears on his album, *Erica Levine and Friends* with twelve other original compositions. Other performers who have recorded the song to date include Kim Wallach and Frankie Armstrong. "The Ballad of Erica Levine" was featured at the 1983 Edinborough Folk Festival.

### The Ballad of Erica Levine

When Er-i-ca Le-vine was sev-en and a half
Up to her door came Ja-son Met-calf— And he said, "Will you mar-ry me,
Er-i-ca Le-vine?" And Er-i-ca Le-vine said,
"What do you mean?" "Well my fa-ther and my mo-ther say a
fel-low ought to mar-ry, And my fa-ther said his bro-ther, who is

my Un - cle Lar - ry, Nev - er mar - ried and he said Un - cle

Lar - ry is a dope— So will you mar - ry me?" Said

Er - i - ca, "Nope.""My pi - an - o teach - er's smart, and she

nev - er had to mar - ry, And your fa - ther may be right a - bout

your Un - cle Lar - ry, But not be - ing mar - ried is - n't

what made him a dope. Don't ask me a - gain, 'cause my

an - swer's "Nope."

2. When Erica Levine was seventeen
   She went to the prom with Joel Bernstein,
   And they danced by the light of a sparkling bobby sock,
   'Cause the theme of the prom was the history of *rock*.
   And after the prom, Joel kissed her at the door,
   And he said, "Do you know what that kiss was for?"
   And she said, "I don't know, but you kiss just fine."
   And he said, "What it means is that you are *mine*."
   And she said, "No I'm not!" and she rushed inside,
   And on the way home, Joel Bernstein cried.
   And she cried, too, and wrote a letter to "Ms.," saying,
   "This much I know: I am mine, not *his*."

208    HERE'S TO THE WOMEN

3.  When Erica Levine was twenty-three,
    Her lover said, "Erica, marry me.
    This relationship is answering a basic need,
    And I'd like to have it legally *guaranteed*.
    For without your precious love I would truly die,
    So why can't we make it legal?" Said Erica, "*Why?*
    Basic needs, at your age, should be met by you;
    I'm your lover, not your mother—let's be careful what we *do*.
    If I should ever marry, I will marry to grow,
    Not for tradition, or possession, or protection. *No*.
    I love you, but your needs are a very different issue."
    Then he cried, and Erica handed him a *tissue*.

4.  When Erica was thirty, she was talking with Lou,
    Discussing and deciding what they wanted to *do*.
    "When we marry, should we move into your place or mine?
    Yours is rent-controlled, but mine is on the green *line*."
    And they argued, and they talked, and they finally didn't care,
    And they joined a small cooperative near Central *Square*.
    And their wedding was a simple one. They wanted it that way.
    And they thought a lot about the things that they would choose to *say*.
    "I will live with you and love you, but I'll never call you mine."
    Then the judge pronounced them married, and everyone had *wine*.
    And a happy-ever-after life is not the kind they got,
    But they tended to be happy more often than not.

## 79. YOUNG AND ALIVE

Betsy Rose is especially concerned with what growing up in the nuclear age does to teenagers. Apathy is common today among young people and adults, and the feeling of helplessness in the nuclear age is hardly unwarranted. As Rose says in this song, however, these feelings should not be allowed to take over our lives. The song puts into words the reasons why the world needs everyone's involvement to make it a better place.

Betsy Rose is a renowned songwriter from Cambridge, Massachusetts, writing songs on those subjects of great interest to people in every phase of their lives, addressing both global and personal issues. For her biography, see p. 160, with the song, "Coming into My Years," on the subject of growing older. She works with young people, and is affiliated with Educators for Social Responsibility.

### Young and Alive

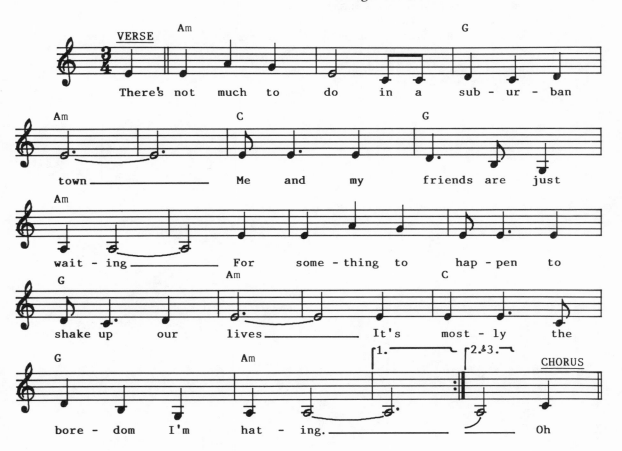

those were the times to be young and a - live,____ I
wish I'd been with them back then _____ It
seems like there's no - thing left worth fight-ing for _____ No
bat - tles left for me to win._____

2. It's school all the day and it's TV at night
   My parents and teachers all say
   In the big game of life the future is mine
   But what if I don't want to play?

3. My big sister Annie she marched in the streets
   And my brother resisted the draft
   I remember at night how I'd listen in bed
   To their friends how they argued and laughed.
   *Chorus*

4. My best friend Jill's getting strung out on pills
   She started with uppers last fall
   We used to be close, now I look in her eyes
   Don't know if she's in there at all.

5. And a couple of boys got killed just this spring
   Driving drunk down a busy thoroughfare
   They weren't close to me but I knew them enough
   To know that they didn't much care.

6. Oh Annie, my sister, you've seen more than me
   Tell me why does this world seem so wrong
   I'm just seventeen and I don't want to die
   From drugs or bad driving or bombs.
   *Chorus*

And you had the time to be young and alive
I wish I'd been with you back then
At least you had something left worth fighting for
And battles you thought you could win.

7. A girl down the hall put a sign on the wall
Called a meeting about nuclear war
She says we're the ones who can stop it for good
But I know that they've tried that before.

8. And I don't like meetings, don't like joining crowds
And none of my friends want to go
But I'm thinking that a meeting is where Annie found
All those good friends she had long ago.
*Chorus*

It may be too late to be young and alive
Did it all really end way back then
It seems like there's nothing left worth fighting for
But a nuclear war means the end.

9. There's not much to do in a suburban town
Just kids hanging out, getting high
But Jill said she'd go to the meeting with me
And my friends said they'd maybe drop by.
*Chorus*

And maybe there's time to be young and alive
Maybe it's worth fighting for
Maybe my sister will march by my side
And maybe we'll stop the big war.

## 80. MY MOM'S A FEMINIST

Kristin Lems, an Illinois feminist singer/songwriter, sent us this song. While it seems that peer pressure controls nearly every kid in the country, obviously many (still) observe a mother's example and attitudes.

Lems's songs deal, most often, with *affirmation*. She is a positive, cheerful, outspoken critic of the status quo. Her live album, *We Will Never Give Up*, was recorded at two rallies, with enthusiastic audience participation (see the Discography). On the back of the album she says, "If you've worn green and white (the E.R.A. colors), driven cross country through the night, canvassed your neighbors, recruited your friends, exasperated your family, made a nuisance of yourself to your legislator, emptied your last pocket and donated the last of your paycheck, lost your voice, lost your job for your 'extracurricular activities,' scaled fences, stopped traffic and gone to jail, sung your heart out, and (you've) done things you never dreamed possible, this album is for you. ... " (Look back to the historical notes about the suffragists. Déjà vu!)

Kristin Lems's biography is on p. 129 with her song, "Farmer."

Kristin Lems. Photograph by John Buckley

# My Mom's a Feminist

VERSE

I pulled in-to the load - ing zone ___

Feel-ing ner-vous, I was all a - lone ___

Un-load ing my e -quip-ment be-fore the show

I star-ted wheel-in' it down

___ the hall ___ 'Til I turned, hear-ing a

young man call ___ "Can I help? That must

___ be hea - vy I know, ___

___ I've been look - ing

CHORUS

for-ward to your show." ___ My mom's a

*(Optional chorus, anywhere in song, using "dad" and "he" or even "folks" and "they")

Words and music by Kristin Lems.
© 1983 by Kleine Ding Music.

fem- i - nist,——— so I un- der - stand——

That's why I'm here to - day,———

I've come to lend a hand ——— I was raised on

e - qual rights,——— and fur -ther-more ———

——— She helped me see —— that e -

qual-i - ty—— is a goal worth fight-ing for. ———

2. She decided she could do some good
   Ringing doorbells in the neighborhood
   Not for the Girl Scouts, but for E.R.A.
   Sometimes she takes her friends along,
   She's only ten, but she's already strong,
   She's a mover and a shaker well on her way,
   When they ask what she's doing, this is what she'll say:
   *Chorus*

3. Different questions in the classroom now
   Young seekers asking how
   Things came to be, and how they can change
   Becoming women and becoming men
   May not ever be the same again,
   But the new ways won't be quite as strange
   When people they trust help them get it arranged.
   *Third verse chorus*

   Because you're feminists, so you understand
   That's why you're here today, you've come to lend a hand
   You raise them on equal rights, and furthermore,
   You help them see that equality is a goal worth fighting for.

4. It's worth all the time you take
   What a difference your time can make
   To the new generation still coming along
   If our movement is to last
   We must see that the torch is passed
   So today's young people will grow up strong
   And thousands more will sing this song.
   *Chorus*

## 81. BEST FRIEND (THE UNICORN SONG)

A foremost writer of women's music, Margie Adam's work is a fusion of pop, jazz, classical, and soft rock styles, with strong themes of equality, freedom, and often, political activism. About "Best Friend" ("The Unicorn Song") Adam says, "This song is a prism of personal freedom—colors of independence and affirmation." It is also her best-known song and was recorded by Peter, Paul, and Mary.

Adam was born and raised in California. Her musical education began at age five with the piano, and as a teenager she composed instrumental pieces and a full piano concerto. She graduated from the University of California in 1969, and taught three years before making songwriting her career. Her first performance of her work in 1973 at a women's music festival led to the first album, *Songwriter.* Co-produced with Barbara Price on their own label, Pleiades Records, it includes this now-famous song.

A number of subsequent albums followed, including a solo piano album, *Naked Keys.* In 1984 Margie Adam co-produced and participated in a tape, *Take Hands: Singing and Speaking for Survival,* on which she was joined by Honor Moore, Susan Griffin, and Janet Marlowe. This production of music and poetry was intended to contribute to the national debate on nuclear arms control (see the Discography for all of Adam's work).

Margie Adam comments on her work: "We're a nation in turmoil. Everywhere around us we see the results of conflicting values. For many people, these are lonely, scary times. Music can reinforce hope and offer new alternatives. I want to encourage people to look to themselves for the answers they need."

Margie Adam. Photograph by Joan Biren

# Best Friend (The Unicorn Song)

Words and music by Margie Adam.
© 1974 by Labyris Music Company.
All rights reserved. Used by permission.

2. When I was seventeen, my best friend was the Northern star.
   The others asked, why was I always dreaming?
   But I did not reply; I found my thoughts were very far
   Away from daily hurts and fears and scheming.
   The Northern star and I would share our dreams together—
   Laughing, sighing, sometimes crying, through all kinds of weather,
   And we'd sing:

   > Seeing is believing in the things you see!
   > Loving is believing in the ones you love!

3. And now that I am grown, my best friend lives inside of me;
   The others smile at me and call me crazy.
   But I am not upset, for long ago I found the key.
   I've always known their seeing must be hazy.
   My friend inside and I will wile away the hours
   Playing, dancing, and romancing in the wild flowers.
   And we'll sing:

> Seeing is believing in the things you see!
> Loving is believing in the ones you love!

## 82. MY KIND OF GIRL

Alix Dobkin's song has a different meaning for us than was intended, but we enjoy the song so much that we asked to use "My Kind of Girl" to represent this important singer/songwriter. Although not on any of Dobkin's recordings, it is featured in a collection of her songs and reminiscences, titled *Alix Dobkin's Adventures in Women's Music* (see Songbooks listing).

While written as a joyous woman-to-woman love song, we pointed out that it can also be a song-statement about the good feelings that a mother has for a greatly loved daughter, which is the reason for its inclusion in this section concerning children.

Alix Dobkin is one of the formidable women in lesbian music. Born in New York City of musical parents, her early influences were "Woody Guthrie, Pete Seeger, The Red Army Chorus, Jane Powell, Katherine Grayson, Rogers and Hammerstein, Dave Brubeck, Vic Damone, and Yiddish songs of resistance and humor."

Dobkin became a professional folksinger in Philadelphia while earning a degree from the Tyler School of Fine Arts of Temple University. After graduation, she moved to New York City and became a full-time musician. Her "home base was Greenwich Village and the Gaslight Cafe, birthplace of folk-rock, and rich, creative musical environments." She married the manager of the Gaslight, and they moved to Miami, Florida, where they built a folk club and ran it for nearly a year. Ronnie Gilbert, Odetta, Ian and Sylvia, Gordon Lightfoot, Simon and Garfunkle, and many others played there. They shortly moved back to New York, and in 1970 daughter Adrian was born. Then the couple separated, and Alix Dobkin began writing and singing music consciously for women. Not long after she came out as a lesbian.

Alix Dobkin and her daughter, Adrian, 1978

Kay Gardner and Alix Dobkin produced a landmark album in 1973; *Lavender Jane Loves Women,* and two years later Dobkin made *Living With Lesbians. XXALIX* was released five years later (see the Discography and the Songbooks listing).

Alix Dobkin produces mixed-media lectures called *Women-Hating, Racism and Violence in the Top-40,* which investigates how the music industry reinforces and condones negative stereotypes in lyrics, album covers, and advertising. Violent treatment of women, blacks, and Hispanics are common, as Dobkin points out to students and other groups to whom she speaks.

The extended-play album, *Never Been Better,* Dobkin terms "danceable and mass-marketable rock-pop music," and features Carol MacDonald and her band, Witch. "The goal of the album is to create a connection between all women. It will reinforce the effects women are having on the world with positive power images," Dobkin says.

## My Kind of Girl

2. You're my kind of girl if you
   Think of what you're doing,
   You're my kind of girl if you're
   Doing what you think,
   And if you can think of me as a sister
   Truly, you must be
   My kind of girl.
   *(Bridge)*

3. You're my kind of girl if you
   Like to trust your feelings,
   You're my kind of girl if you
   Feel like you can trust,
   And if you can trust in me as a sister
   Truly, you must be
   My kind of girl.

4. Because my kind of girl loves to
   Know that she is growing,
   And my kind of girl knows that she can grow in love,
   And if she can grow with me as a sister
   Truly, she must be
   Someone to love,
   Truly, you must be
   Someone to love!

# Role Models

Eleanor Roosevelt as U.S. Delegate to the United Nations (1945–51).
31857/United Nations Photo

### 83. HARRIET TUBMAN

It is strange that a nation so imbued with the ideals of liberty and which was formed on the classical concept of individual freedom would subject a race of people in its midst to 250 years of slavery.

The black experience has had to be lived to be understood. Harriet Tubman, the escaped slave called "the Moses of her people," led 19 separate groups of slaves North to freedom, rescuing about 300. She never lost a single person on any of the trips north on the so-called underground railroad leading to Canada. "I think slavery is the next thing to hell," she once said. "If a person would send another into bondage, he would, it appears to me, be bad enough to send him to hell if he could."

In later life Tubman established a home for poor blacks in Auburn, New York. She was especially interested in providing marketable skills to freed women. While she never learned to read or write, a friend wrote down her dictated autobiography. It makes fascinating reading today (see the Bibliography).

Harriet Tubman. Smithsonian Institution, Washington, D.C.

Walter Robinson, the composer of this song, has been a performer of folk, classical, and jazz music, with a specialty in the double bass. In recent years he has concentrated on composition and was the recipient of a research fellowship at the W.E.B. DuBois Institute of Afro-American History at Harvard, where he worked on a folk opera based on the life of the slave revolutionary, Denmark Vesey.

"Harriet Tubman" has been recorded by Holly Near and Ronnie Gilbert on their album, *Lifeline,* and by others (see the Discography).

## Harriet Tubman

*Bridge (sung twice)*

2. Hundreds of miles we traveled onward, gathering slaves from town to town,
   Seeking every lost and found, setting those free that once were bound.
   Somehow my heart was growing weaker, I fell by the wayside's sinking sand.
   Firmly did this lady stand, lifted me up and took my hand, saying,
   *Chorus and Bridge*

   *(Sing the chorus and bridge as many times as you like.)*

## 84. THE LUCRETIA MOTT SONG

Lucretia Mott (1793–1880) organized the first women's rights convention with Elizabeth Cady Stanton in 1848. A founder of the American Anti-Slavery Society, Mott was a delegate to the World Antislavery Convention in London in 1840. Her life story is told in this song, which we found in a small paperback hymnal published by the Quakers, called *Songs of the Spirit* (see the Bibliography). The lyrics are by Margaret Hope Bacon, a fellow Quaker and Mott's biographer (*Valiant Friend: The Life of Lucretia Mott*. New York: Walker and Company, 1980). The prominent scholar and historian is also the author of *Mothers of Feminism: The Story of Quaker Women in America* (Harper and Row, 1986).

The tune of "The Lucretia Mott Song" is "The Battle Hymn of the Republic." It was composed by William Steffe, and dates back to at least 1856, when it was used for a camp-meeting song and later "John Brown's Body." Julia Ward Howe wrote the lyrics to the famous "Battle Hymn" and she, like Lucretia Mott, was a social reformer who wrote and lectured for Negro emancipation, women's suffrage, and world peace.

The use of the terms "thee" and "Friend" as titles reminds us that many of the Quakers (Society of Friends), particularly in the eastern United States, still use their quaint form of address when they speak together. However, we like to slip the old words, "Glory, glory, hallelujah" back into the song and then end the chorus, "And her light still shines for me."

### The Lucretia Mott Song

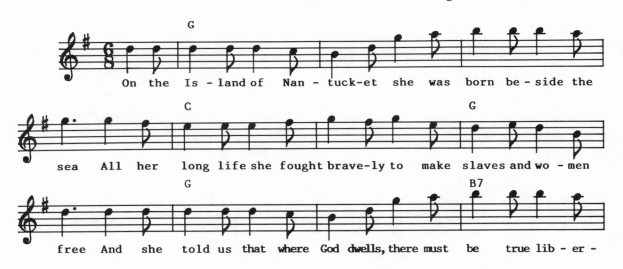

On the Is-land of Nan-tuck-et she was born be-side the sea All her long life she fought brave-ly to make slaves and wo-men free And she told us that where God dwells, there must be true lib-er-

Traditional tune: "Battle Hymn of the Republic" and "John Brown's Body."
Words by Margaret Hope Bacon.
Music by Wm. Steffe.
Permission to print obtained from Margaret Hope Bacon.

ty, And her light still shines for me!

CHORUS

Thank___ thee kind - ly, Friend Lu - cre - tia,

Thank___ thee kind - ly, Friend Lu - cre - tia,

Thank___ thee kind - ly, Friend Lu - cre - tia, For thy

light still shines for me!___

2. In the town of Philadelphia she hid the fleeing slaves,
   For the freedom of her sisters she dared cross the ocean waves,
   And she asked Ulysses Grant to grant a pardon for the braves,
   And her light still shines for me.
   *Chorus*

3. Let's bring an end to poverty, the gentle Quaker pled,
   Let's give the workers all a chance to earn their daily bread.
   Let nations live in peace again, just as our Lord has said,
   And her light still shines for me.
   *Chorus*

4. Throughout the busy cities and across the country-side
   She preached one simple message, O let truth be e'er thy guide.
   —Mind the Light within thee and let love with thee abide,
   And her light still shines for me.
   *Chorus*

## 85. THE DEATH OF MOTHER JONES

Pray for the dead, and fight like hell for the living.

God almighty made the women, and the Rockefeller gang of thieves made the ladies.

—Mother Jones

A heroine among the coal miners, whom she called her children, Mary Harris Jones was born in Ireland in 1830, and at the age of eleven migrated with her family to Toronto, Canada, where she was educated in the "common" (public) schools. The first of her family to graduate from high school and interested in becoming a teacher, she enrolled in the Toronto Normal School. She was unable to get a job as a teacher, however, because her family was Roman Catholic, and she came to the United States.

In Memphis, Tennessee, where she was teaching, she met and married George Jones, an official in the Iron Molders Union. They had four children in four years, then in 1867 her husband and all four children died in a yellow fever epidemic that struck Memphis. She stayed only long enough to help nurse the remaining victims, then packed up and went back to Chicago, where she opened a successful dressmaking shop. In 1871 Mrs. Jones lost every belonging she owned in the great Chicago fire. Never again did she either accumulate possessions or live in a home.

After the fire, Mary Jones began to attend Knights of Labor meetings held in a fire-scorched church. She became an active organizer at forty-two, and worked in the coal mining towns of West Virginia and Colorado and in the mill towns of Alabama, New England, and Pennsylvania. As a member of the United Mine Workers, she traveled from one strike headquarters to another, delivering morale-building speeches, organizing the miners' wives, and helping to take care of the sick and injured. "A fiery speaker, a fearless agitator and organizer, and a great strike strategist," according to Joe Glazer, she could not be frightened away by company thugs or state militia. She was imprisoned for her militancy, but never intimidated.[*]

Mother Jones lived to be 100 years old, fifty of which were spent working for the rights of impoverished working men, women, and children. At the age of ninety-two she started her autobiography with the help of Molly Field Parton. When she was close to death, she confided to a friend: "Die when I may, I want it said of me by those who knew me best, that I always plucked a thistle and planted a flower whenever I thought a flower would grow."

The song "The Death of Mother Jones" was penned by an unknown author and was first heard soon after she died. Gene Autry, the "cowboy" singing star, was apparently the first to record it.

---

[*]Edith Fowke and Joe Glazer, *Songs of Work and Protest* (New York: Dover Publications, Inc., 1973).

## The Death of Mother Jones

The ____ world to-day is mourn-ing ____ the death of Mo - ther Jones; ____ Grief and sor - row ho - ver ____ a - round the mi - ners' homes. ____ This grand old cham - pion of la - bor ____ has gone to a bet - ter land. ____ But the hard - work - ing mi - ners, ____ they miss her guid - ing hand. ____

Anonymous

2. Through the hills and over the valleys, in every mining town,
   Mother Jones was ready to help them; she never let them down.
   In front with the striking miners she always could be found;
   She fought for right and justice; she took a noble stand.

3. With a spirit strong and fearless, she hated that which was wrong;
   She never gave up fighting until her breath was gone.
   May the workers all get together to carry out her plan,
   And bring back better conditions for every laboring man.

## 86. DANCE A REVOLUTION (for Emma Goldman)

"If I can't dance, I don't want to be part of your revolution."

—Emma Goldman

At the turn of the century, Emma Goldman, a Russian Jewish immigrant, began fighting for issues which at the time seemed astounding—shocking. Yet today we embrace her ideals and consider them our inalienable rights.

Trained as a nurse, she was the first to talk about birth control and the right of women to control their own bodies. She advocated women's self-reliance against the tradition of marriage based on women's dependency. She spoke against child abuse and discrimination against homosexuals and prostitutes. She was a labor organizer and fought for unionization, equal pay, and decent working conditions.

Goldman risked and suffered arrest, speaking out at a time when few progressives and even fewer women dared to do so. She called herself, and she was, a revolutionary, because she supported the creation of a system that would favor human rights over property rights. At the same time she decried any attempts at change that would be authoritarian or would not promote true individual freedom.

Linda Hirschhorn, born in New York City, came from a musical home, and she heard Jewish music in particular. After high school she lived in Israel for two years, spending one on a kibbutz, the other in Jerusalem as a student. She returned to the U.S. in 1968 to finish a B.A. in philosophy, and in 1970 she moved to San Francisco to continue music conservatory training. She now lives in Oakland.

Besides writing and performing, Hirschhorn is a licensed marriage and family counselor. She gives voice lessons to people "who think they are tone-deaf," and is a freelance cantor. In performance, Hirschhorn works with viola player Tay Holden.

Linda Hirschhorn's background in Hebrew music brings a Jewish influence to her melody-writing. Her songs draw on themes of peace, personal freedom, feminism, and non-intervention. Poetry can help universalize themes, she says. "Metaphors are lasting; they have meaning beyond the specific instances of their use."

The Emma Goldman song is one in a series of original songs about historically important Jewish women and is based in part on a poem by Derora Bernstein. The song appears on the album, *Skies Ablaze* (see the Discography).

# Dance a Revolution (for Emma Goldman)

CHORUS

And we— will— dance a rev - o - lu - tion to the sound-ing of ____ the ___ drums dance the call ___ of free - dom the call of peace— to come ___ and we— will dance a - way ____ in - jus - tice with the danc-ing of ____ the ___ free and dance un - til ____ we dance a world ___ of hu - man dig - ni - ty _____

VERSE

You came with hud - dled mass - es flee - ing the po - grom search-ing for ____ the har - bor sta - tue and her out - stretched

arm but your name-sake* dis - ap-point - ed you___ child of black bread___ and___ tea___ oh gol-den Em - ma you___ found your gol-den land___ not___ free.___

2. You spoke of sex you talked of birth
   in a world afraid of love
   said human worth could not be measured
   by laws from above
   and to share the profits of our toil
   was every worker's goal
   and emancipation starts inside
   a fighting woman's soul
   *Chorus*

3. Some struggles have been different
   and some like those at hand
   we fight to own our bodies
   and we fight to free the land
   we fight to save the earth the sea
   the future of the sky
   your voice becomes an echo of
   a spirit that won't die
   *Chorus*

*"Namesake" refers to Emma Lazarus, the writer of "Give me your tired, your poor, your huddled masses yearning
  to be free. ... "

## 87. REBEL GIRL

This song was written as a tribute to Elizabeth Gurley Flynn, "the rebel girl" of the Industrial Workers of the World. Flynn was a friend of Margaret Sanger and worked with her to fight the 1873 Comstock Laws, which made it illegal to manufacture birth control devices or to distribute contraceptive information. (Sanger eventually founded what would become the Planned Parenthood Federation of America.)

Even at sixteen, Flynn was a charismatic orator whose role model was Emma Goldman. Flynn helped to raise money for Sanger's defense when she was arrested for trying to get laws passed that would permit doctors to give birth control information "for the cure or prevention of disease." Elizabeth Gurley Flynn's autobiography, *Rebel Girl*, is still in print (see the Bibliography).

Joe Hill, author of "The Rebel Girl," was the bard of the Wobblies. Thirteen of his songs were published in the I.W.W.'s *Little Red Songbook*. In 1915 Hill was shot by a five-man firing squad in Utah after conviction on a murder charge. Many tried to stop the execution, including President Woodrow Wilson and the King of Sweden. Hill may have been killed because he was a Wobbly with a very large following. In a letter to Bill Haywood, the leader of the I.W.W., written just before his death, Hill wrote: "Goodbye, Bill; I die a true rebel. Don't waste any time mourning—organize."

Joanna Cazden, on her tape, *Rebel Girl*, changes the line, "She brings Courage, Pride and Joy / To the fighting rebel boy" to: "She brings Courage, Joy and Pride / To those fighting by her side."

## The Rebel Girl

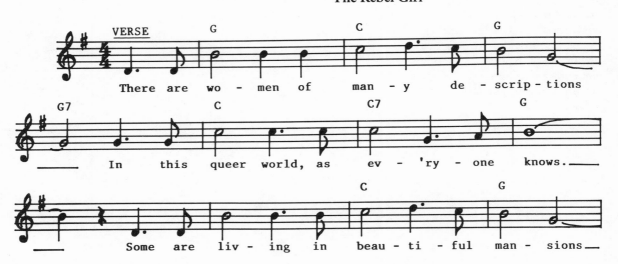

Words and music by Joe Hill.

And are wear-ing the fin-est of clothes.

There are blue-blood-ed queens and prin-cess-es

Who have charms made of dia-monds and pearl But the

on-ly and thor-ough-bred La-dy Is the

Reb-el Girl. That's the

**CHORUS**

Reb-el Girl, That's the Reb-el Girl, To the

work-ing class she's a pre-cious pearl. She brings

Cour-age, Pride and Joy To the

fight-ing Reb-el Boy.* We've had

*Or: She brings Courage, Joy and Pride
    To those fighting by her side.

girls be - fore, but we need some more in the In -
dus - trial Work-ers of the World.＿＿ For it's
great to fight for Free - dom With a
Reb - el Girl.＿＿＿＿＿＿

2. Yes, her hands may be hardened from labor,
   And her dress may not be very fine,
   But a heart in her bosom is beating,
   That is true to her class and her kind.
   And the grafters in terror are trembling
   When her spite and defiance she'll hurl,
   For the only and thoroughbred lady
   Is the Rebel Girl.
   *Chorus*

## 88. UNION MAID

Woody Guthrie, composer of "This Land is Your Land," would never be considered a women's rights advocate, but he was one of our most socially conscious balladeers, and he devoted his life to the causes of the oppressed and poor.

Guthrie was a prolific songwriter who wrote hundreds of songs decrying social injustice wherever he saw it—in the Dust Bowl of his native Oklahoma, in the migratory camps of California, in the political arena, among the vigilantes of the South, in Hitler's Germany, and in the United States' factories and mines. He wrote many up-beat songs as well, some which pay tribute to the beauty of America and to its heroes and heroines. He will always be remembered, too, for his outstanding children's songs.

The influence of Woody Guthrie upon the songwriters and performers of the sixties was incalculable; many consider him the inspiration for the folksong revival of that period. He has been called "the Walt Whitman of song," his music is so imbued with the spirit of America.

Born in 1912 in Okemah, Oklahoma, he left home at seventeen and took to the road as a troubadour, singing in bars, cafes, vaudeville, at union meetings, on the radio, and at political rallies—even in the New York subway—whenever the mood struck him. Although he was a Merchant Marine in World War II, a radical political columnist, a radio personality, a sign painter, artist and poet, he was above all a people's singer and songwriter. He performed with all the great folksingers of his day, including Leadbelly, Pete Seeger, the Almanac Singers and later the Weavers, among others.

Allison Gates at the controls of Caterpillar 950, Front End Loader. Allison is a member of Operating Engineers Local #12, Ventura, California. Photograph by News-Press, Santa Barbara

In 1966, Guthrie was the recipient of an award from the secretary of the Interior, Stewart Udall. A year later he was dead at the age of fifty-five, after fifteen years of battling Huntington's chorea, an inherited and incurable muscular disease for which he was consigned to a sanatorium.

"Union Maid," written in 1941, is Woody Guthrie's tribute to the heroic women who resisted the intimidation of company thugs during an oil workers' strike in Oklahoma City. He dedicated his song to a Southern tenant farmer's union organizer, who, he says in his *Songbook,* he had learned had been "stripped naked and beat up, and then hung to the rafters of a log cabin until she was unconscious."

"Union Maid" became the theme music for the highly acclaimed film of the same name and is the best-known union women's song today. Its tune, from Oklahoma, is the familiar "Redwing."

## Union Maid

There once was a un-ion maid who nev-er was a-
fraid Of the goons and ginks and the com-pan-y finks And the
dep-u-ty sher-iffs who made the raids.— She went to the un-ion
hall when a meet-ing it was called, And when the com-pan-y
boys came 'round, she al-ways stood her ground. Oh, you

can't scare me, I'm stick-in' to the un - ion, ____ ____ I'm stick-in' to the un - ion, ____ I'm stick-in' to the un - ion. ____ ____ Oh, you can't scare me, I'm stick-in' to the un - ion, I'm stick-in' to the un - ion, ____ 'til the day I die. ____

2. The union maid was wise to the tricks of the company spies,
   She couldn't be fooled by the company stools,
   She'd always organize the guys.
   She'd always get her way when she asked for higher pay—
   She'd show her card to the National Guard, and this is what she'd say:
   *Chorus*

Many people have made up more verses to "Union Maid." Here are two:

You women who want to be free, just take a little tip from me:
Break out o' that mold we've all been sold
You got a fightin' history.
The fight for women's rights, with workers must unite—
Like Mother Jones, just move them bones
To the front of every fight!
*Chorus*

A woman's struggle is hard, even with a union card,
She's got to stand on her own two feet
And not be a servant of a male elite—
It's time to take a stand, keep working hand-in-hand,
There is a job that's got to be done
And a fight that's got to be won.
*Chorus*

## 89. AMELIA EARHART'S LAST FLIGHT

Enjoying folksong popularity around the country, this romantic ballad is about the final adventure of the "first lady of the air," in 1937. Its writer is "Red River Dave" McEnery.

Amelia Earhart was the first woman to make solo flights across the Atlantic (1932) and the Pacific (1935), the first woman to fly from Honolulu to the mainland United States, the first woman to fly across the country in both directions, and the first woman to receive the Distinguished Flying Cross. In her attempt to fly around the world in 1937 her plane was lost in the Pacific near Howland Island. She and her partner, Captain Frederick J. Noonan, were never found. The story is in the song.

Born in Kansas, Amelia Earhart studied at Columbia University but dropped out to earn money for her flying lessons. She worked briefly as a social worker, and she wrote *20 Hours, Forty Minutes, The Fun of It,* and *Last Flight* (arranged by her husband, George Palmer Putnam).

Amelia Earhart. San Diego Aerospace Museum

## Amelia Earhart's Last Flight

Well, a ship out on the o-cean,—— just a speck a-gainst the sky, A-me-lia Ear-hart fly-ing that sad day.—— With her part-ner, Cap-tain Noo-nan,—— on the sec-ond of Ju-ly, Her plane fell in the o-cean, far a-way—— There's a beau-ti-ful, beau-ti-ful field—— Far a-way in a land that is fair.—— Hap-py land-ings to

Words and music by Dave McEnery.

you, A - me - lia Ear - hart, ___ Fare -

well, first la - dy of the air. ___

2. She radioed position and she said that all was well,
   Although the fuel within the tanks was low.
   But they'd land on Howland Island to refuel her monoplane,
   Then on their trip around the world they'd go.
   *Chorus*

3. Well, a half an hour later an SOS was heard,
   The signal weak, but still her voice was brave.
   Oh, in shark-infested waters her plane went down that night
   In the blue Pacific to a watery grave.
   *Chorus*

4. Well, now you have heard my story of that awful tragedy,
   We pray that she might fly home safe again.
   Oh, in years to come though others blaze a trail across the sea,
   We'll ne'er forget Amelia and her plane.
   *Chorus*

## 90. MAGGIE KUHN

This song, with the Irish immigrant tune, "Pat Works on the Railway," is our tribute to Maggie Kuhn, the organizer and leader of the Gray Panthers, the group that drew America's attention to the plight of the elderly when it convened in 1972.

The biggest lobby in Washington (barring the Pentagon) is that of the elderly. Older women are now in the political mainstream. The changes wrought by the women's movement have influenced older citizens to work actively for improvements in their economic and social conditions. Maggie Kuhn represents the new militancy of the old, fighting to overcome the concept of useless old age, projecting a positive image of the elderly as fully contributing members of society.

The main concerns of the Gray Panthers are strengthening the Social Security system, raising the mandatory retirement age, seeing that pension increments are keeping up with inflation, and assuring adequate health care and housing for the elderly. A program of daycare centers for the elderly also has the Panthers' support.

Through lobbying, petitioning, and working with members of Congress the Gray Panthers have been instrumental in abolishing the mandatory retirement age for federal employees, fighting the abuses of the elderly in nursing

Maggie Kuhn. Julie Jensen/Photography. Courtesy, Gray Panthers.

homes, and helping corporations restructure their work systems. Their Media Watch Task Force persuaded the National Association of Broadcasters to include age, along with sex and race, as a sensitive area to come under the N.A.B.'s Television Code of Ethics. The group has gained observer status at the United Nations and was made a consultant to the United Nations' Economic and Social Council.

The activities of the Gray Panthers are not limited to the elderly. They have a broad agenda and have built an intergenerational alliance to promote the kind of social, political, and economic changes that will help people of all ages lead better lives.

Born in 1905, Margaret (Maggie) Kuhn served for twenty-five years as a program executive responsible for social education and action in the Presbyterian Church before convening the Gray Panthers.

She was once named Humanist of the Year and until 1983 travelled 150,000 miles each year to give talks and workshops. She shares her home with fifteen people, and it has also been used for offices by the national staff of the Gray Panthers. She lives on her pension and the honorariums received for her speeches, and does not draw a salary from the Panthers.

Listed in *The World Almanac* as one of the twenty-five most influential women in America, the charismatic Kuhn has authored three books: *You Can't Be Human Alone, Let's Get Out There and Do Something About Injustice*, and *Maggie Kuhn on Aging*. In her words: "We should look at life and age and growing old not with fear, but with the hope of fulfillment. We must work to create a more humane society that maximizes the potential of everybody."

## Maggie Kuhn

Oh, Mag - gie Kuhn, oh, Mag - gie Kuhn, We're sing - in' our Gray Pan - thers' tune, Old age need nev - er bring us ruin, A bet - ter day is com - ing soon.

Words by Elizabeth Freilicher.
Tune: "Pat Works on the Railway" (traditional Irish immigrant song).
© 1983 by Elizabeth Freilicher.

*Chorus* (same tune)
> We're leaving that old rocking chair,
> (Cast off depression and despair!)
> We'll join the struggle for what is fair,
> We'll work to gain our equal share.

2. "Weak and crotchety, tired," you say?
   We know we're wiser than ever today,
   And we don't mind being old and gray,
   We're working toward a brand-new day.
   *Chorus*

3. We don't want your pastures or pills,
   Your nursing homes, your old-age mills,
   We're going to cure these terrible ills,
   We'll pass the laws; we have the will.
   *Chorus*

4. We're fighting watchdogs, strong and bold,
   We're breaking out of our old mold,
   Now listen to us—we won't be sold,
   We'll work together, young and old.
   *Chorus*

5. You congressmen and press, watch out!
   Our message to one and all we'll shout,
   We'll picket the White House, and about
   Our future plans we'll leave no doubt.
   *Chorus*

*(Repeat first verse)*

## 91. CORRIDO DE (THE BALLAD OF) DOLORES HUERTA

A ballad is called a *corrido* in Spanish, and it describes a great historical event or an important person. In this case it is Dolores Huerta, the vice president of the United Farm Workers union, working with Cesar Chavez.

Huerta was born and educated in New Mexico, the daughter of migrant farmworkers. She became a teacher and while raising eleven children has worked closely with the United Farm Workers since the early sixties.

"These ballads keep alive the history and traditions and lay the foundations of Mexican and Chicano identity," says José-Luis Orozco, the Berkeley, California, songwriter and performer who writes *corridos*. Orozco was the Director of Multicultural Programs and then became Vice Chancellor at the National Hispanic University in Oakland until 1986. He has published songbooks for children and adults. This song, in Spanish, was sent to us with a literal English translation. The music of Orozco can be heard on his four albums (see the Discography), and the "Dolores Huerta" *corrido* is part of the first one. Two of the albums are for children.

Dolores Huerta. Photograph by Victor Aleman, courtesy of United Farm Workers/AFL-CIO

## Corrido de (The Ballad of) Dolores Huerta

VERSE

Voy a can-tar un cor - ri-do, con gus - to y con e - mo-
ción. Es pa - ra Do - lo -res Huer-ta, mu - jer de gran co - ra-
zón. En Nue - vo Me - xi -co fué, la tier - ra don -de na-
ció, es - ta mu - jer tan va - lien-te que en Ca - li -for-nia cre-
ció. _____ CHORUS ¡Vi - va _____ Do - lo - res
Huer - ta! _____ ¡Or - gul - lo de nues - tra
gen - te! _____ ¡Vi - va la mu - jer del
cam - po! _____ ¡Que en la lu - cha es - tá pre -

1.2.

sen - te!___ Fué ma- lu -cha es -tá pre - sen - te!___

2. Fué maestra de profesión,
   que vió sufrir a los niños,
   trabajando en los campos,
   sin tener un buen destino.

   Luego se unió al campesino
   para luchar por la causa,
   y su presencia le ha dado
   muchos triunfos a La Raza.
   *Chorus*

3. Mujer valiente que luchas
   por defender a los pobres;
   ya por todos los lugares,
   se oye tu nombre, Dolores.

   Quiero terminar cantando
   los versos de esta canción:
   ¡Que viva Dolores Huerta!
   ¡Que lucha con devoción!
   *Chorus*

## The Ballad of Dolores Huerta
### *(A literal translation)*

1. I'm going to sing this song
   with pleasure and emotion.
   It's for Dolores Huerta,
   a big hearted woman.

   It was New Mexico
   the land where she was born,
   this brave woman
   in California was raised.

   *Chorus*
   > Viva Dolores Huerta!
   > Pride of our people!
   > Viva the country woman!
   > Active in our struggle!

2. Teacher by profession,
   she saw the children suffer,
   working in the fields
   with no bright future.

   Then she joined the farmworkers
   to fight for their cause,
   and her presence has given
   many triumphs to La Raza.
   *Chorus*

3. Woman that fights
   to defend the poor
   all around, Dolores,
   your name is heard.

   I want to finish singing
   the verses of this song,
   Viva Dolores Huerta!
   Devoted to the struggle!
   *Chorus*

## 92. RIDE, SALLY RIDE

This song by Casse Culver, a Washington, D.C., singer/songwriter, was written to celebrate an important first for women: NASA launching the first American woman into space. On June 18, 1983, Sally Kristin Ride, a former schoolgirl tennis star and a physicist with the space program, joined four men in the cabin of the space shuttle Challenger. She was one of 8,370 applicants competing for 35 positions as mission specialists. Five other women were chosen at the same time: Judith Resnick, a Ph.D. in electrical engineering, Anna Fisher, an M.D., Kathryn Sullivan, a Ph.D. in geology, surgeon Rhea Seddon, and biochemist Shannon Lucid.

Ride's chief responsibility during the six-day mission was the remote manipulation of a fifty-foot-long mechanical arm used to deploy and retrieve a package of experiments, a job successfully completed.

Sally K. Ride. National Aeronautics and Space Administration

Born on May 26, 1951, Ride received her Ph.D. in astrophysics in 1978 from Stanford University. When asked why she chose astrophysics, she jokingly said, "because I had a bad forehand." Her comment on her venture into space is worth noting: "It's too bad that society isn't to the point yet where the country could just send up a woman astronaut, and nobody would think twice about it."

Casse Culver has been called by Margie Adam, "surly with the fringe on top." Writing provocative feminist songs which she has performed with the Belle Starr Band, Casse continues to write songs and take her music on tour, especially to the various congregations of the Universal Fellowships of the Metropolitan Community Churches.

## Ride, Sally Ride

Words by Casse Culver.
Music by Casse Culver and arranged by Dick Brewer.
© 1983 by Shuttle Songs Ltd., div. of
Sweet Alliance Music BMI, Falls Church, VA.
All rights reserved. Used by permission.

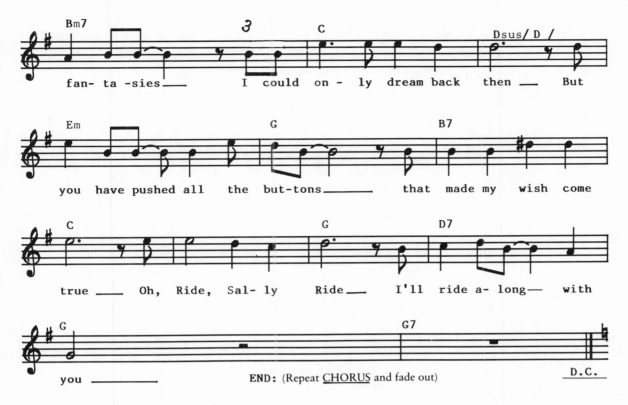

fan- ta -sies ___ I could on - ly dream back then ___ But

you have pushed all the but-tons ___ that made my wish come

true ___ Oh, Ride, Sal- ly Ride ___ I'll ride a- long— with

you ___ **END:** (Repeat <u>CHORUS</u> and fade out)

*D.C.*

2. Mother Earth above you, and your space boots to the Sun
   The freedom of pure weightlessness your determination won
   You have got the right stuff to be an astronaut
   Oh ride, Sally Ride, I'm riding on this shot
   *Chorus*

3. Challenge your tomorrows and who knows what will come
   I'm betting on prosperity and a chance for everyone
   Each walk in space will show us our frontiers never end
   Oh ride, Sally Ride, the future is our friend.
   *Chorus*

# Women Emerging

From *Learning to Rock Climb* by Michael Loughman. Copyright © 1981 by Michael Loughman. Reprinted by permission of Sierra Club Books

### 93. MY LOVE IS A RIDER (THE BUCKING BRONCO)

Cowboy songs, either old traditional ones or the commercial successes that followed, have been sung for generations in the United States. They portray the romantic image of women, the sweet girl the cowboy plans to marry after "the last roundup in the fall."

"My Love Is a Rider" is usually attributed to the pen of the notorious Belle Starr. The prim point of view she expresses somehow tarnishes our vision of Ms. Starr as the Texas outlaw we are told she was. We wonder about her not-so-subtle domination of her cowboy sweetheart who gives up the rodeo just for her sake. Would Belle ever have given up cattle rustling because her *man* demanded it? (The question is merely rhetorical; she married another cattle thief.)

Jennie Metcalf, *another* outlaw. Western History Collections, University of Oklahoma Library

## My Love Is a Rider (The Bucking Bronco)

My love is a ri - der, wild hor - ses he breaks, But he's prom - ised to give it up just for my sake. One foot he ties up and the sad - dle puts on, With a leap and a jump he is moun - ted and gone.

2. The first time I saw him was early last spring,
   He was riding a bronco, a high-headed thing.
   He tipped me a wink as he gaily did go,
   For he wished me to notice his bucking bronco.

3. The next time I saw him was early last fall,
   He was swinging the ladies at Tomlinson's ball.
   We laughed and we talked as we danced to and fro,
   And he promised he'd ne'er ride another bronco.

4. He made me some presents, among them a ring.
   The return that I made him was a far better thing.
   Twas a young maiden's heart and I'll have you all know,
   He has won it by riding his bucking bronco.

5. Now listen, young maidens, where e'er you reside,
   Don't listen to the cowboy who swings the rawhide.
   He'll court you and kiss you and leave you and go
   Up the trail in the spring on his bucking bronco.

This song is attributed to the pen of Belle Starr.
Traditional.

## 94. I WANT TO BE A REAL COWBOY GIRL

We have always assumed that "I Want to Be a Real Cowboy Girl" was written by the Girls of the Golden West, Mildred and Dorothy Good. Stars of old-time radio, they sang many of the commercially successful "cowboy songs" of the thirties, including this one. Millie tells us, however, that the composer is unknown. In the past several years a number of groups have recorded this song (see the Discography).

"The Girls of the Golden West," Millie and Dolly Good, 1934

## I Want to Be a Real Cowboy Girl

Traditional

belt that is four in-ches wide,_____ And
ride like the deuce on a buck-skinned cay-use, With the
cow-boy I love by my side._____ O da
lay-ee-ee oh, ah lay oh lay-ee dee-oh, lee-oh
lay-ee, ay-ee, ay-dee-oh; lee-oh
lay-ee dee-oh, oh-lee-oh lay-ee dee-oh, lee-oh
layee oh, d'-layee oh, d'-layee-o, d'-lay-ay-ee.

The quirt, I can hear it singin',
And I can see lariats swingin',
And my heart is always happy
At the rodeo.
*Chorus*

2. I dream of the song, and it lingers,
In my heart I can hear all the singers,
As they sing of love and friendship
At the rodeo.

How I'd love to ride in the open,
On a great big cayuse just a-lopin',
I'd be happy with my cowboy
From the rodeo.
*Second chorus*

    I want to be a real cowboy girl,
    And wear all the buckles and straps,
    And know how it feels to have spurs on my heels,
    Then strut about in my chaps.
    I want to wear a ten-gallon hat,
    And a belt that is four inches wide,
    Then bulldog a steer at the fair every year
    And jump on my pony and ride.
    *(Yodel)*

## 95. I'M GONNA BE AN ENGINEER

This is Peggy Seeger's liberation masterpiece which tells of the obstacles faced by the woman learning to do a "man's job."

The term *engineer* in Great Britain means a person who operates heavy machinery. In the original words of the song our engineer is a turret lathe operator. We have changed a few words to make her an "engineer" in the American sense of the word.

Peggy Seeger, the daughter of Ruth Crawford Seeger, pianist, composer, and arranger, and Charles Seeger, the well-known musicologist, was brought up in Washington, D.C. Her parents encouraged her interests in folk dance and folk music, and she feels she is "a unique product of two musical traditions."

Peggy Seeger. Photograph by David Gahr

She attended Radcliffe College, then dropped out to travel, and eventually settled in England in 1958. She was, even in the fifties, a specialist in ballad singing, accompanying herself on banjo and guitar. Almost immediately she began working and living with Ewan MacColl, the Scots singer/songwriter. They have appeared together on television and radio programs as a team playing traditional music. They write their own music in the folk tradition. They have written and performed in a series of important "radio ballads" for the BBC, documentaries on workers, handicapped persons, and other important social concerns, interspersing songs and interviews into the scripts. Jointly they have recorded three dozen albums.

Seeger and MacColl have raised three children. Peggy writes more and more topical songs, especially concerning women. Her life is a combination of singer, housewife, and mother.

In the Discography we list her albums for children and those which are specifically oriented toward women. In all, however, she has made fifty albums.

### I'm Gonna Be an Engineer

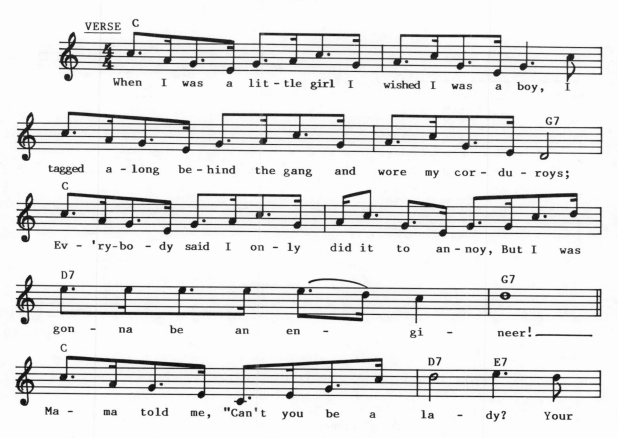

When I was a little girl I wished I was a boy, I tagged along behind the gang and wore my corduroys; Ev-'ry-bo-dy said I only did it to annoy, But I was gonna be an engineer! Mama told me, "Can't you be a lady? Your

Words and music by Peggy Seeger.
© 1976 by Stormking Music Inc.
All rights reserved. Used by permission.

du - ty is to make me the moth - er of a pearl;
Wait un - til you're old - er, dear, Then may - be
you'll be glad that you're a ___ girl." ___

CHORUS
Dain - ty as a Dres - den sta - tue, ___
Gen - tle as a Jer - sey cow, ___
Smooth as silk, ___ gives cream - y milk, ___
Learn to coo, ___ learn to moo, ___
That's what to do to be a la - dy now. ___

2. When I went to school I learned to write and how to read,
   Some history, geography and home economy,
   And typing is a skill that every girl is sure to need,
   To while away the extra time until the time to breed;
   And then they had the nerve to say, "What would you like to be?"
   I says, "I'm gonna be an engineer!"

No, you only need to learn to be a lady,
The duty isn't yours, for to try and run the world;
An engineer could never have a baby,
Remember, dear, that you're a girl.

3. So I become a typist and I study on the sly,
   Working out the day and night so I can qualify,
   And every time the boss come in, he pinched me on the thigh,
   Says, "I've never had an engineer!"

   You owe it to the job to be a lady,
   It's the duty of the staff for to give the boss a whirl;
   The wages that you get are crummy, maybe,
   But it's all you get, 'cause you're a girl.

   > She's smart! (for a woman)
   > I wonder how she got that way?
   > You get no choice, you get no voice,
   > Just stay mum, pretend you're dumb;
   > That's how you come to be a lady today!

4. Then Jimmy come along and we set up a conjugation,
   We were busy every night with loving recreation;
   I spent my days at work so he could get his education,
   And now he's an engineer!

   He says, "I know you'll always be a lady,
   It's the duty of my darling to love me all my life;
   Could an engineer look after or obey me?
   Remember, dear, that you're my wife!"

5. As soon as Jimmy got a job, I studied hard again,
   Then, busy at the drawing board a year or so, and then,
   The morning that the twins were born,
   Jimmy says to them, "Kids, your mother was an engineer!"

   You owe it to the kids to be a lady,
   Dainty as a dish-rag, faithful as a chow,
   Stay at home; you got to mind the baby;
   Remember, you're a mother now.

6. Every time I turn around there's something else to do,
   Cook a meal or mend a sock or sweep a floor or two,
   Listen to the morning show—it makes me want to spew;
   I was gonna be an engineer!

   I really wish that I could be a lady,
   I could do the lovely things that a lady's s'posed to do;
   I wouldn't even mind if only they would pay me,
   And I could be a person too.

What price—for a woman?
You can buy her for a ring of gold,
To love and obey (without any pay),
You get a cook or a nurse, for better or worse;
You don't need a purse when a lady is sold!

7. But now that times are harder, and my Jimmy's got the sack,
I went down to Delco, they were glad to have me back;
I'm a third-class citizen, my wages tell me that,
But I'm a first-class engineer!

The boss he says, "I pay you as a lady,
You only got the job 'cause I can't afford a man;
With you I keep the profits high as may be,
You're just a cheaper pair of hands!"

You got one fault! You're a woman,
You're not worth the equal pay,
A bitch or a tart, you're nothing but heart,
Shallow and vain, you got no brain;
Go down the drain like a lady today!

8. I listened to my mother and I joined a typing pool,
I listened to my lover and I sent him through his school;
If I listen to the boss, I'm just a bloody fool,
And an underpaid engineer!

I been a sucker ever since I was a baby,
As a daughter, as a wife, as a mother, and a dear;
But I'll fight them as a woman, not a lady;
Yes, I'll fight them as an engineer!

## 96. MOTHER'S DAY SONG

While we hear a lot of talk today about "shared parenting," the reality is that most women with children spend a quarter of a lifetime in mothering. Rosalie Sorrels, who went on the road as a performer with five children in tow, knows all about this.

Unless the primary caregiver is someone else, mothers have to realize their work is necessary, underrated, worthwhile, and rewarding—maybe not every minute—but a good deal of the time. The importance of maintaining an independent identity is almost as important as keeping a sense of humor. Along with this song, we would also like to recommend a wonderful book on the subject of thwarted creativity: Tillie Olsen's *Silences* (available in a Dell paperback).

"Mother's Day Song" was included in Rosalie Sorrels' charming anthology of songs and poetry by women, *What, Woman, and Who, Myself, I Am* (see Songbooks listing).

Growing up in Boise, Idaho, Rosalie Sorrels recalls her colorful grandfather, a preacher to the Indians who taught her Shakespeare soliloquies as a little girl, and her father, "a storyteller who loved Balzac and Rabelais." Sorrels' mother ran the local bookstore in Boise, so Sorrels comes by her storytelling ability naturally.

### Mother's Day Song

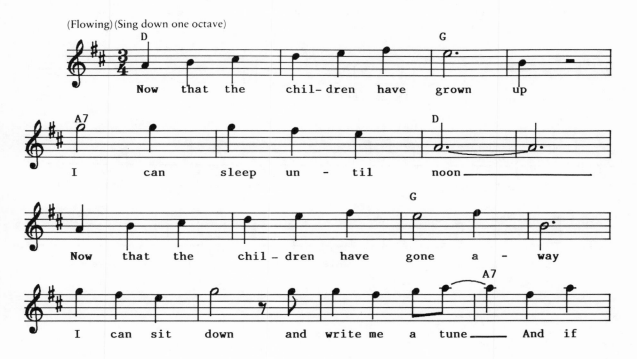

Words and music by Rosalie Sorrels.
© 1980 by Grimes Creek Music.

2. Now that the children have grown up
   Of course I don't sleep until noon
   I worry about where all of them might be
   And if they'll call up or check in pretty soon
   And the nice man who wanted to take me away
   Has married someone young and thin and
   I'm over forty and I'm overweight
   And he'll never ask me again
           tra la la

3. Now that the children have grown up
   I can sleep until noon
   Now that the children have gone away
   I can sit down and write me a tune
   And if I finish paying for all that they broke
   I can buy me a new dress
           tra la la
   And if some nice man asks me to run away
   I might well say yes!

## 97.  I GOTTA LEARN TO SING

Carol Hanisch was born in Havelock, Iowa, and has a B.A. in journalism from Drake University in Des Moines. She has been active in the women's liberation movement since its inception. A founding member of New York Radical Women, and later a member of Redstockings, she contributed to many early movement publications and books and was an editor of the Redstocking's volume, *Feminist Revolution*. Hanisch also originated the idea for the first Miss America Protest ("Myth America") which helped to put women's liberation into the public consciousness in 1968.

Hanisch worked in the Mississippi Civil Rights movement, to which she attributes much of her political insight; she is now active in the anti-apartheid movement.

She was the editor of *Meeting Ground: For the Liberation of Women and Workers*. In the mid-seventies Carol Hanisch began to write songs. From her songbook, *Fight On Sisters!* (see Songbooks listing) we include "I Gotta Learn to Sing" and "Bedroom Backlash," p. 16.

### I Gotta Learn to Sing

folk or rock and roll. But
now I got-ta pluck my own ban-jo strum my own guitar. I got-ta play on my own fid-dle
put my-self in there. 'Cause some-how look-in' on
ain't e-nough if you got-ta make the raft-ers
ring. A wo-man can go look-in' on for-
ev-er and nev-er learn to sing.

2. Now I'll always have a weakness for a guitar man
   'specially if he can sing.
   And I'll always have a weakness for a banjo man
   if he can really pluck those strings.
   And I'll always have a weakness for a fiddle man
   if he can play with soul
   country, western, rhythm and blues
   folk or rock and roll.

   But I'm gonna pluck my own banjo
   strum my own guitar.
   I'm gonna play on my own fiddle
   put myself in there.
   'Cause somehow lookin' on ain't enough
   I wanna make the rafters ring.
   I can't go lookin' on forever
   I'm gonna learn to sing.

## 98. STANDING BEHIND A MAN

Jane Voss's songwriting retains the directness and simplicity of old-time music. The influence of the Carter Family is clear in her first album, from which we have taken two songs for this book.

"Standing Behind a Man," she says, "represents a clarification and strengthening of my own resolve, as well as an explanation of myself and my stance to the world at large. I tried to cast my own experience in the light of, or in contrast to, the cultural norm—the conventional expectations for women's lives. . . . At an early age I determined that my life was my own, that it was all I had, and I'd better make the most of it. Nobody else could make my decisions or do my living for me. . . . Still, the longing for love can sometimes lead one down a rose-strewn path to hell. For women, it can mean landing ourselves in a dangerously compromised situation."

"Standing Behind a Man," like "Keep in Mind (That I Love You)" are both from Jane Voss's *An Album of Songs* (see the Discography).

Jane Voss grew up in Toledo, Ohio, and moved to San Francisco in 1969, where she promptly began her performing career, and by the mid-seventies was widely recognized for her authentic interpretation of old-time country music when her first record, *An Album of Songs,* was given high acclaim. Together with Hoyle Osbourne, a brilliant interpreter of early jazz and ragtime styles, she has also recorded two albums: *Pullin' Through* and *Get to the Heart.* The latter won the *Stereo Review* Record of the Year Award.

## Standing Behind a Man

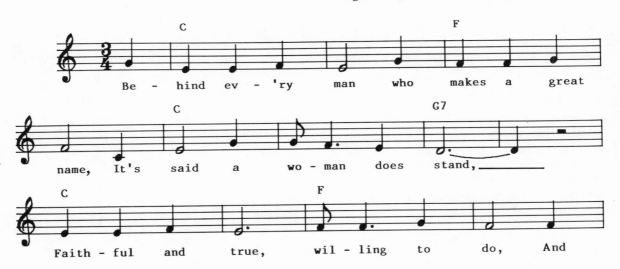

play an - y part in his plan._____ Oh,

how man - y lives have been lived out that way, As

some - bo - dy el - se's right hand?_____

How man - y wo - men with-out fa - ces or names,

Stand - in' be - hind_____ some man._____

2. Once upon a time, I called a man mine,
   And I waited at his every whim.
   In worry and fear, cried many a tear
   In the long nights waiting for him.
   Oh, the time that I wasted, the love that I lost,
   Measure it nobody can.
   I sold my birthright for a warm bed at night
   To be standin' behind some man.

3. Now the love of a man is a beautiful thing,
   A joy and a comfort so fine.
   But if the lovin' you crave just makes you a slave,
   You're sellin' yourself down the line.
   Each person must have their own work to do,
   Each life its own special plan,
   And a woman is lost who pays the great cost
   To be standin' behind some man.

4. If you take a butterfly by the wing
   You know it will never more fly.
   If my life must be some small captive thing,
   You know that I'd sooner die.
   Lovers may come, and lovers may go,
   But I only have what I am,
   And I'd rather be flyin' lonesome and free
   Than be standin' behind some man.
   *(Tag)*

   You know, I'd rather be flyin' lonesome and free
   Than be standin' behind some man.

## 99. I'M SETTLED

Marcia Deihl was co-editor with Joyce Cheney and Deborah Silverstein of the important feminist songbook, *All Our Lives*, published in 1976 by Diana Press and unfortunately now out of print.

Raised by her liberal Presbyterian minister father and her ex-opera singer mother in upstate New York, Deihl received her B.A. in music history and education from Boston University, then an M.A. in Feminist Studies in Folk Music from Cambridge Goddard. She helped to organize the New Harmony Sisterhood Band, a "progressive, radical feminist" string band, which produced the record "*... and Ain't I a Woman?*" (see the Discography).

Since their disbanding after six years, Deihl has performed solo and with country and old-time bands, and also as part of a "political satirical duo." She has contributed to various recordings and tapes as either instrumentalist or songwriter, and she presents her song-lecture, "Adventurers, Shrews and Agitators: The Unsung Women of Folk Music," at local colleges.

About the song "I'm Settled," she says, "The kettle in the song was, in fact, a delicate Chinese teapot, which I did receive along with many beautiful and useful household items, in 1979." She adds that she is "settled in Cambridge, Massachusetts, and (has) no hubby, no house, no car, no kid," as the song says. She lives with a cat, has "many spinster friends," and is "a YUBBIE—a young urban Bohemian." To encourage what she calls "outrageous culture," she gives an annual Bizarre Song Contest. Marcia Deihl has begun to explore performance art. She writes reviews, articles, and poetry, and is co-music editor of *Sojourner*, Boston's monthly feminist journal.

It is becoming a new trend to give house-warming parties for single people in order to ease the cost of furnishing a home. The event also serves to acknowledge today's popular choice of the single lifestyle as valid and worthy.

"I'm Settled" appears on a tape by Betsy Rose and Cathy Winter titled *Strong Singers* (see the Discography), and "is also quoted in a vegetarian cookbook."

### I'm Settled

CHORUS (Sing down one octave)

I'm set-tled,_____ (woa,)_____ I'm set-tled,_____

No hub-by, no house, no car, no kid, And no re-grets for what I did-n't or I did, I'm set-tled yeah, in-deed, I'm set-tled, And when I turn thir-ty gon-na give a big par-ty Just to say, "I de-clare, I'm set-tled!"

VERSE

When I was just a lit-tle girl I was-n't dressed in pink, But there were al-ways sub-tle things To make me stop and think; One day up in the at-tic My folks spied a fine old ket-tle "It's

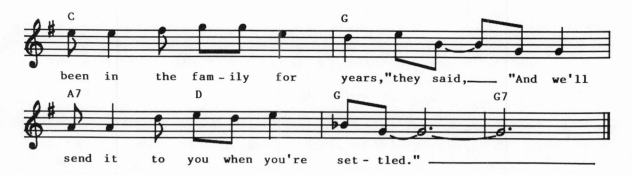

been in the fam – ily for years," they said,___ "And we'll

send it to you when you're set – tled." _____

(*Spoken\*:* I have a sneaking suspicion they meant *married*)

*Chorus*

2. Some folks I know are married,
   And some've untied that knot,
   And when I look at all of them
   Some are "settled," and some are not.
   It's not a piece of paper,
   It happens deep inside,
   You shake hands with your choices,
   Then sit back—enjoy the ride.
   *Chorus*

3. It ain't that I'm a rambler,
   Or I'm too tough to care,
   There's friends I love and work to do
   And a worn-in easy chair.
   Need I explain? Just let me be,
   No cause to worry or meddle,
   Bring on the crockpots, silver and towels,
   I'll put them in my home and get settled!

(*Spoken:* Married folks get *all* the loot.)

*Chorus*

*The spoken sentences are optional.

## 100. SONG OF MYSELF

Peggy Seeger says, "I've written five or six songs that are very close to me, that deal with my personal life. I wrote a song about becoming forty—a song for each of my children. ... This one I wrote driving home by myself, 200 miles from an engagement. In the dark, with a spiral notebook in my lap, I wrote an idea, turned the page, and wrote another. When I arrived home I had 200 pages, each with a line, an idea on it. It took very little time to get it together." This song can be heard on her album, *Penelope Isn't Waiting Anymore: An Album of Women's Songs* (see the Discography). A biography of Peggy Seeger appears on pp. 264–265.

"Song of Myself" is a kind of musical odyssey. It occurs to us that some of our readers might also like to set down on paper such an autobiographical account and philosophy of life. Women play many roles, so an exercise in sorting out one's "real" self can be an artistic challenge and an eye-opener for discovering the direction one's life is taking. (A poem of this nature might be set to either an original tune, as Peggy's is, or to a traditional one.)

Finding time to do this kind of creative work is difficult, yet it is important. Traditionally, women tend to be what Tillie Olsen calls "enablers": those who give the gift of their own time to allow other people to be creative.

"All Gertrude had to do was be a genius."

—Alice B. Toklas

Cora at 86. Photograph by Susan Jørgensen

# Song of Myself

(Unaccompanied and sung freely)

I love those who la-bor, I sing of the far-mers And wea-vers and fish-er-men and mi-ners as well; Now all you who hear me, I pray you draw near me — Be-fore you grow wear-y, I'll sing of my-self.

2. I was brought up in plenty until I was twenty,
   A joy to myself as but children can be;
   A joy to my father, a joy to my mother,
   The pain of my country was nothing to me.

3. My school days being over, I became a rover,
   To Russia and China, to France and to Spain—
   I lived at my leisure, I lived but for pleasure,
   And so, none the wiser, to England I came.

4. I thought it no danger to follow a stranger,
   But with time changing a friend he became;
   For the joys of a lover can equal no other,
   Forever anew—and yet always the same.

5. Good fortune attending, we don't lack a living,
   Our children a blessing our joy to renew—
   But to live amid plenty can only torment me
   When the wealth of the many belongs to the few.

Words and music by Peggy Seeger.

6. I join with the angry, I join with the hungry,
   For long years of anguish the price will be paid—
   To hate and to anger I am not a stranger,
   I welcome the danger—and yet I'm afraid.

7. For I fear the fate of the rebels and fighters
   Who ransom the future with torture and pain;
   As the trial comes near, if I find I can dare it,
   With joy I will share it, no longer afraid.

8. For I've learned to be angry, I've learned to be lonely,
   I've learned to be many, I've learned to be one;
   I've earned all my friends, even foes will commend me,
   I stand with the many, I am not alone.

9. In the presence of fighters I find a new peace,
   In the company of others replenish myself—
   Of miners and weavers, of rebels and dreamers:
   When I sing of my brothers, I sing of myself.

# Discography

Listed below are the contributing songwriters, with the recorded sources of their music represented here. *L* indicates their inclusion in the *Ladyslipper Catalogue,* an invaluable source for music by and for women. Ladyslipper carries more than fifteen hundred titles. We have provided sources for the music not in the catalogue, with company addresses. The traditional music of the songbook is mentioned in this section when it has been recorded by these contemporary songwriters. Rounder, Folkways, and Folk Legacy companies handle much of the traditional material sung by the early songwriters.

Adam, Margie. "Best Friend" ("The Unicorn Song") is found on the album, *Songwriter* (Pleiades LP 2747 or cassette PC 2747). Adam is a renowned and prolific songwriter. *L.* Peter, Paul and Mary have also recorded "Best Friend."

Allen, Linda. "Here's to the Women" and "Ballad of the Welfare Mother" are both from *Mama Wanted to be a Rainbow Dancer* (LP Nexus 103 or cassette C 103). *L.*

Alsop, Peter. *Wha'd Ya Wanna Do?* is the album featuring the song "My Body" (LP Flying Fish 298). The cassette and album, *Uniforms* (FF 90256) has the song, "It's Only a Wee-Wee." The latter, however, is *not* a children's album. Both are on the Flying Fish Records label.

Arnold, Linda. "Sleepyhead" is from the album *Nine Months/Songs of Pregnancy and Birth* (Folkways 6270) *L.* "No Place to Hide" is on a small 33 rpm with four other songs about peace and disarmament called *Sweet Mother Earth* (Ariel AR 2111). The title song was featured with the film, *The Last Epidemic.* (Box 2999, Santa Cruz, CA 95063).

Blue, Bob. His song is from his album, *Erica Levine and Friends* (Black Socks Press). Both Frankie Armstrong and Kim Wallach have recorded "The Ballad of Erica Levine" at this writing. Either the Wallach and Blue recordings can be obtained from 63 Webster Park, W. Newton, MA 02165. Armstrong's version is on the album, *I Heard a Woman Singing* (Flying Fish 332) with many other good women's songs from this favorite British Isles singer. *L.*

Buell, Ruth. From Uncle Ruthie's first album, *Take a Little Step* (UR01) comes "The Family Song." Distributed by Paradigm. *L.*

Cazden, Joanna. "Bombs Away!" is from the album, *Hatching* (Sister Sun 02). *L.* "The Left-Handed Song for Human Rights" is from *Live and Well* (Sister Sun 03). *L.*

The I.W.W. song by Joe Hill, "Rebel Girl," is sung by Cazden on her tape of that title (Sister Sun 04). *L.*

Christian, Meg. "Ode to a Gym Teacher" is from Christian's first album, *I Know You Know* (LP Olivia LF 902 or cassette Olivia LC 902). Christian is a major exponent of women-identified music. (See the Songbooks listing). *L.*

Cox, Ida. There are many blues singers popular among feminists today, although most of their love songs are neither gender-free nor victimless. The producer of many of the great blues singers' albums, Rosetta Reitz, has made a point of featuring *independent* blues singers on her Rosetta Records label. "One-Hour Mama," by Ida Cox, is a cut from *Mean Mothers—Independent Women's Blues Vol. I* (RR 1300). An anthology of a number of famous "classic blues" performers, Cox's song was recorded in 1939. *L.* A one-woman album, *Wild Women Don't Have the Blues* was recorded by Cox in 1961. (LP Rosetta 1304 or cassette Rosetta C 1304) *L.* Cox can also be heard on Vanguard's two-record anthology, *From Spirituals to Swing* (VSD 47/48). A contemporary singer reviving "Wild Women" is Ginni Clemmens (LP Open Door 1004 or cassette Open Door C 1004). *L.*

Culver, Casse. "Ride, Sally Ride" (Sweet Alliance 45-2) is a 45 rpm record. All of Culver's work is available. *L.* Her unique Christian music is available from Sweet Alliance Ministries: 2920 A Rosemary Lane, Falls Church, VA 22042.

Deihl, Marcia. "I'm Settled" is on The New Harmony Sisterhood Band's album, *"... and Ain't I a Woman?"* (Paredon 1038). (The record also includes "Sojourner Truth," not in this collection, but an important women's song.) *L.* Cathy Winter and Betsy Rose recorded "I'm Settled" on their *Strong Sisters* tape (Origami ORI-C231). *L.* Lifeline's *We Have Seen the Future* also features the song, along with "Harriet Tubman" (Opportunity C-1). *L.*

Dickens, Hazel. Her songs have been recorded by many singers; Dickens herself has made solo albums and two duet albums with Alice Gerrard. "Rambling Woman" is from *Hazel Dickens and Alice Gerrard* (Rounder 1154). Four of Dickens's songs also appear on *They'll Never Keep Us Down: Women's Coal Mining Songs* (Rounder 4012), on which The Reel World String Band also performs "What She Aims to Be," by Sue Massek.

Dobkin, Alix. "My Kind of Girl" is from Alix Dobkin's *Adventures in Women's Music* (see Songbooks listing). Dobkin is a pioneer in lesbian music; her *Lavender Jane Loves Women* album is a classic of its kind and enjoyable by anyone's standards. (Women's Wax Works A001C). *L.*

Fink, Sue and Joelyn Grippo. The often-sung "Take Back the Night" is an early anthem for women's rallies against rape, but surprisingly, seems not to have ever been recorded. Sue Fink's LP is *Big Promise*. (Ladyslipper LR 201 or cassette LRC 201.) *L.*

Gerrard, Alice. *Hazel and Alice*, which features bluegrass duets by Hazel Dickens and Alice Gerrard, has the song "Custom-Made Woman Blues" (Rounder 0027). *L.* The recordings of the New Lost City Ramblers include more of Alice Gerrard, as do the Harmony Sisters' recordings.

Good, Dolly and Millie. *The Girls of the Golden West* (Sonyatone 143). The song, "I'm Gonna Be a Real Cowboy Girl" is included in this reissue of this old-time duo, and it can also be heard on Any Old Time stringband's *Lady's Choice* (Bay 217).

Hardy, Lyn. "Something I've Been Meaning to Tell You" is from *Putnam String County Band* (Rounder 3003).

Hirschhorn, Linda. "Dance A Revolution" is from the album *Skies Ablaze* (Oyster C111). *L.*

Kahn, Si. This important songwriter's records appear on several labels. "Truck-Driving Woman" is on *New Wood* (June Appal 002. June Appal Records: P.O. Box 743, Whitesburg, KY 41858). Bobbie McGee recorded "Truck-Driving Woman" on her album, *Bread and Raises: Songs for Working Women* (LP Collector 1933 or cassette) (Collector C-1933). *L.* Singers and groups performing working women's music often record Kahn's songs. He appears with many feminist musicians: Cathy Fink, The Reel World String Band, and others. While other albums are on Flying Fish, all of Kahn's records are available from June Appal. The double album, *Carry It On* (Flying Fish, FF104), has six songs found in *Here's to the Women:* "Union Maid," "I Am a Union Woman," "Which Side Are You On?," "Harriet Tubman," "Bread and Roses," and "I'm Gonna Be an Engineer." Si Kahn, Pete Seeger, and Jane Sapp are the performers.

Lems, Kristin. Both "Farmer" and "My Mom's a Feminist" are from 45 rpm recordings, and each has "The Ballad of the ERA" on the reverse side (Carolsdatter 45-1 and 45-2). *L.* "My Mom's a Feminist" also appears on Lem's album, *We Will Never Give Up!* (Carolsdatter C-K003), and she sings Bonnie Lockhart's "Witch Song" on the same album. *L.*

Lockhart, Bonnie. The co-editor of *Out Loud! A Collection of New Songs by Women* (see Songbooks listing), Lockhart performs "The Witch Song" on the Plum City Players' *Plum Pudding* album (Sisters' Choice LP 365 or cassette, C-365). Kristin Lems also recorded "The Witch Song." "Still Ain't Satisfied" has been recorded by Robin Flower on *More Than Friends* (Spaniel 1916) *L,* and by Rosy's Bar and Grill on their album of that title (Biscuit City 1326). *L.*

Massek, Sue. The Reel World String Band records on both Vetco and Flying Fish. "What She Aims To Be," about coal-mining women, is from Reel World's *Long Way to Harlan* album (Vetco LP 521). *L.* It is also on the album of coal-mining songs of women, *They'll Never Keep Us Down* (Rounder 4012). Other songwriters on the latter album are Hazel Dickens, Si Kahn, Mary Lou Layne, Sarah Ogan Gunning, Florence Reese, Jean Ritchie, Billy Edd Wheeler, and Deborah Silverstein. *L.*

McClatchy, Debby. "Best of Friends" was originally recorded on an album apparently no longer in print, *Homemade Goodies* (Fretless 101). Green Linnet Records carry McClatchy's *Lady Luck* (GL1017) and *Debby McClatchy with the Red Clay Ramblers* (GL1003).

Near, Holly. A singer whose name is almost a household word, Holly Near has many albums to her credit. "Old-Time Woman" is a song from *A Live Album* (Redwood C3700). *L.* "Hay Una Mujer" was originally recorded on *Imagine My Surprise!* (Redwood C401). *L.* It was updated with its new ending on the album *Lifeline* (RR404), where Holly Near and Ronnie Gilbert sang it as a duet. (The new ending was transcribed from their performance for this songbook.) *L.* The reader may also wish to note that Redwood is carrying albums by new Nicaraguan singers, not so much feminist as they are intercultural. Information is available from Redwood Records Cultural and Educational Fund, 478 West MacArthur Blvd., Oakland, CA 95609.

Orozco, José-Luis. "The Ballad of Dolores Huerta" appears on an album titled *160 Anos del Corrido Mexicano y Chicano* (Bilingual Media Productions, Inc./Babel Inc., 255 E. 14th St., Oakland, CA 94606). Also hear *De Colores*, a latin band's version of "Dolores Huerta" (Pajaro Records MC500). For Orozco's album of Hispanic folklore, see the children's recordings.

Reagon, Bernice Johnson. A number of albums are available by the fine lead singer of the ensemble, Sweet Honey in the Rock. *Folksongs of the South* (Folkways 2457) *L* is a solo album of work songs and spirituals; "Give Your Hands to Struggle," in this songbook, is on the album of the same title (Paredon 1028), where all four parts of the a capella harmonies are Reagon's. *L.* "Oughta Be a Woman" is from Sweet Honey in the Rock's *Good News* (Flying Fish 245). *L.*

Reynolds, Malvina. Four of Malvina Reynolds's songs appear in this volume. "If You Love Me" appears on *Malvina Held Over* (CFS 3688); "We Don't Need the Men" is also a cut from that album. *L.* "Mario's Duck" is on *Mama Lion* (CR 050) *L*, and "What Have They Done to the Rain?" has become a folk favorite. Joan Baez recorded it on Vanguard (VSD 2122) and *In Concert* (Vanguard 54.5). *L.* See children's albums and songbooks lists for more of Malvina Reynolds's work.

Ritchie, Jean. *None But One* (Greenhays 708) is issued through Folkways and June Appal and has the song, "Black Waters." *L. High Hills and Mountains* (marketed by Flying Fish) has many of the songs in her fine songbook, titled *Celebration of Life* (see Songbooks listing).

Robinson, Walter. "Harriet Tubman" is sung as a duet on Holly Near and Ronnie Gilbert's album, titled *Lifeline. L.* Others have also recorded the song: the first is probably Kate Taylor, and later the group Bright Morning Star, among others.

Romaine, Anne. "Georgia Cotton Mill Woman" is from Romaine's album, *Gettin' On Country* (Rounder 3009). *L.* (She recorded Joe Hill's "Rebel Girl" on *Take a Stand* [Flying Fish 323] *L.*)

Rose, Betsy. "Coming Into My Years" is on her solo album, *In the Very Front Row* (LP Paper Crane 5455 or cassette, Paper Crane C-5455), and also recorded on the earlier *Strong Singers,* with Cathy Winter (Origami 231. Tape only). *L.* Judy Gorman-Jacobs recorded "Coming Into My Years" on *Right Behind You in the Left-Hand Lane* (One Sky 02). *L.* Betsy Rose's song, "Young and Alive" has not been recorded.

Rubin, Ruth. While her song about the Triangle fire is not recorded, Folkways has several of Rubin's albums available (8720, 8740, and 3801). Ruth Rubin is possibly the greatest American collector of Jewish songs. (See the Songbooks listing.)

Sainte-Marie, Buffy. "The Universal Soldier" and "Now That the Buffalo's Gone" are among her earliest songs. Both appear on the recording titled *Spotlight on Buffy Sainte-Marie* (Spot 1018), a double album with twenty-four of her best songs. *L.*

Schimmel, Nancy. "Turkeys" is yet unrecorded, but the album *Plum Pudding,* with stories and songs for children, is in print (Sister's Choice C 365). *L.*

Seeger, Peggy. With fifty albums to her credit, we mention only her particularly feminist records: *Different Therefore Equal* (Folkways 8561). *L;* and *Penelope Isn't Waiting Anymore* (Rounder 4011). *L.* The latter lists "I'm Gonna Be an Engineer," "The Housewife's Lament," and "Song of Myself"—all in one album. Many performers have recorded "Engineer": Kristin Lems, Willie Tyson, and Pete Seeger, among others.

Small, Fred. Small is interested in the movement called "Changing Men," (as are Willie Sordill and Peter Alsop); his material is particularly supportive of women. "Talking Wheelchair Blues" is from Small's album, *The Heart of the Appaloosa* (Rounder 4014). Small and Sordill both can be heard in the anthology, *Walls to Roses: Songs of Changing Men* (Folkways FTS 37587). *L.*

Small, Judy. Three albums in a short time are credited to Judy Small of Australia (and no relation to Fred Small). The song "Mothers, Daughters, Wives" appears on two: *A Natural Selection* (Good Things C-1), and *Mothers, Daughters and*

*Wives* (Redwood C-3100). *L.* Ronnie Gilbert also has it on her first recording made in twenty years: *The Spirit Is Free* (Redwood C-408). *L.*

Smith, Janet. "Talking Want Ad" was on a now out of print record, *Virgo Rising: The Once and Future Woman.* Peggy Seeger also recorded "Want Ad" on *Penelope Isn't Waiting Anymore* (Rounder 4011). *L.*

Sordill, Willie. Sordill, who appears on the *Walls To Roses* album, has two solo records at this writing: *Please Tip Your Waitress* (Folkways 37582), and *Silent Highways* (Folkways 37585). Both emphasize themes of social justice. The latter presents the topic of Central American–U.S. relations (and features Latin guitar rhythms). *L.*

Sorrels, Rosalie. This renowned singer/songwriter/storyteller has many volumes to her credit. "Brigham, Brigham Young," a traditional folksong in this collection, appears on Sorrels' *Songs of Idaho and Utah* (Folkways 5343). *L;* our arrangement here is very similar. See *Miscellaneous Abstract Record No. 1* for a wonderful discussion of Aunt Molly Jackson and other determined women (Green Linnet 1042). *L.*

Tyson, Willie. *Debutante* (Urana WWE-82) is nearly out of print at this writing. It is a fine album, with the song "Debutante Ball" and Peggy Seeger's "I'm Gonna Be an Engineer." Tyson's other albums are available. *L.*

Voss, Jane. "Standing Behind a Man" and "Keep in Mind (That I Love You)" are songs from her first record, *An Album of Songs* (Bay 207. Address: 1516 Oak Street, #302, Alameda, CA 94501). *Get to the Heart* (Green Linnet SIF 1031) has an original song for Bessie Smith; *Pullin' Through* (GL SIF 1044), again accompanied by the fine ragtime and early jazz performer, Hoyle Osborne, is also full of humor, and the songs are remarkably victimless. Jane Voss has a considerable ability to interpret music of a given era in a faithful fashion. The songs on her first album are reminiscent of the Carter Family; the music on the last two are in the "city" jazz and barrel-house blues styles of the twenties and thirties.

West, Hedy. This important singer has few recordings available at the present. Her banjo playing is peerless. The "single girl" set of songs was from a now-rare record on Vanguard: *Hedy West* (Vanguard VRS 9124). The album *Love, Hell and Biscuits* contains the song, "Babies in the Mill," by Dorsey Dixon, published in the labor section of this songbook. See also *Old Times and Hard Times* (Folk Legacy 32). *L.*

Winter, Cathy. *Breath On My Fire* (Flying Fish 342), her first solo album, has "Sure Am Glad To Know." *L.* See her other albums and tapes with Betsy Rose, as well as her children's tape, also with Rose. *L.*

# Songbooks

F EW women's songbooks exist, and most of the songbooks listed below pertain to the history in this volume rather than to women. A few *are* for women, however, or contain a significant number of songs for or about women. They are starred. *L* indicates their inclusion in the *Ladyslipper Catalogue*.

*Adam, Margie. *Songwriter Songbook*. *L*. These are songs from Adam's first album.

*Allen, Linda. (comp.) *Rainy Day Songbook*. Published by the Whatcom Museum of Bellingham, Washington (121 Prospect Street, zip 98225), this is a good regional songbook. The *Linda Allen Songbook*\* has original songs and is available from Nexus Records, P.O. Box 5881, Bellingham, WA 98227.

*Alloy, Evelyn. *Working Women's Songbook*. New England Free Press, 1976. The Free Press no longer exists, but the book is worth the search, since it is a very useful collection of women's labor songs.

Arnett, Hazel. *I Hear America Singing*. New York: Praeger, 1975. This is one of several volumes to come out during the Bicentennial containing historical songs.

Baez, Joan. *The Joan Baez Songbook*. New York: Ryerson Music Publishing, Inc., First published 1964. Now distributed by Music Sales Corporation, 33 W. 60th Street, New York, NY 10023.

Brand, Oscar. *Songs of '76*. New York: Evans Company, in association with J. P. Lippencott, New York and Philadelphia, 1972.

*Christian, Meg. *I Know You Know Songbook* (Olivia SB). *L*. These are songs from Christian's first album.

*Cheney, Joyce, Marcia Deihl, and Deborah Silverstein. *All Our Lives*. Baltimore, MD: Diana Press, 1976. Long out of print, a few copies still exist of this good women's songbook.

Cheney, Thomas E. *Mormon Songs From the Rocky Mountains*. Publication of the American Folklore Society, University of Texas Press, 1968, Vol. 53.

Collins, Judy. *The Judy Collins Songbook*. New York: Grosset and Dunlap, 1969. Now distributed by Music Sales Corp., New York.

Cunningham, Sis. *Songs of Our Times*. (From the pages of *Broadside Magazine*.) Out of print.

*Dobkin, Alix. *Alix Dobkin's Adventures in Music*. Tomato Publications. *L*. This collection includes "My Kind of Girl," and other songs by Dobkin, with autobiography and pictures.

Edwards, Jay. *The Coffee House Songbook*. New York: Oak Publications, 1966.

Foner, Philip S. *American Labor Songs of the 19th Century*. Urbana: University of Illinois Press, 1975.

*Fowke, Edith, and Joe Glazer. *Songs of Work and Protest*. New York: Dover Publishing, 1973 (in cooperation with the Labor Division, Roosevelt University, Chicago, 1960). This fine collection of labor songs includes a number about women. The historical notes are excellent.

Glazer, Tom. *Songs of Peace, Freedom and Protest*. New York: David McKay, Inc., 1971.

Greenway, John. *American Folksongs of Protest*. New York: A. S. Barnes; University of Pennsylvania Press, Perpetua Edition, 1960.

Guthrie, Woody. *A Tribute to Woody Guthrie*. New York: Ludlow Music, Inc. in association with Woody Guthrie, Inc., 1968.

Hall, Patty. *Growin' Songs*. Containing twenty originals, including "Organic," Hall's book is available from Skimpy Productions, 1000 Natchez Road, Franklin, TN 37064.

*Hanisch, Carol. *Fight On, Sisters!*. Available from P.O. Box 7, New Paltz, NY 12561, the songs include "Bedroom Backlash" and "I Gotta Learn to Sing."

*Henderson, Kathy, with Frankie Armstrong and Sandra Kerr. *My Song Is My Own: 100 Women's Songs*. London: Pluto Press, 1979. This is a British collection of feminist songs, with an inordinately large number of traditional songs about man/woman relationships: "Don't Let Me Die An Old Maid," "The Gypsy Laddie," etc. One entire section is titled, "I Long to Have a Young Man." Many songs are in dialects. The book features a good section of work songs. ("We were unable to find any gay women's songs from this country that stood up beside the rest. We hope that others will fill in our gaps," says Henderson in her Introduction.)

*I.W.W. Songs to Fan the Flames of Discontent*. Chicago: Industrial Workers of the World, 1976. A relatively recent edition of the "Little Red Songbook."

Kornbluh, Joyce. *Rebel Voices*. An anthology of I.W.W. songs. Ann Arbor, Michigan: University of Michigan Press, 1968.

Lawrence, Vera Brodsky. *Music for Patriots, Politicians and Presidents*. New York: MacMillan, 1975.

Leventhal, Harold, and Marjorie Guthrie. *The Woody Guthrie Songbook*. New York: Grosset and Dunlap, 1976.

Lomax, Alan. *Folk Songs of North America*. New York: Doubleday, 1960.

Lomax, Alan. *Hard-Hitting Songs for Hard-Hitting People*. New York: Oak Publications, 1967.

Lomax, John and Alan. *Folk Song U.S.A.* New York: Signet Book, 1966.

*Near, Holly, and Jeff Langley. *Words and Music*. Hereford Music, 1976.

*Out Loud! A Collection of New Songs by Women* (Comp. by the Berkeley Women's Songbook Project; ed. Bonnie Lockhart, Laurie Olsen, and others.) Oakland, CA: Inkworks Press. Out of print, it features music of mainly west coast feminist songwriters and has a strong lesbian emphasis. Its excellent politically aware introduction explains the need for songs for women involved in the then-new freedom movements.

Reynolds, Malvina. *Songbook*. The volume contains sixty-three of her favorite songs. L.

Ritchie, Jean. *Celebration of Life*. Geordie Music Publishing: Box 361, Port Washington, NY 1971. A visually beautiful book, it features many photos of Jean Ritchie's Kentucky home and her family. Her songs, though originals, are written in the "old style."

Rubin, Ruth. *Jewish Folksongs in Yiddish and English*. New York: Oak Publications/ Music Sales Corporation, 1965 and 1980.

Sainte-Marie, Buffy. *Songbook*. New York: Grosset and Dunlap 1971.

*Seeger, Pete, and Bob Reiser. *Carry It On*. New York: Simon and Schuster, 1985. A well-written labor songbook. Thirteen of the songs overlap with those in this volume. The commentary is from contemporary accounts (newspapers, etc.); the volume features an unusual collection of photos.

Silber, Irwin. *Lift Every Voice*. New York: People's Artists, Inc., 1955.

*Silverman, Jerry. *The Liberated Woman's Songbook*. New York: Collier Books, 1971. Out of print, this well-produced women's songbook contained only one or two contemporary songs, and many of the choices were of questionable interest to women. Nonetheless, it was one of only two or three collections that could be termed "song anthologies for women" to be published during the entire decade of the 1970s in the United States.

*Sing Out! Published by the Sing Out Corporation, Box 1071, Easton, PA. *The* folk-song magazine (although smaller regional folksong magazines are published around the country), *Sing Out!* presents a great deal of material about and by women. A number of the songs of this collection appeared in *Sing Out!* either before or after the research for this volume was completed.

Small, Fred. *Breaking From the Line*. Cambridge, MA: Yellow Moon Press: P.O. Box 1316, Cambridge, MA 02238. Fred Small is an outstanding songwriter; his "Wheelchair Blues" is included in his songbook.

*Songs of the Spirit*. Published by the Tempe (Arizona) Friends Meeting, 1520 Race Street, Philadelphia, PA 19102. A small spiral bound paperback hymnal, *Songs of the Spirit* is used by Quakers, Unitarian-Universalist, and other groups. It contains many folk songs, spirituals, and Shaker tunes. Also this little hymnal has songs by Pete Seeger, Malvina Reynolds, Sidney Carter; even some old-fashioned hymns, many with new words, and also old, nearly-forgotten carols. We found the "Lucretia Mott" song in this outstanding little book.

*Sorrels, Rosalie. *What, Woman, and Who, Myself, I am*. Dist. by Music Sales Corp., NY, 1976. A small collection of twenty-eight songs, half of them by Sorrels, and poetry, also by women. Beautifully illustrated.

*Wasn't That a Time?* This book of songs of historic struggles, published by People's Artists, Inc. is long out of print.

*Williamson, Cris. *The Changer and The Changed Songbook* (Olivia SB 904). *L.*

# Records, Tapes, and Songbooks
## for Children

W E have developed this selected list of records, tapes, and songbooks for children to help augment the material for women. There is considerable interest today in producing nonsexist literature and songs for young people, and offering children an alternative to the continual violence and trauma to which they are exposed on television. The entries below deliberately point in the opposite direction: most offer children a chance to hear and learn about their own musical heritage, and many give them a glimpse of other cultures. Always the emphasis is on humor, good will and fairness, and thoughtful and creative play.

Alsop, Peter, *Wha'd Ya Wanna Do?*. Alsop's record has "My Body" and other good songs he has written for children. Many are incredibly silly, but all of them rely on children's innate sense of their own foibles, and Alsop never gets preachy, even when he's teaching a moral.

Buell, Uncle Ruthie, *Take A Little Step* (UR01). Uncle Ruthie's first album features nice back-ups by Marcia Berman and other performers experienced in working with small children. "The Family Song" is included. *L.*

Challis, Evelyn. *Jumping, Laughing and Resting.* New York: Oak Publications/Music Sales Corporation, 1974. A fine collection of children's songs, many known, many unusual ones; some in Spanish. Some of the great folksong writers are included: Woody Guthrie, Malvina Reynolds, and Tom Paxton, among others.

Clemmons, Ginni. *Sing A Rainbow* (Folkways (7637). A record of good singalongs with children. *L.*

Cline, Dallas. *Cornstalk Fiddle and Other Homemade Instruments.* New York: Oak Publications/Music Sales Corporation, 1976. With a little help, children can follow directions for making simple folk instruments at home. There are some good songs included that will please even small children.

Fink, Cathy. *I'm Gonna Tell* (007 Rooster: RFD 2, Bethel, Vermont 05232). One of the best children's albums, and one that adults will not be able to resist, due in large part to the quite bizarre recitations of Peter Paul Van Camp (never heard of since). Cathy Fink's second album for children, *Grandma Slid Down the Mountain*, features this two-time winner of the West Virginia Old Time Banjo Contest teaching kids to yodel (LP Rounder 8010, or cassette, Rounder C 8010). *L.*

The Folkways Children's Series, with many albums from Ella Jenkins, Pete Seeger, Woody Guthrie, Jean Ritchie, and others can be found in the Folkways catalogue.

Jenkins, Ella. With too many albums to name, Jenkins is an important woman in children's music. She especially emphasizes Black and Jewish (urban) cultures. *L.*

Jones, Bessie. *Step It Down: Games for Children* (Rounder 9004). The great Georgia Sea Island singer won the National Library Association's Record of the Year Award in 1980 for this album. *L.*

Petric, Faith. *Sing A Song, Sing Along* (A Gentle Wind Cassette, C-1015). *L.*

Reynolds, Malvina. All three children's albums are fine. The titles alone are charming: *Artichokes, Griddle Cakes and Other Good Things; Funnybugs, Giggleworms and Other Good Friends;* and *Magical Songs. L.* The songbooks are presented to different age groups. The youngest children will enjoy *Tweedles and Foodles for Young Noodles.* The songs have pleasing piano arrangements and guitar chords. *There's Music In the Air* is for the "middle young," with "Magic Penny," "You Can't Make a Turtle Come Out," and other favorites. The albums, records, and songbooks can be ordered from Sisters' Choice, Schroder Music Company, 1450 Fifth Street, Berkeley, CA 94710.

Ritchie, Jean. *Marching Across the Green Grass and Other American Children's Game Songs* (Folkways, 7702). This album features traditional music from Kentucky. *L.*

Seeger, Mike and Peggy. *American Folk Songs for Children.* These three albums are considered classics (Rounder 8001, 8002, 8003).

Schimmel, Nancy. *Plum Pudding.* Stories and songs with the Plum City Players, a group of women from the Bay area of California. *L.*

Thomas, Marlo, and Friends. *Free to Be ... You and Me.* This delightful rock music album is one of the first consciously feminist and nonsexist records. (Arista AB4003). *L.*

Winter, Cathy, and Betsy Rose. *As Strong As Anyone Can Be* (Cassette only. A Gentle Wind 1010.) *L.*

# Catalogs and Other Publications

*LADYSLIPPER* is the major distributor of women's music, with fifteen hundred titles. We have indicated throughout the Discography and Songbook sections with *L* whenever the catalog can be consulted. Below are the addresses for Ladyslipper and four record companies that are mentioned frequently. When *L* does not appear, the book or record may be obtained directly from the record company. Some music stores will order albums, as well. All catalogs are free.

FLYING FISH
1304 W. Schubert
Chicago, IL 60614

GREEN LINNET RECORDS
70 Turner Hill Road
New Canaan, CT 06840

LADYSLIPPER, INC.
P.O. Box 3124
Durham, NC 27715

REDWOOD CULTURAL WORK
P.O. Box 10408
Oakland, CA 94610

ROUNDER (also distributor for
    FOLKWAYS)
One Camp Street
Cambridge, MA 02140

Also see: *HOT WIRE: A JOURNAL OF WOMEN'S MUSIC AND CULTURE,*
5210 N. Wayne, Chicago, IL 60640.

A teach-yourself tape, with portions of 23 songs from *Here's to the Women*, including "I'm Gonna Be an Engineer," "One-Hour Mama," "Talking Want Ad," "We Don't Need the Men," "Corrido de Dolores Huerta," and "Ride, Sally Ride" is available from:

> Heidi-Ho Music Productions
> P.O. Box 42516-T
> Santa Barbara, CA 93140

Please write for order information.

# Annotated Bibliography

Addams, Jane. *Twenty Years at Hull House.* New York: MacMillan, 1910, reissued 1945. This volume represents the second of a two-part autobiography by the founder of the famous settlement in Chicago.

Bacon, Margaret Hope. *Valiant Friend: the Life of Lucretia Mott.* New York: Walker and Company, 1980. A well-known Quaker of our time is the biographer of the great reformer, abolitionist, and suffragist, Lucretia Mott.

Banner, Lois. *Women in Modern America: A Brief History.* New York: Harcourt, Brace, Jovanovich, 1974. A respected historian has provided a well-illustrated, entertaining, and informative volume.

Baxandall, Rosalyn, Linda Gordon, and Susan Reverby, eds. *America's Working Women: A Documentary History from 1600 to the Present.* New York: Random House, 1976. The work women have performed throughout U.S. history is described in contemporary accounts.

Berg, Barbara J. *The Remembered Gate: Origins of American Feminism: the Woman and the City.* New York: Oxford University Press, 1978. American women's participation in reform, benevolence, and later women's movements is traced from their early need to break the bonds of women's "sphere."

Blassingame, John W., ed. *Slave Testimony.* Baton Rouge: Louisiana State University Press, 1977. A very important collection of accounts of slavery by those who lived under it.

Boston Women's Health Collective. *The New Our Bodies, Ourselves.* New York: Simon and Schuster, 1984 ed. This comprehensive volume contains essential information about women's health and their sexuality, childbearing, birth control, and other aspects of women's bodies and minds. "Learning to understand, accept, and be responsible for our physical selves," is the stated goal of the 1976 edition.

Bradford, Sarah. *Harriet Tubman: The Moses of Her People.* Chevy Chase, MD: Citadel Press/Corinth Books, 1961. (Originally published 1886.) This is the dictated autobiography of the great escaped slave and conductor of the Underground Railroad, Harriet Tubman.

Buhle, Mari Jo and Paul. *The Concise History of Woman Suffrage: Selections from the Classic Work of Stanton, Anthony, Gage and Harper.* Urbana, IL: University of Illinois Press, 1978. Major writings of four important suffragists are included in this important source book.

Chafe, William H. *The American Woman: Her Changing Social, Economic and Polit-*

*ical Role—1920 to 1970.* New York: Oxford University Press, 1972. A respected historian discusses women's roles after suffrage was attained.

Chevigny, Bell Gale. *The Woman and the Myth.* (Margaret Fuller's life and writings.) New York: The Feminist Press, 1976. This is the life of the visionary nineteenth-century transcendentalist and utopian, who believed in the total equality of the sexes.

Cone, James. *The Spirituals and the Blues.* New York: Seabury Press, 1972. The author discusses the origins of black music.

Cott, Nancy F. *The Bonds of Womanhood: "Woman's Sphere" in New England, 1780–1835.* New Haven, CT: Yale University Press, 1977. The early separation of the roles of men and women are explored.

Davis, Rebecca Harding. *Life in the Iron Mills.* Old Westbury, NY: The Feminist Press, 1972. This novel, first published in 1861, depicts the exploitation of laborers, and the tragedy of wasted talent.

Degler, Carl. *At Odds: Women in the Family in America from the Revolution to the Present.* New York: Oxford University Press, 1980. Degler is by all accounts one of the most important of the historians writing about American women today.

DePauw, Linda Grant. *Founding Mothers: Women of America in the Revolutionary Era.* Boston: Houghton-Mifflin Company, 1975. The crucial roles of women in the social, political, military, and economic life of colonial America is brought to light. The author presents a particularly good chapter on the Daughters of Liberty.

_____ , Conover Hunt, and Miriam Schneir. *Remember the Ladies: Women in America, 1750–1815.* New York: Viking Press, 1976. The roots of feminism are explored. The title comes from a quotation by Abigail Adams, often considered America's first feminist.

Ehrenreich, Barbara, and Deirdre English. *For Her Own Good: 150 Years of the Experts' Advice to Women.* Old Westbury, New York: The Feminist Press, 1977. The history of the (male) medical establishment's power over women is detailed.

_____ . *Witches, Midwives and Nurses.* New York: The Feminist Press, 1973. This is a well-documented and entertaining history of women healers.

Eisler, Benita, ed. *The Lowell Offering: Writings by New England Mill Women, 1840–1845.* New York: Harper and Row, 1980.

Flynn, Elizabeth Gurley. *The Rebel Girl.* New York: International Publishing, 1973. The autobiography of the radical crusader for the I.W.W. and the working class (and Joe Hill's heroine).

Foner, Philip S. *The Factory Girls.* Urbana, IL: University of Illinois Press, 1977. An important labor historian writes on the life and struggles of factory workers in New England in the 1840s.

_____ . *Women and the American Labor Movement.* New York: The Free Press (a division of MacMillan), 1979.

Forster, Margaret. *Significant Sisters: The Grassroots of Active Feminism, 1839–1939.* New York: Knopf, 1984. Forster presents eight portraits of important feminists of the past (including Margaret Sanger), with their words and her own.

French, Marilyn. *Beyond Power: On Women, Men and Morals.* New York: Summit Books, 1985.

Friedan, Betty. *The Feminine Mystique.* New York: Norton, 1963. Friedan was the first contemporary writer to make transparent the glorification of femininity perpetuated by men, and to say that historically women have traded their individuality for security.

Frym, Gloria. *Second Stories*. San Francisco: Chronicle Books, 1979. The author conducted interviews with ten women whose artistic careers began after age thirty-five, including a frank discussion with Malvina Reynolds.

Gaillard, Frye. *Watermelon Wine: The Spirit of Country Music*. New York: St. Martin's Press, 1978. This volume contains good information about the evolution of Nashville music and includes some lyrics.

Garland, Phyl. *The Sound of Soul*. Chicago: Henry Regnery Company, 1969. Motown and its roots are the subject of this book.

Genovese, Eugene. *Roll, Jordan, Roll: The World the Slaves Made*. New York: Pantheon Books, 1974. Because this is one of the few volumes to discuss slave women as a separate group, Genovese's book is an important addition to the literature.

Giele, Janet Zollinger. *Women and the Future: Changing Sex Roles in Modern America*. New York: The Free Press (a division of MacMillan), 1978. Strategies for effecting a more egalitarian society are the subjects of Giele's volume.

Gilman, Charlotte Perkins. *The Yellow Wallpaper*. Old Westbury, NY: The Feminist Press, 1973. (First published in New England Magazine, Boston, January, 1892.) Gilman was a radical feminist whose life bridged the 1900s and the early part of the twentieth century. This famous story is about a would-be writer driven mad by the prevailing social pressures and medical treatment commonly imposed on women of that time.

Gray, Madeline. *Margaret Sanger: A Biography of the Champion of Birth Control*. New York: Marek and Company, 1980. While this is one of more than a dozen biographies of Sanger in print, it is especially interesting for including many details of Sanger's personal life, which could easily be the subject of a novel.

Green, Archie. *Only a Miner: Studies in Recorded Coal-Mining Songs*. Champaign, IL: University of Illinois Press, 1972. This well-researched volume was written a decade or so before 3,000 to 5,000 women entered the coal mining occupation.

Gurko, Miriam. *The Ladies of Seneca Falls*. New York: MacMillan, 1974. The story of the first Women's Rights Convention in 1848 is told in an especially absorbing way.

Hahn, Emily. *Once Upon a Pedestal*. New York: Thomas Crowell, 1974. This informal book shows how women have been viewed throughout our history.

Harris, Sheldon. *The Blues Who's Who: A Biographical Dictionary of Blues Singers*. New Rochelle, NY: Arlington House, 1979. An important resource book for information about the lives of Bessie Smith, Ida Cox, and many others.

Hartmann, Susan M. *The Home Front and Beyond: American Women in the 1940s*. Boston: G. K. Hall, 1982. Women entered the labor force on a massive scale during World War II to take the place of men. This account tells how they took over "men's jobs" and what happened to working women after the war was over.

Holiday, Billie, with William Dufty. *Lady Sings the Blues*. New York: Lancer Books, 1956. "Lady Day" wrote a famous—and frank—autobiography full of information about the life of the blues singers of the era when blacks first entered the business of nightclub performance.

Holland, Ruth. *Mill Child*. New York: Crowell-Collier Press, 1970. The plight of the child laborers, the "mill mites" of the nineteenth century, is chronicled.

Honey, Maureen. *Creating Rosie the Riveter: Class, Gender, and Propaganda During World War II*. Amherst, MA: University of Massachusetts Press, 1984. The author's research recounts World War II's effect on women's opportunities for formerly male-oriented jobs in industry.

Hunter College Women's Collective. *Women's Realities. Women's Choices*. New York: Oxford University Press, 1983.

Janeway, Elizabeth. *Man's World, Women's Place: A Study in Social Mythology*. New York: William Morrow, 1971. Janeway's volume concerns sex discrimination.

Jones, Hettie. Big Star Fallin' Mama: Five Women in Black Music. New York: Viking Press, 1974. The biographies of five black singers are presented.

Jones, Mary Harris ("Mother" Jones). *The Autobiography of Mother Jones*. Chicago: Charles H. Kerr Publishing Company, third edition, 1976. (First published in 1925.) Written at an advanced age, this is the great labor organizer's own story.

Kahn, Kathy. *Hillbilly Women*. New York: Doubleday, 1972. This is a unique study of "hillbilly" cotton mill workers in which words are recalled from the early "miners' bards" as well as from contemporary workers. The book is illustrated with many photos.

Keepnews, Orin, and Bill Grauer, Jr. *A Pictorial History of Jazz*. New York: Crown, 1955. Long out of print, but still available, this is a classic picture book full of rare photographs of the early jazz era.

Kessler-Harris, Alice. *Out to Work: A History of Wage-Earning Women in the United States*. New York: Oxford University Press, 1982. This book explores the transformation of women's work into wage labor.

_____ . "Where Are the Organized Women Workers?" *Feminist Studies* 3, Fall 1975. The author discusses the obstacles to unionization of women.

_____ . *Women Have Always Worked*. Old Westbury, NY: The Feminist Press, 1980. This is an introduction to women's work inside and outside the home.

Kuhn, Margaret E. (Maggie). *Maggie Kuhn On Aging: A Dialogue*. Philadelphia: Westminster Press, 1977. The revered leader of the Gray Panthers imparts her philosophy about the organization and about getting older.

Larcom, Lucy. *A New England Girlhood*. New York: Reprinted from 1889 by Corinth Press, 1961. The author writes of her own experiences as a factory girl in the Lowell Mills in the early years of the Mill, when labor there was viewed as an attractive option.

Lerner, Gerda. *The Female Experience: An American Documentary*. New York: Bobbs-Merrill Company Inc., 1977.

_____ . *The Grimké Sisters of North Carolina: Rebels Against Slavery*. Boston: Houghton-Mifflin, 1967. This is an absorbing account of the famous lecturer/abolitionists of the pre-Seneca Falls era.

_____ . *The Majority Finds Its Past: Placing Women in History*. New York: Oxford University Press, 1979. The "invisible majority" is made visible.

Lumpkin, Katherine, and Dorothy Wolff Douglas. *Child Workers in America*. New York: International Publishers, 1937. Child labor laws were not effected nationwide until the late thirties. This book explores the subject of children as workers.

Melder, Keith E. *Beginnings of Sisterhood: The American Women's Rights Movement, 1800–1850*. New York: Schoken Books, 1977. A historian discusses the evolution of the country's earliest social movements into the later more sophisticated and important ones.

Morgan, Edmund S. *The Puritan Family: Religious and Domestic Relations in Seventeenth-Century New England*. New York: Harper and Row. Revised 1966. Morgan's volume describes the influence of religious belief on the domestic life of the Puritan family.

Neidle, Cecyle. *America's Immigrant Women*. Boston: Twayne Publishing (a division of G. K. Hall), 1975. Neidle discusses the economic and social contributions of immigrant women.

Norton, Mary Beth. *Liberty's Daughters: The Revolutionary Experience of American Women, 1750–1800.* Boston: Little, Brown, 1980. Among other subjects, the author evaluates the role of the Daughters of Liberty.

Olsen, Tillie. *Silences.* New York: Dell Publishing Company, 1965. "We who write are survivors." A classic volume about women's thwarted creativity from the viewpoints of many important writers, both men and women.

O'Neill, Nena and George. *Open Marriage: A New Lifestyle for Couples.* New York: M. Evans, 1972. This book endorsed extramarital sex for both partners and was a major influence on the sexual revolution.

O'Neill, William. *Everyone Was Brave: A History of Feminism in America.* Chicago: Quadrangle Books, 1971. The evolution of women in politics is analyzed in this highly regarded volume.

Parker, Gail, ed. *The Oven Birds: American Women on Womanhood, 1820–1920.* New York: Anchor Books, Doubleday, 1972. This is a fine collection of early feminist essays.

Raines, Howell. *My Soul is Rested: Movement Days in the Deep South Remembered.* New York: Putnam, 1977. The Civil Rights struggle is recounted here.

Robinson, Harriet Hanson. *Feminism: The Essential Historical Writings.* New York: Vintage Books/Random House, 1972. Again, writers from early days are presented.

Rossi, Alice. "Equality Between the Sexes: An Immodest Proposal." Reprinted in a volume edited by Robert J. Lifton, *Woman in America.* Boston: Houghton-Mifflin, 1965. Rossi proposes some social measures to be taken to assure equality of the sexes: daycare, for example; also non-sexist early childhood education, involving people specially trained to be the paid caretakers of children.

———. (comp.) *The Feminist Papers: From Adams to de Beauvoir.* New York: Columbia University Press, 1973.

Rowbotham, Sheila. *Hidden from History: Rediscovering Women in American History From the Seventeenth Century to the Present.* New York: Pantheon/Random Books, 1974.

Ryan, Mary P. *Womanhood in America: From Colonial Times to the Present.* New York: New Viewpoints, 1975. This is a well-known women's history.

Shulman, Alix Kates, ed. *Red Emma Speaks: Selected Writings and Speeches by Emma Goldman.* New York: Random House/Vintage Books, 1972. The volume contains "The Traffic in Women" and "The Tragedy of Women's Emancipation."

Southern, Eileen. *The Music of Black Americans: A History.* New York: Norton, 1971. This is a scholarly and richly informative account of the earliest black music and instruments, tracing them through all phases of their unique evolution during 250 years.

Spargo, John. *The Bitter Cry of the Children.* A reprint of the 1906 edition. New York: Quadrangle/New York Times Book Company, 1968. The history of child labor in the United States is explored by an early critic.

Steinem, Gloria. *Outrageous Acts and Everyday Rebellions.* New York: Holt, Rinehardt, 1983. The founder of *Ms.* magazine, Gloria Steinem is the author of this collection of articles written since the 1960s.

Thompson, Mary Lou. *Voices of the New Feminism.* Boston: Beacon Press, 1970. An editor at Beacon Press produced one of the earliest and still most important collections of mid-twentieth century feminists' writings.

Truth, Sojourner. *Narrative and Book of Life.* Chicago: Johnson Publishing Company, 1970. The autobiography of the great abolitionist and suffragist is in print today.

Wald, Lillian. *The House on Henry Street.* New York: Henry Holt, 1915. The founder of a great settlement which met the needs of the immigrant poor tells of its history and her work.

Walker, Alice. *In Search of Our Mothers' Gardens*. San Diego, New York and London: Harcourt Brace Jovanovich, 1983. "Listen to the voices of Bessie Smith, Billie Holiday, Nina Simone, Roberta Flack and Aretha Franklin . . . imagine those voices muzzled for life." The nameless black women of the American past have made possible the creative expression of great black artists of today.

Welks, Edward. *The Lowells and Their Institute*. Boston: Little, Brown, 1966. The owner of the early Lowell mill in 1821 planned for an educational institute to better the lives of his early female cotton mill workers. As cheap immigrant labor supplanted the New England farm girls, the idealism was abandoned.

Wertheimer, Barbara Meyer. *We Were There: The Story of Working Women in America*. New York: Pantheon Books, 1977. In this fine history of working women, Wertheimer demonstrates the relationship of trade unionism among women to the labor movement at large.

# Index of Titles and First Lines

Song titles are listed in **boldface.**

# Index

The seven topical sections of the book are listed in **boldface.**

War protest, 210–12
Washburn, Nannie, 108
Washington State Women's History Project, 114
Waters, Ethel, 18
Weavers, The, 73
Welfare mother, xxxii, 151–52
Welfare rights, 22, 151
West, Hedy, 7, 95, 287
West, Lillie Mulkey, 7
Wiggins, Ella Mae, xxviii, 99, 103
Willard, Frances, 53
Williamson, Cris, 27, 291
Winter, Cathy, 85, 184, 287, 294
Witchcraft, xxxiii, 202–203
"Wobblies." *See* Industrial Workers of the World
Wollstonecraft, Mary, 49
Woman suffrage. *See* Suffrage, woman
Woman's rights conventions, xxvii, 49, 58
**Women Emerging,** xxxiv, 257–82
Women's Bureau, xxx
Women's Christian Temperance Union (WCTU), xxvii, 53–54. *See also* Prohibition; Temperance movement

Women's leadership, xxi
Women's liberation, xx, xxiii, xxvi, xxxiv, 11–12, 32, 264, 272
Women's movement, xx, xxv, 32, 272; men in support of, 124
Women's multiple roles, xxxv*n*, 115–17, 265
Women's property rights, xxvii, 49
Women's rights, 49, 58–59
Women's rights conventions, xxvii, 49, 58
Women's right to vote. *See* Suffrage, woman
Women's roles, xxi, 44. *See also* Sex roles
Women's Trade Union League (WTUL), 112
Working conditions, xxviii–xxxi, 63, 95, 101, 103, 111–12, 235
World Antislavery Convention (1840), 49, 58, 230
World War II, xxix

Young, Brigham, xxxi, 144